8 / 96

The
Third
World

opposing viewpoints®

Other Books of Related Interest in the Opposing
Viewpoints Series:

The Third World

opposing viewpoints®

David Bender & Bruno Leone, *Series Editors*

Jonathan S. Petrikin, *Book Editor*

OPPOSING
VIEWPOINTS
SERIES®

Greenhaven Press, Inc., San Diego, CA

Greenhaven Press, Inc.
PO Box 289009
San Diego, CA 92198-9009

Library of Congress Cataloging-in-Publication Data

The Third World : opposing viewpoints / Jonathan S. Petrikin, book editor.
    p.   cm. — (Opposing viewpoints series)
    Includes bibliographical references and index.
    Summary: Presents opposing opinions on such questions concerning the Third World as why it is poor, how it can achieve economic development, and what forms of government would best serve its needs.
    ISBN 1-56510-250-9 (lib., acid-free) — ISBN 1-56510-249-5 (pbk., acid-free).
    1. Developing countries. [1. Developing countries.] I. Petrikin, Jonathan S., 1963–   . II. Series: Opposing viewpoints series (Unnumbered)
HC59.7.T45473   1995
909'.09724—dc20   94-41911
                                           CIP
                                           AC

"Congress shall make no law . . . abridging the freedom of speech, or of the press."

First Amendment to the U.S. Constitution

The basic foundation of our democracy is the First Amendment guarantee of freedom of expression. The Opposing Viewpoints Series is dedicated to the concept of this basic freedom and the idea that it is more important to practice it than to enshrine it.

Contents

Why Consider Opposing Viewpoints?

"The only way in which a human being can make some approach to knowing the whole of a subject is by hearing what can be said about it by persons of every variety of opinion and studying all modes in which it can be looked at by every character of mind. No wise man ever acquired his wisdom in any mode but this."

John Stuart Mill

In our media-intensive culture it is not difficult to find differing opinions. Thousands of newspapers and magazines and dozens of radio and television talk shows resound with differing points of view. The difficulty lies in deciding which opinion to agree with and which "experts" seem the most credible. The more inundated we become with differing opinions and claims, the more essential it is to hone critical reading and thinking skills to evaluate these ideas. Opposing Viewpoints books address this problem directly by presenting stimulating debates that can be used to enhance and teach these skills. The varied opinions contained in each book examine many different aspects of a single issue. While examining these conveniently edited opposing views, readers can develop critical thinking skills such as the ability to compare and contrast authors' credibility, facts, argumentation styles, use of persuasive techniques, and other stylistic tools. In short, the Opposing Viewpoints Series is an ideal way to attain the higher-level thinking and reading skills so essential in a culture of diverse and contradictory opinions.

In addition to providing a tool for critical thinking, Opposing Viewpoints books challenge readers to question their own strongly held opinions and assumptions. Most people form their opinions on the basis of upbringing, peer pressure, and personal, cultural, or professional bias. By reading carefully balanced opposing views, readers must directly confront new ideas as well as the opinions of those with whom they disagree. This is not to simplistically argue that everyone who reads opposing views will—or should—change his or her opinion. Instead, the series enhances readers' depth of understanding of their own views by encouraging confrontation with opposing ideas. Careful examination of others' views can lead to the readers' understanding of the logical inconsistencies in their own opinions, perspective on why they hold an opinion, and the consideration of the possibility that their opinion requires further evaluation.

Evaluating Other Opinions

To ensure that this type of examination occurs, Opposing Viewpoints books present all types of opinions. Prominent spokespeople on different sides of each issue as well as well-known professionals from many disciplines challenge the reader. An additional goal of the series is to provide a forum for other, less known, or even unpopular viewpoints. The opinion of an ordinary person who has had to make the decision to cut off life support from a terminally ill relative, for example, may be just as valuable and provide just as much insight as a medical ethicist's professional opinion. The editors have two additional purposes in including these less known views. One, the editors encourage readers to respect others' opinions—even when not enhanced by professional credibility. It is only by reading or listening to and objectively evaluating others' ideas that one can determine whether they are worthy of consideration. Two, the inclusion of such viewpoints encourages the important critical thinking skill of objectively evaluating an author's credentials and bias. This evaluation will illuminate an author's reasons for taking a particular stance on an issue and will aid in readers' evaluation of the author's ideas.

As series editors of the Opposing Viewpoints Series, it is our hope that these books will give readers a deeper understanding of the issues debated and an appreciation of the complexity of even seemingly simple issues when good and honest people disagree. This awareness is particularly important in a democratic society such as ours in which people enter into public debate to determine the common good. Those with whom one disagrees should not be regarded as enemies but rather as people whose views deserve careful examination and may shed light on one's own.

Thomas Jefferson once said that "difference of opinion leads to inquiry, and inquiry to truth." Jefferson, a broadly educated man, argued that "if a nation expects to be ignorant and free . . . it expects what never was and never will be." As individuals and as a nation, it is imperative that we consider the opinions of others and examine them with skill and discernment. The Opposing Viewpoints Series is intended to help readers achieve this goal.

David L. Bender & Bruno Leone,
Series Editors

Introduction

"For those who would understand and/or promote international development, the late twentieth century must be seen as both the best of times and the worst of times."

—*Jan Knippers Black*

When President Harry Truman said in his 1949 inaugural address that the largest part of the world consisted of "underdeveloped areas" in need of American help, he launched an idea that would profoundly affect the entire world. Since that time, *development* of the Third World (also called the South, or the developing world) by the First World (also called the North, or the developed world) has been a controversial undertaking—praised by some for raising living standards and blamed by others for exacerbating poverty.

Most discussions of Third World development center on the economic development programs sponsored by the World Bank and the International Monetary Fund (IMF)—the two primary international lending organizations. These institutions provide loans and other assistance to Third World countries in an attempt to spur economic growth. Governments receiving this aid are required to institute free-market reforms—or "structural adjustments"—that include cutting government spending, relaxing price controls, privatizing state industries, eliminating trade barriers to imports, and promoting exports. These reforms are intended to stimulate economic growth in Third World countries by reducing government intervention in their economies and by increasing their participation in the international trading system.

Some critics argue that these reforms have hindered, rather than promoted, development. For example, Walden Bello, Shea Cunningham, and Bill Rau write in the Winter 1993 *Food First Action Alert* that

> economies under [structural] adjustment are stuck in a low-level trap, in which low investment, increased unemployment, reduced social spending, reduced consumption, and low output interact to create a vicious cycle of stagnation and decline, rather than a virtuous cycle of growth, rising

12

employment, and rising investment, as originally envisaged in World Bank theory.

Consequently, the authors argue, in Latin America, "the numbers of people living in poverty rose from 130 million in 1980 to 180 million at the beginning of the 1990's." And in Africa, "the number of people living below the poverty line now stands at 200 million of the region's 690 million people."

Bello, Cunningham, Rau, and others contend that this poverty is not inadvertent, but an intentional result of the World Bank and IMF programs. These programs, critics argue, are the latest tactic employed by the First World in its historical practice of enriching itself at the expense of Third World peoples. They equate modern development with the colonialism of the late nineteenth and early twentieth centuries, when the major industrialized nations of Europe dominated much of the Third World, extracting raw materials and penetrating new markets for their manufactured goods. In a similar way, they contend, development programs require Third World countries to export their primary resources, which bring low returns on the international market, while importing higher-priced finished products from the First World. Because Third World countries are forced to perpetually spend more on imports than they make on exports, critics argue, the world's wealth flows one way: from the Third World to the First World. According to Jeremy Seabrook, author of *Victims of Development*, this system is designed "to maintain the flow of wealth from global poor to rich."

Others reject the contention that development programs constitute a new form of colonialism. Amy L. Sherman, author of *Preferential Option: A Christian and Neoliberal Strategy for Latin America's Poor*, argues that Third World poverty has been caused not by neocolonialism, but by the statist regimes that assumed control of many Third World countries as colonial rule declined in the 1950s and 1960s. Statist governments, by definition, favor heavy government involvement in their economies. According to Sherman, this government intervention—which includes state control of industry and regulations on labor and trade—precludes the operation of free-market processes. For this reason, and because economic power was placed "in the hands of government bureaucrats" who were often corrupt and inefficient, economic growth has been stymied. Sherman insists that the structural adjustment programs prescribed by the IMF and the World Bank, which call for reduced government intervention, are needed to reverse the damage done by these counterproductive administrations.

Some assert that market-oriented reforms have proven successful in many Third World countries. In 1991, Michel

Camdessus, the managing director of the IMF, reported that Third World countries that had instituted reforms such as spending cuts and deregulation had experienced significant growth: "Look at the 35 or so countries that have steadfastly implemented stabilization and reform strategies over the medium term—which together account for about half of developing country output. These 35 countries have recorded a truly impressive performance." And many critics credit trade-oriented reforms for the drastic economic growth of the four Asian "tigers"—Hong Kong, Singapore, Taiwan, and South Korea —since the 1950s and 1960s, and of China and Sri Lanka since the late 1970s. Of the Asian "tigers," author Alvin Rabushka writes, "Never before in history [have] four nations moved from Third World to First World status in one generation."

The debate Truman sparked in 1949 continues to this day. While some view development programs as attempts to subjugate and exploit Third World nations, others see them as the only viable route to improved living standards in the developing world. These divergent viewpoints are among those represented in *The Third World: Opposing Viewpoints*, which includes the following chapters: Why Is the Third World Poor? How Can Third World Development Be Achieved? Is Democracy a Workable Form of Government for the Third World? What Is the U.S. Role in the Third World? What Is the Future of North/South Relations? These chapters reveal that debate over the Third World often centers on the First World's perceived role in causing and/or alleviating the problems that confront the world's "underdeveloped areas."

Why Is the Third World Poor?

The
Third
World

Chapter Preface

When delegates convened at the September 1994 United Nations Conference on Population and Development in Cairo, Egypt, one of the main issues discussed centered on the relationship between population and poverty.

Heading the U.S. delegation to Cairo was Vice President Albert Gore Jr., who notes that in his own lifetime "we have gone from a little more than 2 billion to almost 6 billion people"—a trend, he says, that will carry the human population to 10 billion by 2050. Annually adding a population the size of Mexico to the world, Gore argues, is destroying the environment as more people try to eke out a living on a rapidly declining amount of arable land. In the cities, he adds, "population growth . . . almost always holds wages lower than they would otherwise be." What these trends mean for the Third World, where over 90 percent of population growth is now occurring, is that already one in eight people does not have enough to eat, according to the United Nations Population Fund.

Others dispute the idea that population is the cause of Third World poverty. According to Julian Simon, a teacher of business administration who has written on population, current research suggests "no statistical evidence of a negative connection between population increase and economic growth." In fact, Simon contends, some of the wealthiest countries—such as Japan and Hong Kong—are also the most densely populated. Among those who agree with Simon is Sheldon Richman, senior editor at the Cato Institute, a libertarian public policy research group. "Population growth and high density . . . promote progress by allowing a more elaborate division of labor, which raises productivity and incomes, and by creating economies of scale," Richman explains. "Contrary to the vice president," he asserts, "we don't need to impose population control to head off a struggle for survival."

The Cairo conference spotlighted the contentious debate over the effects of population growth in developing countries. This and other issues are discussed in the following chapter on the causes of poverty in the Third World.

"[The Third World] is a putrefying state of existence perpetually in the grip of a plague deadlier than anthrax: the burgeoning human race."

Third World Overpopulation Causes Poverty

Malcolm W. Browne

The Third World suffers from a multitude of plagues, famines, and wars, which, according to journalist Malcolm W. Browne, all have a single cause: overpopulation. Overpopulation in the Third World wipes out local resources, the author argues, causing the severe poverty that many Third Worlders try to escape through immigration. Browne warns that Third World overpopulation is spreading like a cancer over the planet, the ability of which to support the human population must surely fail. Browne, a Pulitzer Prize–winning correspondent for the *New York Times*, reports on science and environmental issues. He is the author of *Muddy Boots and Red Socks*, a memoir of his reporting experience in wartime Vietnam and other Third World nations.

As you read, consider the following questions:

1. What examples does Browne use to support his assertion that life is cheap in the Third World?
2. What characteristics of human population growth does Browne say are shared with the growth patterns of bacteria and cancer?
3. What does the author suggest should be done to curb humanity's burgeoning population?

I have seen the future and it doesn't work. It's the Third World, and it's coming our way, as inexorably as the Africanized killer bees from Brazil.

When I lived in South Asia I discovered that a Bengali or Indian or Sri Lankan could fetch more money chopped into pieces and sold as laboratory specimens than he or she could as a live person. The reason for this horrible reality is that medical specimens are always in demand, while there is always a surplus of people in places like the Indian subcontinent.

In just a few months in 1971, war and monsoon floods combined to kill about one million people in East Pakistan, and the Bengali landscape in 1971 looked like a medieval allegory of the Apocalypse. But though death seemed to reign supreme, birth swiftly overtook it. United Nations demographers I knew, whose detailed census produced the first really reliable estimate of population growth in Bengal, computed that another one million people were being created every eighty-four days. Put another way; in less than three months, Bangladesh replaced all the million human beings whose corpses choked its rivers, floodplains, villages and wells. And since then, the time needed to grow a million Bengalis has been cut in half.

Unneeded and Unwanted

The brutal fact is that most of the people of Bangladesh—indeed, most of the people living in the Third World—are unneeded and unwanted by the rest of the human race, and living in lands that simply cannot sustain them. Chronic optimists cluck and say, well, all we need do is teach the benighted people of South Asia, Africa and Latin America to produce more and to limit their consumption.

Produce what? And limit what consumption? Hordes are starving already. And are we to tell the Indians and Bengalis and Chinese and Somalis and Andean peoples that they must curb their appetites for refrigerators, cars and television? Have we the right?

To me, Bengal is the Ghost of Christmas Yet to Come, for it shows what can happen anywhere in the creeping Third World.

The Bengali Example

Bengal once supplied the world's jute market, but today's producers of grain ship their products in bags made mostly of synthetic fibers, and the market for Bengali jute has largely dried up. The country sells its only other major crop, Basmati rice, to China. This brings in some badly needed foreign exchange, but in return, Bengal often imports inferior Chinese rice to feed its own people. Bangladesh and China, in effect trade rice for rice.

With neither any industry worthy of the name nor a profitable agricultural base, Bangladesh has few jobs, and the poverty of its people is beyond belief. The average person is a liability to his or her community, not an asset. The only consolation is that most people die young.

Behrendt/ Cartoonists & Writers Syndicate, used with permission.

But there has long been a brisk market for human skeletons, skulls, brains, livers and other odds and ends. Human parts are used in the West by medical schools, laboratories and pharmaceutical manufacturers for a variety of purposes, and the cadaver trade has been largely supplied by India, Sri Lanka and Bengal. (These countries have all outlawed the export of human remains and reduced the flow—unwisely, in my opinion—but a living can still be made from the human flesh market.)

It's hardly surprising, then, that a lot of poor people have come to value the contents of their nation's graves and rivers more than their own living kin. The price of a human skull in America can feed a Bengali family for a year!

A Putrefying Existence

When I speak of the Third World, I mean something more than a range of latitudes or distinctive colors on a map, some-

19

thing that goes beyond the numbers describing gross national product, literacy, infant mortality and the other indices of good fortune. I mean a collective state of mind.

The label "Third World" is a euphemism for a domain embracing the urine-drenched sidewalks of New York City and Los Angeles slums, as well as the villages of the Nile Delta, the festering hamlets of Africa, Latin America and Asia, and all the other places where cruelty, intolerance and superstition rule. The Third World is not a "developing" culture. It is a putrefying state of existence perpetually in the grip of a plague deadlier than anthrax: the burgeoning human race.

For the last dozen years I have devoted most of my reporting to science, including the sciences applied to environmental problems. I have become convinced that until population growth can be controlled, all other environmental problems will remain insoluble.

The Environmental Scorecard

We hear and read quite a lot about these problems—acid rain, depletion of the ozone layer, "greenhouse" planetary warming, the fouling of the seas and the proliferation of waste of all kinds.

Meanwhile, biologists tell us that as we chop away at the wilderness we are killing thousands of species a year simply depriving them of habitat, and that the greatest mass extinction in the planet's history is now taking place, not because of the impact of an asteroid or the drying up of inland seas, but because of unchecked human reproduction. We are destroying the global gene pool, a resource that might not only have made our planet more interesting but which has given us some potent defenses against disease and starvation.

Some world leaders have begun to worry particularly about the torrent of carbon dioxide we pour into the atmosphere, which may end up warming the whole earth, with devastating effects on agriculture and life.

But rarely do the politicians mention that all human beings exhale carbon dioxide from their own lungs, not just from their chimneys and the tail pipes of their car. We each foul the global nest merely by breathing.

People Are the Problem

Moreover, every human being consumes energy, resources and food. We all also produce vast amounts of waste, and something physicists call entropy, an entity that reflects the disorder of systems. Scientists who study environmental problems are in wide agreement that until we do something about unchecked human reproduction, piecemeal attacks on chloro-fluorocarbons and carbon dioxide and desertification and all the other man-made scourges will always be inadequate. Our biggest problem is people.

That simple and seemingly obvious fact is indigestible. News directors don't like it much more than does the Vatican, or the mullahs of Saudi Arabia, or any who believe that more is better when it comes to population.

The Third World, like AIDS and killer-bee swarms, gropes outward with persistent tendrils, like the tender roots of plants that pierce even concrete sewer pipes. The branch of medicine called epidemiology has turned up evidence that the Third World has something in common with bacterial cultures and cancerous tumors.

The Human Bacterial Colony

In a bacterial culture, organisms propagate exponentially and without limit, as long as they have food and room to dump their wastes. Given the chance, they will consume every last molecule of the nutrient medium in which they live. But when the nutrients are exhausted and waste products increase without limit, a population crash in the colony inevitably occurs, as every freshman bacteriology student knows.

Less well known is the fact the expanding cities at the close of the twentieth century have come to resemble bacterial colonies that are on the verge of depleting their nutrient media to extinction.

Scientists have noticed similarities, for instance, between the changing shape of Los Angeles as seen by space satellite, and the changes visible in petri-dish cultures inoculated with *E. coli* bacteria, organisms that live in animal guts. Both the bacterial and human colonies expand in intricate fractal patterns, gradually filling the spaces surrounding them. Judging from satellite pictures, human beings in Los Angeles exhibit no more ability to control their own collective growth than do the *E. coli* germs.

Human reproduction also has some disturbing similarities to cancer. In an analysis he published in 1990 in the journal *Population and Environment*, Warren M. Hern, an anthropologist at the University of Colorado, noted some striking clinical parallels between a typical urban community and a malignant neoplasm, a cancerous tumor. They share rapid, uncontrolled growth, they invade and destroy adjacent tissues, and cells (or people) lost their differentiation, the concerted specialties and skills needed to sustain a society or a multicelled animal.

In his monograph, Dr. Hern included photographs taken from space satellites showing the growth of Baltimore and the colonization of the Amazon basin, side by side with photomicrographs of cancers of the lung and brain. They were hard to tell apart.

"The human species," Dr. Hern wrote, "is a rapacious, preda-

tory, omniecophagic [devouring its entire environment] species"
that exhibits all the pathological features of cancerous tissue. He
grimly concluded that the human "cancer" will most likely destroy its planetary host before dying out itself.

Many would disagree with that assessment, but for what it's
worth, my own experience as a journalist bears it out.

Facing the Population Facts

It seems astounding that there have been people making the argument that the planet has room for a steadily increasing population and that governments should stay out of the population management business. . . .

Some facts lend emphasis to the situation. Oil and fossil fuels
won't be replenished; trees take time to grow; and humans take
time to find means of making them grow faster. Polluted water
demands either high-level human organization (to prevent pollution) or high technology and expense to clean. Nuclear waste
simply can't be buried and forgotten. With the human race increasing at [an alarming] rate . . . *all* land will be needed shortly.

It is clear that changes in culture will be required if humans are
to survive the population crisis. Rural and agricultural civilizations needed more hands in the pretechnology age. They don't
any more, and the cultural premises that underlie this thinking
have to change. Ancient religious dogma also will have to accommodate that aspect of 21st-century life. Such change won't be
easy. Culture is imbedded in family socialization. Children learn
early and more by seeing than by reading. Population management policy, made by governments, will have to reach into the
home.

Llewellyn D. Howell, *USA Today*, September 1994.

And as we contemplate the social, political and economic
needs of, say, Somalia, it may be well to remember that kindly
instincts may do more harm than good when the real ogre is
overpopulation.

In 1990 *The Lancet*, Britain's leading medical journal, included
a paper and an accompanying editorial that shocked some readers by saying what public health experts have long acknowledged: there are things worse than merciful death.

The author of the *Lancet* paper, Dr. Maurice King of the department of public health medicine at the University of Leeds,
England, has devoted his career to saving lives, and he is no cal-
lous crank. But he has observed how excess population inflicts
famine and other curses on many parts of the Third World—and

how the population plague is engulfing more countries every year. Dr. King believes that for people caught in the demographic trap, there are only four possibilities.

They can stay where they are and die of starvation and disease; they can flee their homelands to seek salvation in more prosperous countries; they can kill themselves off by war or genocide; or, finally, they can live on foreign aid, "first as emergency relief and then, perhaps, indefinitely."

In countries racked by cholera and dysentery, many of the infants who in the past would have been doomed to die of dehydration can now be saved by oral rehydration, Dr. King noted. But when a nation afflicted by cholera is also dying of hunger, a thoughtful public health official must make Solomonic decisions. "Such . . . measures as oral rehydration should not be introduced on a public health scale," Dr. King wrote, "since they increase the man-years of human misery, ultimately from starvation."

In other words, millions of the world's people today would be better off dead, in Dr. King's opinion. Another British scientist, A.V. Hill, asked the following question in an address before the British Association for the Advancement of Science: "If ethical principles deny our right to do evil in order that good may come, are we justified in doing good when the foreseeable consequence is evil?"

No Stabilizing of Population

The conservative editors of *The Lancet* endorsed Dr. King's shocking conclusions.

"Global population grows by a remarkable 1 million more births than deaths every four days," the journal said. "If a bomb as destructive as the one that destroyed Hiroshima had been dropped every day since August 6, 1945, it would not have stabilized human numbers. . . .

"Through an unhappy combination of indecision, political cowardice, scientific illiteracy and bureaucratic myopia, will human numbers simply drift toward 15 billion?" *The Lancet* asked.

Among the answers proposed for the population bomb are an intensive campaign to educate and emancipate Third World women; a crash program to reduce the economic gulf between the rich and poor nations; and bounty to any man or woman willing to undergo sterilization.

But many scientists believe such measures will inevitably be too little and too late. One ingenious alternative that some experts are pondering would exploit a harmless virus to spread an epidemic of human sterility for a few years . . . long enough, perhaps, for the planet to catch its breath.

The scheme would depend on the meshing of two biological techniques, both of which are under investigation. This first is the development of an antifertility vaccine that would immunize a man or woman against conception for a few years, just as people are protected by vaccines against tetanus, smallpox and many other diseases.

The other prong of the new therapy would be the development of a bacterial or viral carrier that would make the antifertility factor infectious—capable, that is, of spreading throughout the human race on its own. Infection of a few individuals with the sterility bug might produce an epidemic that might spread widely enough to reduce the global birthrate for a while, until human beings became immune and resumed breeding.

An Unimaginable Solution?

One of the pioneers in this little-known but potentially important field of research is Dr. Cecil Hugh Tyndale-Biscoe of the Australian government's Commonwealth Scientific and Industrial Research Organization. He and other scientists are currently looking into the feasibility of springing something like this on Australia's overabundant rabbits. But the scientists involved are very much aware that the technique might work for humans as well, although, as Dr. Tyndale-Biscoe put it, "I can't imagine the government of Australia or any other nation authorizing such an approach to human population control."

I suppose journalists should be grateful to the Third World for supplying us with much of the dramatic misery we are able to pass on to our readers and viewers. But since most sensible people would want to avoid personal contact with the Third World, here are some of the warning symptoms I have observed that can tell us when the Third World is nigh:

- People refuse to stand in line for anything—buses, bread, railroad tickets, economic recovery, lifeboats—anything. Altruism toward strangers disappears, and devil-take-the-hindmost public behavior eclipses common decency.
- The clan take precedence over collective society in all matters, even while strolling the sidewalks. Friends or relatives fan out as they walk along, obstructing the way to strangers.
- Unenforced laws and edicts proliferate as rapidly as worthless money.
- Police take to carrying automatic weapons.
- Locally made products break, and the busiest and most prosperous artisans are the handymen and fixers.
- Range wars, wars for water rights and wars for simple living space become endemic.
- A pervasive religious hierarchy—priests, mullah or witch doctors—dominates society and suppresses dissent.

One reason the Third World illness is so hard to treat is that people persist in kidding themselves with euphemisms like

"Third World" and "developing." Argentina, for instance, is classified today as a "developing" country despite its retrograde progress over the past half century. In the 1930s, economists ranked Argentina as "developed," because of the riches it earned from its pampas, the vast grasslands that once produced enough cattle to feed a large part of the world. But because of the hemorrhaging of Argentine capital into foreign investments—and because of the country's backward social and political practices—Argentina has declined, and bankers now call it a "developing" country.

Why do otherwise reasonable people tolerate such distortions of language?

Now we have another misnomer called the "North-South Dialogue," a shouting match between the underprivileged nations of the Southern Hemisphere (a.k.a. "The Group of 77") and the alleged economic exploiters of the Northern Hemisphere, especially the United States. The North-South Dialogue has no more chance of a friendly resolution than the Hundred Years War, but it does, at least, provide work for diplomats and journalists.

Every Man for Himself

Elusive though a good definition of the Third World may be, I think it boils down to an overall lack of commonweal, a collective unwillingness to work for anything larger than a family or clan.

Like Pleistocene society, the Third World is violent. It offers constant work for people like my friend Clyde Collins Snow, a forensic anthropologist and defender of human rights, who travels far and wide searching for bones of the victims of Third World pogroms. Snow and his colleagues even sometimes manage to finger the state-sanctioned murderers themselves, for all the good it does them.

Experts like Dr. Snow have some interesting insights into human behavior. For many years Snow was employed by the Federal Aviation Agency as an expert in the identification of bodies from airplane crashes. He examined the pitiful bones of thousands of crash victims, and from them, he came to an appalling conclusion: in virtually all airliner crashes that leave any survivors, the passengers who pull through tend to be sturdy, active men—frequent-flyer business travelers, for the most part. Women and children don't survive crashes very often. The clear evidence, which the FAA tried at one time to suppress, is that in a crash, it's every man for himself, even if this means putting a heel in some child's face to get through the exit door.

That, to my mind, is the essence of the Third World.

"The 'problem' of population ceases to be one if there is adequate distribution of food supplies."

First World Overconsumption Causes Third World Poverty

Ivy George

Overpopulation is not the reason for Third World poverty, argues Ivy George in the following viewpoint—Japan, Holland, and Belgium are all densely populated, she observes, yet they are affluent. The problem is mainly distributional, George contends: The First World uses too much of the earth's resources, which it obtains through the market-based exploitation of the developing world. George concludes that future relations between First World and Third must be based on a solidarity that puts people first. George, a native of Madras, India, is professor of sociology at Gordon College in Wenham, Massachusetts.

As you read, consider the following questions:

1. How does the author say that birth rates were reduced in the Indian state of Kerala? How is this approach different from that employed by international organizations like the World Bank?
2. According to Rosa Luxemberg, cited by the author, what is a constant necessary condition for capitalist growth?
3. What kind of development does George want to see at both the individual and international levels?

Excerpted from Ivy George, "The Propaganda of Prosperity," *Sojourners*, August 1994. Reprinted with permission from *Sojourners*, 2401 15th St. NW, Washington, DC 20009. (202) 328-8842.

"My people are tired of development, they just want to live" was a sentiment expressed by Mexican author Gustavo Esteva in his remarks at a conference of the Society for International Development in 1985. Today as we are surrounded by the propaganda of prosperity, it is exceedingly difficult to ponder the exhaustion and exasperation contained in that statement. The 1980s and 1990s have witnessed expanded investment in countries that have relaxed foreign investment restrictions. The friendly logos of Western corporations are seen all over the world from neon-lit billboards to cars, from electronic items to television programs. In Eastern Europe, Marx is out and Ronald McDonald is in, and in Maoist China, Russian prostitutes are available for services.

The size of the global village is shrinking, the middle classes everywhere are swelling their ranks, the course of capitalism is secure and the "free" market has triumphed once and for all. That the gods of the West have won is the gospel of globalism. While this appears to be the surface picture in the popular press, there are nagging realities that continue to beleaguer the prosperous world—the ecological crisis and the population "problem." The two issues are closely related; I will take up the subject of population and consider how it fits in the global context.

Control of What?

What of the population question? What is so problematic about human population that we have to "control" it? Is talk of "population control" a semantic subterfuge for control of poor people, women, and other "inferior" peoples (frequently those of color)?

Is there a Darwinian urge to engage in triage—a medical practice in wartime when physicians save the strong and leave the weak to die? Is it a strategy for the rich and powerful everywhere to carry on as usual with no thought to control themselves and their numbers? Should we not extend the categorical link between poverty and population to include wealth as part of this triangle of crisis? No doubt these are some of the questions I might ask if my class or tribe of people were the targets of some top-down plans to control growth among our numbers.

The world, with more than six billion people, continues to see population increases in the two-thirds world despite a decline in total fertility rates there. From the standpoint of simple formulae, galloping birth rates and lagging economic growth rates are detrimental for social welfare. Economists and demographers see excessive population growth rates as direct threat to economic development, the maintenance of the environment, food security, and family health and welfare.

In light of this crisis, international development organizations,

27

the World Bank, foreign governments, and Third World governments have long encouraged and instituted family planning programs to reduce the numbers. Yet rapid population growth in and of itself has not always been a problem. Europe welcomed an increase in population during the Industrial Revolution, as did the United States in the 19th century.

The Population "Problem"

Besides the search for natural resources and raw materials, the value of human resources was also a factor in the rampages of colonialism in the past. Today governments such as those of Singapore and the United States welcome the growth in select populations through their family planning programs and immigration policies. Why then is growth in some segments of the population seen as a drag on development—especially if the world's food supply is adequate for the feeding of its people, as experts in the United Nations' Food and Agriculture Organization and other development agencies have attested to over the years?

The "problem" of population ceases to be one if there is adequate distribution of food supplies. The economist Amartya Sen defines the issue in terms of "entitlement," meaning there are large numbers of people who have no access to food because of their social locations. Mahatma Gandhi said, "There is enough in the world for everyone's need, but not for some people's greed."

At this juncture one asks, What is the link between population density and poverty? Is the relationship cyclical? While countries like Japan, Holland, and Belgium are densely populated, little energy is spent on the control of their populations and their people don't rank among the world's nutritionally needy. They trade their electronic goods for food. Conversely, the Indian state of Kerala (which, if classified as a separate country, would be ranked as the ninth poorest country in the world) has low birth rates compared to the rest of India and other low-income countries. Bolivia, with five people per square kilometer, is susceptible to famine.

Overpopulation or Overconsumption?

How many people is too many people? Is the "too many" in reference to their food needs? Are those who are concerned with needs and resources equally concerned with too few people having access to too much, such as Americans who represent 6 percent of the world's population and consume 35 percent of the world's resources? Further, is there a connection between overconsumption and overpopulation? In other words are consumptivitis and "over"-population two squares on the rubik's cube of social questions?

Analysts vary in their explanations of poverty and population.

Nigel Twose of Oxfam argues that while poverty that deprives poor people of access to contraceptives is the reason for large families, the poor themselves are reluctant to have large families. Demographers like Paul Demeny suggest otherwise—that poor families are not keen to plan families because children provide social security for their parents.

By permission of Chuck Asay and Creators Syndicate.

Regardless of the correctness of their conclusions, the implication is that reducing poverty will lead to the automatic reduction of population. However, as pointed out previously, there are other intervening variables in the equation. In Kerala, despite low per capita income, birth rates have fallen due to a series of redistributive measures undertaken by the government. These measures were enacted in the areas of land reform, price controls on food and other basic needs, free or inexpensive medical care, public housing, educational services, and various social and economic policies to improve the position of the poorest groups in the population.

Research on Kerala and the other Indian states reveals a weak connection between income and birth rates. Rather, studies show that the states' redistribution of wealth and provision of basic health care contributed significantly to changing birth rates. Demographer K.C. Zachariah notes that the shifts in birth rates were brought about in the following sequence: "reduction in infant and child mortality, followed by or along with an increase in female education, followed by redistributive policies, and finally the official family-planning programme."

Questioning Development

This cameo illustration of Kerala leads us to put the subject of population in a larger framework, one in which population is not treated in isolation from the more critical and imperative discussion of development and human welfare. Such an approach rids us of our perception of God's creatures as a "problem" we must "control." If we see that *all* societies are developing, our discussion of human population growth will cease to be in the oppositional categories of us and them, rich and poor, Christian and pagan, First World and Third World.

The imbalance of demographics exists in a more cosmic imbalance of power relations at multiple levels in the global community. *All* are enmeshed in this gridlock of power, hence it is counterproductive for the long term to isolate population growth and treat it as mere cause or effect.

"My people are tired of development, they just want to live." What is the experience of development that provokes such a response? Essentially, "development" is a post-colonial terminology and program that has emerged from the West to identify and evaluate itself and others on the basis of the success of Western industrial capitalism. The assumption behind development thought is that Western economic categories of "needs," "growth," "efficiency," and "productivity" are inherent goods in themselves and are thus universally applicable to all human societies. The post-colonial era in most non-Western societies has been one of adopting, accommodating, and adjusting to this model of "development"—otherwise known as progress.

Development's Colonial Heritage

There is one snag of chimerical proportions in this paradigm of "development"—the suggestion that development can be had without the colonization of "other" peoples, cultures, and ecologies. Historical and contemporaneous dishonesty abounds in the neglect of this reality among advocates of development. Rosa Luxemberg has pointed out that colonialism is a constant necessary condition for capitalist growth. Thus, while development produces certain forms of wealth, there is an attendant creation of particular forms of human misery and marginalization. It is this "maldevelopment" that Gustavo Esteva laments.

When development is enlarged beyond its conventionally economic connotations, we move toward developing in concert with the entire creation—not only economically, but socially, politically, ecologically, and spiritually. Stated simply, an alternative perspective on development is that it is relational. It is the process of becoming fully human in relation to God and all creation.

Beyond the "Simple Fix"

Although we expect the South to double its population by the year 2050, while the North's remains constant, this will only affect local conditions. The North will still consume twice as much as the South.

After we finish consuming, our garbage creates a major dilemma for the environment. . . .

A survey completed by the Organization for Economic Co-operation and Development of 20 industrialized countries found that industrial and municipal waste amounted to 1.6 tons per person per year—about 10 times that produced in developing countries.

Many argue that as the population grows, there is less land available to house and feed people. However, the problem is not simply family size, but the amount of land available for the poor. In Brazil, for example, a piece of privately-owned land the size of India sits untilled, while 20 million rural peasants are landless. . . .

Those who want to work to improve the quality of our environment and ascertain that resources will be available for all must look beyond the "simple fix" of population. Reducing our numbers won't be half as effective as reducing our consumption and redistributing land and resources so that everyone has a piece of our planet.

Ellen Dorsch, *Toward Freedom*, March 1993.

This scheme will resist the creation and objectification of poor people whereby they are turned into commodities subjected to the whims of others, or to the cruelties of impersonal forces. Development is about choice and responsibility for the individual that frees her to grow personally and socially. Development is about facilitating the individual to embark on twin journeys—an inner journey of spiritual realization and an outer journey of affecting structures around her. Development is about the twin goals of love and justice.

The Balance Sheet on Development

My use of the female pronoun with regard to development is not only to be gender inclusive but it is also to state the fact that women in the two-thirds world have been victims of development. Alongside her stand all indigenous people and nature. Scores of studies show that her workload has increased, her family structure has been split (with the men leaving to find employment), her control of and access to family resources has decreased, the "goods" of development such as health, education, and credit have all been systematically denied to her. This was the unanimous conclusion at the end of the U.N. Decade for Women in the 1980s. Two-thirds world feminists argue that development is a project of modern Western patriarchy.

However, it seems too late in the day to carry on earlier arguments about colonialism, capitalism, the West, and development. It is beyond dispute that Western values have a far-reaching impact on the destinies of poor people and the Earth. While the impact has been largely mixed, it is clear that rich and poor countries are inextricably intertwined in their relationship of dependence. This relationship of dependence is unequal, with the rich and powerful everywhere exploiting the poor to their advantage.

While communism was a reaction to the failings of capitalism, it too has been a flawed model. Both systems have failed to reckon with the ontological considerations of human nature operant in them. It is human nature to exploit, to overpower, and to subdue. It is equally in the nature of humans to resist evil in their dealings with power. Thus for all the homogenization brought on by globalization and development, resistance is also spawned from its recipients. Material prosperity has not been able to root out the universal desires to pursue or preserve values of community, language, culture, kinship, and religion.

In this heyday of global capitalism, there is no evidence at all that people everywhere will find work, shelter, food, clothing, health, education, and all the supercilious "goods" that the multinationals taunt in their faces. There is a widening gap between the haves and the have-nots globally. Increasing numbers of poor people and their children are part of this gap, and it will be these marginalized groups that will challenge the colonialism of development.

An Alternative Vision: Solidarity

Even as the virus of consumptivitis has caught the imagination of the rich and the poor alike, so also the dream and work of solidarity with God and creation grips a critical remnant of people age after age everywhere. This consciousness for solidarity does not stem from the hubris of having a "solution" to the "problem" of population or poverty. Rather, it rests in the knowledge that love, peace, and justice come about in the freedom of the subordinate partner—whereby all subordination is ended.

One does not merely have to imagine the possibilities. We have already been taken over by creative imagination. The recent report of the young boy in California who was embarrassed by hair loss from cancer treatment and the response of his teacher and several of his classmates to shave their heads in solidarity with him illustrates our capacity to give up freely. My husband is witness daily to the extraordinary care rendered to young gay AIDS patients by their partners, gay nurses, and others from the gay community. . . .

The process of solidarity is ongoing and unending—in our personal, national, and international relations we must understand the virtues of temperance and acceptance. The task of solidarity is a universal one. It is not merely for the First World in its relationship to the Third World, but it is also a challenge for the ruling elites in the Third World in their relationship to the marginalized.

Bound Together for Better or Worse

As the century draws to a close, calls for personal and collective introspection are a distant wail in a wilderness burgeoning with materialism. Poor Indian parents are driven to sell their children into bonded labor to nearby carpet factories that export their product to the United States. Little children in a south Indian fishing village are turning blind for want of vitamin A, as the fish caught by their parents are transported to satisfy the dietary whims of faraway consumers. Thai parents would rather gamble with the AIDS virus than with hunger as they send their little boys and girls off to Bangkok to satisfy the sexual fancies of tourists.

The complicity of the rich (from the megastructures of finance and trade to their personal acquisitiveness) in this violence is less than tenuous. In the main the rich would rather not lose their appetite, and so they flip the channel on the poor in their midst. They blame the victims and their "irresponsible" breeding behaviors with little discussion of their own responsibility in the tragedy.

My own hope for the future well-being of our world flags and flails as I see the overwhelming capacity of free-market capitalism and entrepreneurial Christianity to sway and "save" the world. I am moved by a diary entry by Min Chong Suk, a South Korean sewing-machine operator who works from 7 a.m. to 11:30 p.m. in a garment factory (perhaps she was the seamstress of my blue jeans!). She wrote, "We all have the same hard life. We are bound together with one string."

> *"The promise of the West that it will show the rest of the world how to attain its levels of affluence is simply an illusion."*

External Development Strategies Impoverish Third World Countries

Jeremy Seabrook

Western development of the Third World, argues Jeremy Seabrook, is simply a mutated form of colonialism that is as exploitative and destructive as its predecessor. The Southern, or developing, countries buy into this capitalist theology, the author explains, because they desire the luxury they see in the North. What they do not realize, he contends, is that the North's wealth is based on the South's exploitation. Development for Third World citizens means being deprived of their self-sufficient, land-based economies in order to be taken advantage of and impoverished in the cities, he concludes. Seabrook has worked as a teacher, lecturer, social worker, and journalist. He has written numerous stage, television, and radio plays and is the author of 20 books, including *The Unprivileged, What Went Wrong?, The Leisure Society*, and *The Myth of the Market*.

As you read, consider the following questions:

1. Why were the goals of colonialism subsumed under the guise of development, in Seabrook's account?
2. What does the author say has been the effect of capitalism on people's lives in the developed countries?

All over the world, more and more people are being disadvantaged by a version of development which, even as it creates wealth, leaves them with a sense of loss and impoverishment. When they resist the violence done to them in the name of development, they are often branded by their own governments as 'extremists', 'criminals', 'wreckers'; at best, enemies of progress and modernization.

Among the people marginalized in this way are many indigenous communities; the inhabitants of forests and uplands, evicted by loggers and mining companies; those forced from ancestral lands, who have no choice but to live in squalid city slums. There, they die of grief for their defunct way of life, or they destroy themselves with the destructive consolations of alcohol and drugs, which industrial society offers them for their loss. Nomads, pastoralists, fishing communities, those ousted from subsistence or self-reliant farming, are seen as obstacles to development, as indeed are the urban poor themselves. The urban poor had fled to the harsh refuge of the cities precisely because they could no longer earn a living from devastated lands. Many had been compelled to give up farming by the rising costs of inputs or the pressure of agribusiness. Even when they arrive in the urban centres, they find no peace; their fragile shelters are routinely broken up by police and the military; the land they occupy is required by a different kind of 'developer'. There are, worldwide, more and more environmental refugees, developmental displaced persons, those caught up in wars, many of which are caused by a struggle for resources or ethnic differences between people who had lived without conflict for hundreds of years. Indeed, the victims of development are far more numerous than those removed from their habitat by megaprojects like dams, hydroelectric schemes, airports and military installations. Upheaval, displacement and endless moving on are part and parcel of processes which have at their heart the subversion of self-reliance, the undermining of sufficiency, the destruction of satisfactions, which are found outside an expanding global marketplace.

What Kind of Development?

For what is this version of 'development' if not the export model of an economistic ideology, which has served the West so well for over two hundred years? Anisur Rahman says that 'development' was originally a Western promise to the South, designed to counter the danger of socialism. 'It was the threat of Bolshevik revolution inspiring social revolutions in the Third World that was countered by a promise of "development" and "development assistance" to help underdeveloped societies to catch up with the "developed". Development was exclusively defined as economic development, reducing the degree of progress and maturity in a society to be measured by the level of its production. The attraction of massive external finance and thrilling technology generated client states in the "underdeveloped" world, where oligarchies able to capture the organs of state could enrich and empower themselves as a class relative to the wider society, to whom "development plans" one after the other at the national level, and subsequently, at the global level, were offered as a perpetual hope for prosperity.

'The result: the economic benefits of such development have not even trickled down to the vast majority of the people in most countries honourably referred to as "developing". But the most fundamental loss has been the obstruction of the evolution of indigenous alternatives for societal self-expression and authentic progress.'

The Western—it should perhaps be called global, now that alternatives to it have been declared both inefficacious and unnecessary—economic system is an ideological construct. It is a mechanism for transforming all the varieties of wealth on earth into money; for concentrating it in the hands of those who already have it; and finally, for legitimizing the process that provides so happy an outcome. It is a rationale for global social injustice and institutionalized exploitation. The union of the logic of capitalist expansion and the furtherance of a Western tradition of colonialism is consummated.

From Colonialism to Development

Economics is neither science nor art, but ideology. Its system of accounting is extremely selective about what it includes and what it omits, in terms of both costs and benefits, profits and forfeits, advantages and penalties. This partial and fragmented view of human affairs is now the focus of an evangelizing fervour by Western governments and financial institutions.

Indeed, the ideological underpinning of its economic system is now the bearer of a far older universalizing mission of the West. Formerly, this mission was carried in a less sophisticated, and now officially discredited, belief; namely, that it was the destiny of the West to civilize and convert the backward peoples of the earth to the truths vouchsafed to the West alone. The certitudes that animated earlier generations of missionaries, colonists and bringers of enlightenment now work through far more effective vehicles of domination. The IMF [International Monetary Fund], the World Bank, the GATT [General Agreement on Tariffs and Trade] negotiators, the transnational corporations and those Western governments that insist that the recipients of their aid must provide evidence of 'good governance' and 'sound economic policies' are now the eager transmitters of messages of

36

economic salvation. Within the Western countries themselves, the ideology of economics is so deeply rooted that even radicals and dissidents rarely call into question those revelations that have deserted Bibles and scriptures, and have taken up their abode in the prescriptions and edicts of economists, those masters of what they call 'the real world'.

A Criminally Unequal System

The workings of capitalism constantly produce criminal misuse and distribution of the world's wealth. Just one nuclear U.S. aircraft carrier costs more than the Gross National Product in 53 countries. Tremendous wealth is spent to enforce the world's status quo, while 20 million children in the Third World die each year from hunger and malnutrition.

Stores in cities like Paris and New York routinely offer handbags and watches for $1,500, while each of these luxury items costs more than the average person lives on *for a whole year* in over 40 countries.

In the imperialist countries there is about one doctor per 400 people and an explosion of unnecessary cosmetic surgery for the rich. In oppressed countries, there is an average of one doctor for 7,000 people and *hundreds of millions* of people die from easily preventable diseases.

In short, the labor of billions of people has steadily increased the *basis* for eliminating poverty, hunger, and suffering—but the workings of world capitalism have systematically created more and more suffering *in the midst of more and more wealth*.

Revolutionary Worker, July 24, 1994.

The sanctification of the 'science' of economics serves to conceal the narrow, partial and, above all, fiduciary nature of its accounting system. The exclusions, the violence and dispossessings which the Western system now inflicts on the South are seen by its votaries as nothing more than the unfortunate byproducts of processes that are as necessary as they are ultimately benign. Yet it simply eliminates everything that is inconvenient to its version of profit and loss—the ruin of the resource-base of the earth, the reduction of biodiversity, the injury to a large proportion of the world's people, the multiple forms of impoverishment which accompany its limited vision of riches. These consequences of its workings are referred to as 'externalities', that is, as having nothing to do with economics; and yet economics continues to colonize and expand over more and more areas of our experience.

The quasi-religious element in the economic dogmas of the IMF and World Bank is scarcely new. The 'hidden hand', whereby the pursuit of private gain is transmuted into public virtue, was always, presumably, the hand of God.

The laws of political economy were seen as a regulatory mechanism, whereby a fallen human nature could none the less redeem itself through the creation of wealth. These convictions, hardened, concealed beneath the self-justifying, opaque and impenetrable calculations of economics, underlie the sweeping, universalizing doctrines now being imposed on the whole world, notwithstanding the human and environmental desolation they cause. Thus, the IMF looks approvingly on 'the timely and decisive policy reforms of India'. The British prime minister, John Major, agrees to limited forgiveness of Third World debt, on condition that the countries thus favoured submit to the advice of the IMF. His foreign secretary, Douglas Hurd, insists that the conditions for disbursement of the EC [European Community] aid budget should be 'the pursuit of sound social and economic policies'. Indeed, during the negotiations between the government of India and the IMF in the summer of 1991, one of the 'conditionalities' of the loan, which the government resisted, was a cut in food subsidies. (The word 'conditionalities' is an interesting euphemism; it sounds less harsh than 'laying down conditions', which is what victors usually do to the vanquished.) That the representatives of the Western financial institutions should even consider the option of reducing food subsidies in a country where as many as 40 per cent of the people do not have sufficient purchasing power to provide themselves with an adequate diet indicates something of the priorities of the IMF. It is clear that hunger, if not starvation, has become an instrument of economic adjustment.

A More Subtle Domination

Earlier justifications of Western dominance obviously had to change. Assumptions of a civilizing mission based on racial superiority suffered a severe setback in the middle years of the twentieth century, as a result of the devastation wreaked by Nazism and Fascism in the heartland of Western civilization itself. That these excesses were no temporary aberration in the ideology of the West may be understood by anyone familiar with the apologies offered for Western violence against those people whom centuries of colonists and empire builders had sought to subdue militarily. 'The coolie, though fond of money, prefers perfect idleness, and it is frequently necessary to drive him out of his village to force him to earn a good day's wages on the neighbouring railway works,' they said with a candour which their descendants have learned to avoid. After the Second

38

World War, however, the open expression of that form of arrogance ceased to be a respectable vehicle for the continuing mission of bringing the backward and recalcitrant peoples of the world to an acknowledgement of their own inferiority, dependence and subordination.

A more subtle and efficient form of domination was required. And what could have been more acceptable and benign than a promise to share with the whole world the secret of the West's spectacular capacity for self-enrichment? That this secret involved centuries of subjugation and plunder of the South has not deterred many Third World governments from eager acceptance of the advice, instructions and, indeed, orders now issuing from the IMF, World Bank and Western governments. As decayed Communist regimes and disillusioned, sometime independent former colonial territories alike hasten to implement these prescriptions, we are clearly in the presence of mass conversions of an order and scope to which those other bearers of revelation, the Marxists, could never, in their wildest, most scientifically socialist dreams, aspire. Their transforming visions were, by comparison, the most idle of utopias. Anisur Rahman describes how, under the promise of 'development', 'the vast majority of the people were classified as "poor", and therefore as objects of sympathy, paternalistic intervention and assistance. Many of these people, under the blinding light of compassionate observation which was flashed upon them, have internalized this negative self-image. Perceiving themselves is "inferior", they have sought to be "developed" by the "superiors", surrendering their own values, cultures, their own accumulated knowledge and wisdom. Others have been forced to do so by the sheer power of "development" effort, which itself has concentrated power and privilege and wealth in a few hands with the ability to subjugate and exploit the broader masses; and which has uprooted vast masses of people from their traditional life and lifestyles *to become inferior citizens in alien environments*. Thus they have suffered not only economic impoverishment, but also a loss of identity and ability to develop endogenously, authentically, within their own culture and capabilities; *a deeper human misery* which as economists we were not trained to recognize.'

The Triumph of Western Ideology

The exuberant and self-confident advice now being tendered to the countries of the South by the IMF and World Bank should be seen as part of Western rejoicing over the death of all rivals to its definition of development. It is certainly no celebration of the end of misery and injustice. Far from it. It is simply that misery and injustice no longer appear to have the power to pose a threat to Western interests; which suggests that new, unimagined poverties may still be in store for those who already see themselves with nothing. Indeed, so powerful has the West become, that seductive voices are raised once more, declaring not only that inequality and social injustice are irremediable, but that they are necessary, even an essential prerequisite, for the creation of that form of wealth whose showy iconography has seized hold of the imagination of the people of the world.

That we are confronted by blind faith in the 'miracles' of Western economics is clear from the fact that it is not disconfirmed by mere evidence. Those countries that have faithfully followed IMF structural adjustment plans and corrective macroeconomic policies (and how mechanistically Marxist some of these sound, as though the ideological winners had learned a thing or two from those they have vanquished)—Brazil, Peru, the Philippines, for example—have seen their landscapes ravaged, their resources gutted, in their effort to service fathomless debts; they have seen their forests felled, their cities teeming with refugees, the indices of ill-health, malnutrition and mortality worsening. This has not prevented other, desperate Third World governments from following the same path, hoping perhaps that they will somehow be delivered from the inescapable consequences of their imposed policy 'choices'. . . .

Nothing now apparently stands in the way of Western expansionism in the world. Nothing can prevent its violent incursions into lives and livelihoods, its evictions and uprootings of people, its forcible refashioning of custom and tradition, in order to maintain the flow of wealth from global poor to rich. For the promise of the West that it will show the rest of the world how to attain its levels of affluence is simply an illusion. That experience of the West, which has crucially depended on centuries of exploitation and plunder, and the sustained transfer of riches from South to North, is not replicable in those countries now following Western prescriptions. There, we can expect to see only intensified social dislocation, further excesses of violence, secessionism and terrorism, casteism and class conflict, kidnappings, bombings and repression. This will be viewed in the North as evidence only of corrupt rulers, instability and the inferiority of those people afflicted by it. Its model of development will remain untainted; its faith in its ideology will not be impaired by the rumblings of distant atrocities and televized brutality; its unquiet enjoyment of poisoned privilege will be untouched. . . .

The Cost of Greening the West

At the same time, the West expresses its dedication to cleaning up an environment which it has recklessly polluted for two centuries. This can be understood only in terms of its intentions towards the South. What is not spoken in this project is that it can be accomplished only at great cost. And while the West restores and landscapes and ritually cleanses its own damaged and degraded industrial sites, it is at the same time passing on the costs of sustaining business as usual to other, less defended parts of the world, precisely in the name of 'development'. This is the meaning, not only of the dumping of toxic wastes in the Two-Thirds World [i.e., the Third World], but also of the export of dangerous technology prohibited in the United States or Japan, of the more intensive resource-culling of the seas, the forests and fertile lands of the South, of the accelerated ransacking of the earth. The deepest dishonesty lies in persuading the people of the South—or at least its leaders—that by following the path pioneered by the West, their people, too, can freely partake of the fruits of industrial growth, which the people of the West so conspicuously enjoy.

The poor cannot have what the rich have without irreparable damage to the resource-base. The promise that they can is an illusion; and while the credulous leaders of the Two-Thirds World seek to accommodate themselves to the exhortations and advice coming from the West, their people, especially the poorest, are paying the costs of this lie. The spread of the West's dogmas cannot liberate these countries. For under the influence of these, the people of the South will have to reduce their claims on their own resources in order that the West may continue in the way of life to which it has become accustomed; indeed, upon which its people have developed a terrifying dependency. The conspicuous environmental improvements in the West, like its conspicuous and continuing extravagant life-style, are paid for by the ousting of the peoples of the South from the sites where valuable minerals lie, by the evictions from the forests of Sarawak [Borneo], Indonesia or the Philippines; by the impoverishment of Lima [Peru], the violence of São Paulo [Brazil], the slums of Calcutta [India]; by the chaotic growth of Lagos [Nigeria], Cairo [Egypt] or Nouakchott [Mauritania]; by the poisoning of the peoples of South-East Asia by Japanese technology, the appropriation of the natural beauty of Penang [Malaysia] or Goa [India] for tourists.

The Colonialist Monstrosity

The role of the South in the new world order proves to be a very old one: to be suppliers of labour, cash-crops, amenities, playgrounds for the rich. It used to be called colonialism, but continues under the—until now—less controversial designation of 'development'. The servicing of debt, the flow of wealth from poor to rich, the terms of trade, the brain drain, transfer pricing and the multiple manipulations of the transnationals are a few of the mechanisms whereby older patterns of conquest and domination have mutated into more efficient and more opaque

41

forms, now ennobled by being allied to economic necessity.

More and more people are caught up in this monstrosity as it rolls over the earth, laying waste, not merely the face of the planet, but all human societies and relationships that stand in its way, all other ways of answering need, all customs and traditions that are an obstacle to its further expansion. What we see is a confrontation between an aberrant version of riches and a grotesque form of poverty in a world which could—which still could—furnish all humanity with a decent, and even noble, sufficiency.

*"The keys to using and maintaining a
transplanted technical system are . . . to be found
. . . in the education . . . of the user."*

Internal Conditions
Perpetuate Third
World Poverty

Jean-Jacques Salomon and André Lebeau

There are many internal problems in developing countries, such
as overpopulation and a lack of an educated citizenry, that make
economic development difficult, explain Jean-Jacques Salomon
and André Lebeau in the following viewpoint. Many developing
countries have found it hard to import Western technology and
graft it on top of societies that are not adequately prepared for it,
Salomon and Lebeau contend. An increasingly uneven distribution of income often results, the authors conclude, along with
popular resentment for the Western system that produced these
dislocations. Salomon is professor at the Conservatoire Nationale
des Arts et Metiers (CNAM) in Paris. Lebeau is head of the
French Weather Bureau, and is also a professor at CNAM.

As you read, consider the following questions:

1. What do Salomon and Lebeau say separates the development
   experience in Asia from that of many African nations?
2. How is technology a "social process," according to the authors?

43

Anyone who travels in the Third World or reads the reports of the international organizations is aware that remarkable progress has been made, yet the results differ so widely that it is unwise to use them to make general predictions about the future. There are still too many places where food production lags behind population growth, even though many more countries than before have managed to increase their level of self-sufficiency thanks to the spread of high-yield crops and of agricultural advisory services.

Neither India nor China, for example, is in the least what it was less than a quarter century ago, when both suffered from frequent famines, epidemics, and natural disasters. The introduction of new varieties of grain and the improvement in farming methods generally in India, Pakistan, and Indonesia have speeded up their transformation into producers of surpluses. In China, after the upheavals of the Cultural Revolution, the stimulus of a moderate dose of private enterprise and competition helped a large section of the rural population to improve its position by at least 50 percent between 1980 and 1984.

Some Technical Successes

These spectacular results derived above all from better irrigation (more efficient pipes and channels, many more pumps installed on wells and riverbanks) and the huge increase in the number of high-yield varieties of wheat and rice. Between 1950 and 1980, the irrigated area in India rose from 50 to 100 million acres and in China from 40 to 80 million. Countries as different as Burma (now Myanmar), South Korea, Pakistan, and the Philippines doubled the area under irrigation. These results also depended upon the quality of the people running the agricultural sector and whether they encouraged the spread of new techniques arising out of agricultural research. Another contribution came from the implementation of a more efficient grain policy based on better management of stocks and some intervention as regards prices and markets (in China this meant in fact a limited reintroduction of free-market mechanisms).

These successes in Asia are in sharp contrast to the equally spectacular failures in Africa. Nevertheless, thirty years ago it was about the desperate food shortages in overcrowded Asia that the experts were raising the alarm, whereas the situation in Africa, where population growth was slower, did not worry them as much. Both the assessment of the current situation and the forecasts made by Edouard Saouma, head of the United Nations Food and Agriculture Organization (FAO), in a report published in 1986 are catastrophic: Although they were virtually self-sufficient 25 years ago, most African countries cannot now feed themselves; unless there is a radical shift in the policies of the countries concerned, along with massive aid from the richer nations, the situation can only get worse by the end of the century. Since 1961, per capita food production has fallen by almost 20 percent and the population explosion is frightening: over 3 percent per annum on average.

Internal Obstacles to Success

Why are there empty stomachs in one area and full storehouses in another? Virtually all the experts now agree in seeking the main reasons in the social and cultural background of the countries and in policies detrimental to agriculture. This does not mean we should discount the physical constraints imposed by climate and geography or the consequences of fluctuations in the prices of primary products. Nevertheless, drought and the deteriorating terms of trade are useful alibis to disguise problems that have nothing to do with the state of the heavens or of the commodity markets. The *internal* explanations for the setbacks, which are beginning to be recognized by the countries themselves, are far more weighty than any others: the contempt for food crops, exhaustion of good soils, destruction of forests (10 million acres per year!), lack of trained people to educate and advise farmers, rural institutions stifled by overgrown bureaucracies, the attraction of the cities and of work in service industries, too many officials, political instability, governments without political legitimacy, and so on.

Nonetheless, taken overall, the developing countries have made undeniable progress. Between 1960 and 1984, the average annual increase in gross domestic product (GDP) per capita was about 2.8 percent (not including China and some oil-exporting countries). As for the oil-importing countries, the highest growth has been in Latin America and the Far East, with rates well above the overall average of 3.4 percent for all the developing countries taken together. These rates have been 50 percent higher for a quarter century than was the case for today's industrialized nations during a whole century of development: 2.7 percent on average between 1850 and 1960.

Different Success Rates

Clearly there are enormous differences among countries and regions. The lowest rates of growth (2.9 to 1.8 percent) are found in the poorest countries of Africa and Asia. The rise in oil prices and the recession in the 1980s made the economic situation of some countries even worse than before. In Africa and Latin America, at least a decade of increase in per capita income seems to have been lost for this reason. In Asia, on the other hand, many countries have achieved impressive rates of growth (8.6 percent annual average increase throughout the period 1960–1982).

From the disasters in Ethiopia and the Sahel region, to stagnation if not decline in Ghana or Zaire, to the encouraging results in countries like India, Brazil, Indonesia, Malaysia, or, more recently, China, the disparities in the growth rates of per capita incomes reflect the range of situations as regards population growth, resources, and above all the choice of economic and political strategies. Nevertheless, twenty-seven countries more than doubled their per capita GDP between 1960 and 1982: Ten are oil exporters (Algeria, Ecuador, Egypt, Indonesia, Iraq, Libya, Mexico, Nigeria, Saudi Arabia, and Syria), and five are classed as newly industrialized countries, or NICs (Brazil, Hong Kong, Singapore, South Korea, and Taiwan).

Bureaucracy Hinders African Development

Soon after they gained independence, many countries in Africa rejected the political and economic systems that they had inherited from their colonial rulers and adopted institutional frameworks which they believed would provide the state with the wherewithal to provide for national development. Several of the new African rulers argued that in order to bring together the multitude of ethnic groups in existence in their countries and provide for economic growth and development, it was necessary to have strong central governments. . . .

Over three decades of state control of economic activities has failed to rid African societies of mass poverty and deprivation. Massive state control has instead encouraged and advanced nepotism, bureaucratic and political corruption, and constrained the development of viable and sustainable economic and governmental systems. When the decade of the 1990s began, Africa was still the poorest and least developed continent in the world. Despite massive flows of development assistance, the standard of living of most Africans has either declined since the 1960s or has improved only marginally. The significant economic potential that could have been used to improve human conditions in the continent has been squandered through perverse economic policies, bureaucratic corruption, and financial mismanagement.

John Mukum Mbaku, *The Journal of Social, Political & Economic Studies*, Summer 1994.

Economic growth has (far) outstripped the forecasts generally proposed twenty-five years ago. In spite of the recession, at the beginning of the 1980s the developing countries were producing six times their 1950 output of goods and services, and their manufacturing output at the beginning of the 1990s reached a figure eight times that of 1950. These countries' manufactured products increased their share of the Organization for Economic

Cooperation and Development (OECD) market from 7.1 percent in 1955 to 17.8 percent in 1981. In human terms, the average life expectancy in developing countries rose from 42 to 59 years between 1950 and 1980 (from 40 to 56 years if China is excluded), while infant mortality among children under the age of four fell from 28 to 12 percent (including China).

The Reasons for Difference

These improvements in the Third World as a whole cannot be denied, even if the enthusiasm of the applause should vary to take account of the considerable differences among countries and—above all within each country—between those social groups that have genuinely benefited and those that have been left behind. Herein lies the essential difference between the industrialized and developing countries: In the 1950s and 1960s, growth in the industrialized nations substantially reduced the incidence of poverty, whereas in the developing countries growth has increased it. Policies aimed at development, in those instances where they were followed resolutely, have been hindered by the twin problems of a soaring birthrate and a highly skewed income distribution.

The true outcome is therefore not clear-cut, and the successes remain tiny in comparison with the scale of problems still to be solved. Full storehouses on their own do not fill empty bellies. Nobody any longer dies as a result of famine in India or China, and that is a major advance; but the general (though unquestionable) improvement does not prevent malnutrition linked to poverty from continuing to exist. The full stores are a sign that the policy of increasing agricultural production has worked, but they do not prove that the crucial challenge of development— the fact that huge sections of the population are close to destitution—has been dealt with. "Neither the growth of agricultural production nor self-sufficiency in food defined by the criterion of imports and exports alone, nor the existence of sizeable stocks is therefore a guarantee that malnutrition has been conquered."

The Wrong Focus

The excessive enthusiasm of most countries for development based on heavy industry, exploitation of mineral resources, and production of consumer goods has in fact made the distortions in their economies and the social disparities all the greater. It was thought that the surest way to economic "takeoff" was to focus on manufacturing, but when this eventually happened, the benefits of growth did not spread to reach most of the population. This choice of priorities, for which the industrialized countries and the international organizations are partly responsible, led to a substantial difference between the rates of growth of manufacturing and agricultural production.

The rate of increase in food production has been totally inadequate in comparison with the enormous population growth in the developing countries (over 1 billion extra mouths, of whom 600 million were in Asia, between 1965 and 1983). Even in those countries where food production grew faster than the population, the poorest people living in rural areas, who make up the majority, were not much better off. And in the cities and towns, the expansion of manufacturing and services has not generated enough new jobs to absorb the increase in the numbers of jobseekers.

Consequently, progress in economic terms did not stop the numbers of poor people from rising. In 1980 the World Bank estimated that about 800 million lived in extreme poverty, almost half of them in India, 130 million in sub-Saharan Africa, another 130 million in South Asia and the Far East, and 140 million in the Western Hemisphere, North Africa, and the Middle East. The problem of poverty in the Third World, whether seen in terms of production or of incomes, is still essentially one of rural underdevelopment, despite the continuing rise everywhere in the proportion of the population working or looking for work in the cities.

Developmental Shortcuts?

It is in the light of this state of affairs with all its contradictions—encouraging in some respects, depressing in others—that questions should be raised about the true scope for possible "shortcuts," that is, the idea that there are ways of catching up to the industrialized countries by quicker routes than the century (at least) that the latter took to industrialize.

The very notion of "catching up" is not that obvious: Is development really a race in which the laggards can hope to draw abreast of the front-runners? Putting the question in these terms does not mean that we regard underdevelopment as unavoidable; rather we are suggesting that there are other routes to development besides those followed by the most highly industrialized countries, and in particular that it is not necessary to rely heavily on the most advanced technologies. The overall progress achieved so far, and by the newly industrialized countries in particular, shows that the struggle to modernize is far from hopeless. But is "the last shall be first" true for the race between nations?

There is, of course, the example of Japan as a country that has made the transition from having a feudal society and a basically rural economy to being among the leading exporters of advanced manufactured products. But this has not happened overnight. Japanese industrial might is not a recent or even a postwar phenomenon; the Japanese had absorbed, and indeed rapidly mastered, Western scientific and technological knowledge well before Pearl Harbor. With the Meiji revolution/restoration (1868), Japan started to industrialize only just after France, and at that time already had acquired the vision, the means, and the discipline to implement what was planned as a long-term effort.

Japan's Secret

Among the components of this effort, none was more crucial in the long run than the policy on education. The Japanese deliberately chose to import, adopt, and adapt the kinds of education and training they felt had proved the most successful for the purposes of industrialization in Europe and the United States. The University of Tokyo was established in 1877, when the first Japanese scientific societies were also created, and the Imperial Academy of Sciences was founded two years later. Japan effectively stepped into the modern world when the samurai, forced to abandon their feudal rights, took the decision virtually collectively to switch their energies to studying science and technology. They were the dominant social group, but there were not enough posts for all of them in government, and only about 10 percent of them could make their careers in public life. Because they could not compete with the other castes in the traditional areas of agriculture, handcrafts, and trade, the former warriors—who had been aware of Western technological superiority ever since Commodore Perry's visit and the opening of the ports—made themselves the pioneers and the supervisors of industrialization.

While it is true that the first graduates of the Imperial University in science and engineering were drawn from the former warrior caste, we should overlook neither the fact that the social and economic organization of pre-Meiji Japan was well suited to the process of industrialization, nor (more important) the role of the education and training policy steadfastly pursued for over a century. From this angle, many European countries did not embark on their Industrial Revolutions much ahead of Japan.

People talk about the "Japanese miracle" as if it sprang from nothing, like Athena from the head of Zeus, fully formed and not needing to mature. In fact, however, the Japanese realized early on that industrialization required coordination between the trends in technical progress and the pace of training a skilled workforce at every level of activity. They were not content simply to concentrate on training or retraining top managers: Economic growth was accompanied by a commensurate increase in the numbers of middle managers and skilled workers. To see a "Japanese miracle" is in fact to be blind to the determination—and the scale—with which Japan planned, implemented, and maintained its policies for education and training *over the long term* in order to meet the growing demands of industrialization.

The real question raised by the strategies of looking for short-cuts is, What are the costs involved? "Leapfrogging" is possible, obviously, but experience shows that this almost always means progress for a tiny group within the country concerned. Efforts to achieve rapid industrialization, connected with the latest technologies, have led everywhere to a substantial increase in the disparities between the few who share the gains and the vast majority of the population who at best can only gather the crumbs. It is hardly surprising if this approach, through which only a small section of the urban population gets the direct benefits, comes up against the inertia of the rural masses, if not signs of resistance and outright rejection. . . .

Technology in Society

Why is it that modern science, as we have known it since the seventeenth century—since Galileo—has developed only in Europe and not in China (or India)? And why is it that until the fifteenth century the Chinese were far more efficient than the Europeans at applying their knowledge of nature to practical human needs? According to Joseph Needham, the great Cambridge scholar who has written a superb history of Chinese science and technology, the answer to both these questions lies above all in the social, intellectual, and economic structures of the different civilizations.

The history of science is not alone in showing that certain societies or civilizations, at particular periods in history, are more efficient than others in their mastery of scientific knowledge and the exploitation of technical progress. In our own time, while people talk about the new technologies (computers, telecommunications, biotechnologies, new materials) as a further stage in the Industrial Revolution, it is obvious to everyone that there are wide differences in the capacities of different societies to take advantage of the possibilities opened up by the new technologies and, even more, in their ability to contribute to the conception, development, and production of new products and processes.

While social and cultural factors—from attitudes and beliefs to economic, political, and social organization—affect the role that science and technology play in a given country, the spread of new knowledge, products, and processes developed thanks to science and technology in turn transforms social structures, behavior, and attitudes. Technology itself is a *social process* among many others: It is not a question of technical development on one side and social development on the other, like two entirely different worlds or processes. Technical change and society constantly interact and alter one another. In this sense, a society is defined

50

no less by those technologies it is capable of creating than by those it chooses to use and adapt in preference to others. . . .

All in all, there is no inevitability in technical change: Neither its pace nor its direction is predetermined (even if it is unwise to underestimate the strength of certain nations or industrial lobbies in imposing their factories or products), and the success of an innovation is never assured. Technology influences economics and history, but it is itself the product and expression of culture. The same innovations can therefore produce very different results depending on the structure and values of the society (or at different periods in the same society). "Technological change is often discussed as if its rate and direction were something predetermined, and as if it were something to which individuals and society could make only rather passive adaptations," Nathan Rosenberg has written. "Actually, these things are largely the outcome of a social process in which individuals and larger collectivities make choices determining the allocation of resources, and these allocations inevitably reflect the prevailing system of values."

When Worlds Collide

Another distinction needs to be drawn, this one between the impact of technical progress on the industrialized countries where these advances are initiated, and the penetration of traditional societies by imported technologies. The local value system in the latter case is in direct conflict with the foreign (often, indeed, alien) values conveyed by the techniques developed according to Western thought processes. Traditional societies have so little freedom to choose the technologies appropriate to their needs that their propulsion into the modern age often seems more endured than desired. Hence arise the limits and sometimes the failures of certain experiments in modernization conducted at headlong speed, without regard for the economic, social, or cultural realities of the societies into which they are being introduced. The utilization of science and technology cannot be reduced simply to inserting know-how, techniques, and methods into a social fabric that has not been prepared beforehand. . . . Transfers of technology require much more than the movement of a physical object from one place to another. Learning to use new technologies has a social dimension: Each new tool involves a new type of organization, a new discipline, a new way of working. The keys to using and maintaining a transplanted technical system are not to be found in the instruction manual provided by the supplier but in the education and training of the user. To think that one can skimp on this training is to run the risk of turning the keys in vain or of breaking the machine.

51

Periodical Bibliography

The following articles have been selected to supplement the diverse views presented in this chapter.

Jan Knippers Black — "Development Jujitsu: Looking on the Bright Side," *Studies in Comparative International Development*, Spring 1993. Available from Transaction, Dept. 4010, Rutgers University, New Brunswick, NJ 08903.

Stephen Budiansky — "Ten Billion for Dinner, Please," *U.S. News & World Report*, September 12, 1994.

Sonia Correa and Rosalind Petchesky — "Exposing the Numbers Game: Feminists Challenge the Population Control Establishment," *Ms.*, September/October 1994.

Sally Ethelston — "Gender, Population, Environment," *Middle East Report*, September/October 1994. Available from 1500 Massachusetts Ave. NW, Suite 119, Washington, DC 20005.

Llewellyn D. Howell — "The Population Bomb Keeps Ticking," *USA Today*, September 1994.

Jodi L. Jacobson — "Gender Bias: Roadblock to Sustainable Development," *Worldwatch Paper 110*, September 1992. Available from Worldwatch Institute, 1776 Massachusetts Ave. NW, Washington, DC 20036.

Robert W. Lee — "The Grim Harvest of Population Control," *The New American*, September 5, 1994. Available from 770 Westhill Blvd., Appleton, WI 54914.

John Mukum Mbaku — "Bureaucratic Corruption and Reform in Africa," *The Journal of Social, Political, and Economic Studies*, Summer 1994.

Brian Robertson — "Third World Bucks U.S. Bid to Mold Policy on Population," *Insight on the News*, August 22, 1994. Available from PO Box 96067, Washington, DC 20090-6067.

Francis Abrahamer Rothstein — "Women's Work, Women's Worth: Women, Economics, and Development," *Cultural Survival Quarterly*, Winter 1992.

Emily Smith — "Cairo: A Victory for Women—and the World," *Business Week*, September 26, 1994.

Toward Freedom — "Redefining Development: For Whom? For What?" October 1992.

How Can Third World Development Be Achieved?

The
Third
World

Chapter Preface

Nineteen ninety-four marked the fiftieth anniversary of the World Bank and the International Monetary Fund (IMF)—two international lending institutions that have had more impact on Third World development than any other organizations. Since the early 1970s, the bank and the fund have instituted structural adjustment programs (SAPs) throughout the developing world. These programs are designed to integrate Third World nations into the world trading system as a means of reducing their debts to Northern banks.

Some believe that structural adjustment programs have condemned Third World nations to poverty. Because these programs encourage countries to increase their exports to pay their debts, critics argue, they result in the depletion of the resources required to meet the basic needs of their citizens. According to Susan George, author of several books on Third World debt, SAPs demand the production of "'tradeables'. . . to the detriment of resources for 'non-tradeables' [such as education and health care], which are more immediately useful to the population." Others, such as Arief Budiman, author of several books on democracy and the Indonesian government, contend that Third World countries suffer a disadvantage in international trade because their only competitive exports are their natural resources, which command a lower price than the manufactured products of the First World.

Proponents contend that SAPs are necessary because the state-controlled economies of many Third World countries impede economic growth. According to Amy L. Sherman, author of *Preferential Option*, many Third World governments in the 1960s tried to withdraw from the market and become industrially self-sufficient, but government control of their economies led to bloated bureaucracies, inefficient enterprises, and budget deficits. Critics of SAPs, Sherman argues, fail "to distinguish between suffering caused by the adjustment measures themselves [and that] . . . caused by the misguided statist policies that made [the] adjustment necessary." Sherman notes that countries that have completed the reform of their economies, such as Chile, are now the wealthiest in the South.

As the IMF and the World Bank celebrated their fiftieth anniversaries, many critics exclaimed, "Fifty years is enough!" Whether SAPs exacerbate poverty or create wealth is among the issues debated in the following chapter on Third World development.

> *"Frustration within the [less-developed countries] and among the international development institutions . . . over the failures of statism have fueled the [economic] reform movement."*

Market Reforms Are Necessary for Southern Economic Development

Amy L. Sherman

Market-friendly reforms that seek to limit Third World governments' control over their economies may be painful for many citizens employed in government-subsidized jobs, admits Amy L. Sherman in the following viewpoint. However, she argues, these reforms are the only way to bring about real economic development by eliminating the inept and corrupt bureaucratic mishandling of Third World resources and instead allowing the market to ensure the smooth running of nations' economies. Amy L. Sherman is the editor of *Stewardship Journal* and the author of *Preferential Option: A Christian and Neoliberal Strategy for Latin America's Poor*, from which this viewpoint is adapted.

As you read, consider the following questions:

1. What evidence does Sherman offer to support her belief that Third World poverty is not the result of exploitative North-South relations?
2. How did the price supports of food have the effect of economically punishing the poor, according to the author?

Excerpted from "Rethinking Development: A Market-Friendly Strategy for the Poor" by Amy L. Sherman. Copyright 1992, Christian Century Foundation. Reprinted by permission from the December 9, 1992, issue of *The Christian Century*. (The *Christian Century* article is adapted from Sherman's book *Preferential Option*, published by William B. Eerdmans, Grand Rapids, Michigan.)

With the fall of the Berlin Wall, worldwide attention has focused on the democratic revolution in world politics. But another revolution, an economic one, is also altering once-familiar territory. Under its influence, other walls—those erected against free markets and free trade in the name of socialist and statist forms of development—are gradually being torn down. Throughout the underdeveloped world and especially in Latin America, governments are trying to convert their state-centered economies into capitalist ones. And just as the political revolution has stimulated much rethinking about East-West issues, so the market revolution requires reassessments of international development and the North-South debate.

Though in some Third World (and formerly Second World) countries economic reforms are more talk than reality, most of the developing world is rethinking economic strategies. The trend is away from state-centered models of development and toward an appreciation of free-market principles. The phrase "structural adjustment," ubiquitous in the late '80s and early '90s, has been coined to capture this transformation. Some less-developed countries (LDCs) have achieved important successes; others are struggling to swallow the bitter medicine of economic austerity. Average citizens in countries undergoing adjustment feel it—some quite keenly. Traveling in Poland and Guatemala in the summer of 1992, I heard plenty of complaints about spiraling food prices and unemployment.

Obvious suffering and hardship in underdeveloped countries struggling to implement market-friendly reforms has some people in the U.S. religious community questioning whether the transition is a good idea at all. With the popular and decisive rejection of socialism throughout Eastern Europe, observers can hardly champion Marxist-oriented strategies that allegedly benefit the poor. But few are willing to embrace the market either. Longed for instead is that attractive but all-too-elusive "third way" between capitalism and socialism that somehow would be both humane and efficient.

No Alternatives

Unfortunately, no such third way exists. Attempts to create one in many LDCs resulted mostly in the establishment of various forms of "statism"—less brutal and usually less ideological versions of a government-controlled economy than their cousin, communism. Statist models, like their relative, have gone bankrupt; indeed, many of the Third World's economic woes today can be traced to their misguided policies. Frustration within the LDCs and among the international development institutions (World Bank, International Monetary Fund) over the failures of statism have fueled the reform movement. To understand why the statist model proved so detrimental to the poor and why market reforms are necessary, it is important to clarify statism and the motives behind it. After all, economic strategies do not emerge in a vacuum but depend on interpretations of economic situations. Economic strategies are implemented in response to these interpretations.

The "statist consensus" grew out of two primary assumptions about the nature of Third World poverty. First, according to this consensus, blame for economic stagnation in the LDCs was assigned largely to exploitive North-South relationships in the global economy. Neocolonial and dependency theory analysis declared that Western colonial powers had first oppressed and pillaged parts of the underdeveloped world and then, after the independence period, continued with such expropriation through unfair trading practices. Development in industrialized countries actually "created" underdevelopment in the LDCs. In other words, the rich countries were rich *because* the poor countries were poor. Moreover, they were kept poor because the industrialized countries controlled the rules and institutions of the global economic order and manipulated them to their advantage. Trading relations between the North and South were beneficial to the former only at the expense of the latter. The South exported cheap raw materials with steadily deteriorating prices but at the same time had to import ever more expensive manufactured goods from the North.

Second, this consensus interpretation maintained that if an LDC's poverty was attributable to problems within its own domestic economy, the chief systemic distortion could quickly be identified as the internal "capitalist" economic structure that benefited wealthy oligarchs at the expense of the masses. Inequitable income distribution was seen as the clearest reflection of this deformation, and unemployment, rural poverty and worker exploitation were counted as its common side-effects.

Half-Truths

These assumptions contained half-truths but missed much of the story. Colonialism brought with it multiple woes but several economic benefits as well—including the development of an infrastructure, the seeds of an education and health system, and new technologies. If colonial policies had produced unmitigated disaster for the colonies, we would expect that the countries with the greatest sustained contact with the Western powers would today be the least well-off. In fact, the poorest LDCs are those that have had the least contact.

Similarly, if trade relations between the North and South were exclusively beneficial to the North, we would expect that those developing countries with the greatest export orientation and extensive trade relations would be most exploited by the global economy. Instead, the economic miracles of the developing world—the countries that, like the East Asian "tigers" of Taiwan, Hong Kong, Singapore and South Korea, have graduated out of underdeveloped status, or the countries like Chile, Malaysia and Thailand that are on the way toward doing so—are those countries that most aggressively traded in the international market.

Market Reforms and the Environment

Building on the synergy between poverty reduction and economic efficiency . . . has a powerful impact on the environment. The World Bank is working with its borrowers to develop policies that can provide both substantial economic and environmental benefits, such as the elimination of subsidies for environmentally harmful activities, clarification of property rights, and liberalization of trade. The elimination of energy subsidies [for logging and charcoal production] in developing countries, for instance, would save governments nearly $230 billion each year with a dramatic impact on air quality. Where the links between poverty and the environment are not so positively related, policy measures can minimize the tradeoffs by targeting environmentally destructive behavior with market-based incentives, such as taxes or charges, or government regulations.

Mohamed T. El-Ashry, *EPA Journal*, April/June 1993.

Nonetheless, the glaring contradiction between the opulence of the industrialized nations and the economic despair of the LDCs inevitably produced a sense that the two are somehow causally related. When idealistic leaders in Africa and Asia came to power in the '50s and '60s they—like those in Latin America a few decades earlier—surveyed the social ills around them and pushed for an activist response.

The Statist Response

On the basis of such diagnoses of their socioeconomic woes, these governments developed a two-part, state-centered response. First, they advocated that LDCs withdraw as much as possible from what they had determined was an exploitive world economy, pursue "self-sufficiency" and emphasize import-substituting industrialization. Agriculture and an export-oriented economy was to be avoided in favor of significant government involvement in the economy, especially in heavy industry. The idea was to produce necessary goods domestically in order to avoid dependence on trade with the rich countries. This meant, second, that market forces could not be left alone to drive investment and production decisions. Rather, central planning and state-led industrialization through public firms would be necessary. Centralization would bring an added benefit, many believed: the government as employer would, unlike greedy private capitalists, see to it that workers would be protected with adequate salaries, safe working conditions and good benefits. The state, perceived as a neutral entity acting in the public interest, would automatically ensure that national development would benefit all of society's members rather than only the economic elites. . . .

Tragically, the policies implemented under statist regimes actually worsened the suffering of the poor and brought about the Third World's current severe economic crisis. Statist regimes of varying stripes (populist and mercantilist) undertook several policy initiatives that at first glance seemed compassionate or favorable to the poor. When the actual consequences of such policies are examined, however, it is clear that whatever the good intentions, many people were killed with kindness.

Statist regimes often enforced numerous regulations on economic activity to protect the poor from potential abuses in the private sector. Governments also tried to shield people from exploitation by multinational companies by strictly regulating foreign investment. These regimes in many cases provided publicly sponsored employment for citizens, taxed the rich heavily to produce funds for social spending on health, education and welfare, and instituted minimum-wage laws to protect lower-income workers.

Opportunities for Corruption

Peruvian author Hernando de Soto was among the first to document systematically the actual effects of such ostensibly "pro-poor" policies. His watershed book *The Other Path* (1989) argued that the government's very efforts to help the poor often did them the most harm. Laws and regulations originally intended to assist the poor and effect wealth redistribution in the society instead led over time to a concentration of economic power in the hands of government bureaucrats. These officials, controlling all sorts of business permits, licenses, registration documents and titling procedures, could trade these economic goodies for bribes or political favors from wealthy and politically connected businessmen. This regulatory system created innumerable opportunities for collusion between corrupt officials and businessmen. Together they could corner markets, establish monopolies and shut out the poor from access to the formal (the legal or above-ground) economy. These tactics had the effect of pushing lower-class "microentrepreneurs" into the underground or informal economy where they lacked the security of property, access to credit, ability to enforce contracts and opportunities for expansion.

To specify how these 20th-century mercantilist economic structures hurt the poor, de Soto devised a number of experiments in which he proposed different avenues that poor families might take to improve their economic situation. In one experiment de Soto's researchers found that a poor family aspiring to legally establish a small garment business would need 289 days to fulfill all the prescribed bureaucratic steps and $1,231 (32 times the average monthly wage) to pay the required fees and bribes. In his analysis, poor families stayed poor because most of them had neither this kind of time nor money. . . .

Overregulation of the economy by state bureaucrats produced innumerable inefficiencies that blocked economic growth. A major source of inefficiency was precisely the government's clout in the economic realm: economic decisions were most often made on the basis of political considerations. Management positions in state-owned enterprises were given not to the most competent individuals but to those who were owed a political favor. Even when the detrimental effects of excessive social spending on public budgets was clear, populist government leaders dependent on the urban, middle-class vote did not dare to cut back and live within the government's means. Meanwhile, legal companies without privileged political access wasted hundreds of hours and dollars bogged down in red-tape procedures that provided make-work for innumerable and unnecessary civil servants. Money that these firms could have used to find new jobs or make better, more competitive products was simply wasted.

Compassionate Destruction

Other allegedly compassionate policies common to nonmarket economies oppressed the poor with similar force. On the premise that the capitalist world economy exploited Third World farmers, populist LDC governments instituted state marketing boards as the sole legal purchasers of domestic crops. This was supposed to provide a sure and steady market for poor farmers. In reality it impoverished them, since they were inevitably offered below-market prices for their goods and were forbidden from selling them in markets where they could obtain a better price. This discouraged agricultural production, encouraged urban migration, and in some instances created food shortages. Under the influence of statist policies, some LDCs that had been net food exporters became net food importers. On the premise that the poor must be protected from exploitation by employers, many governments instituted minimum-wage laws and various other regulations restricting a firm's ability to fire employees. These benefits were a boon to the few employees who could actually get jobs, but exacerbated the problems of the unemployed. Under such regulations firms could not afford to hire as many people as they might have, and inefficient workers had to be kept in order to avoid state-imposed penalties for discharging them. This continued the cycle of business incompetence, economic stagnation and high unemployment.

LDC governments also imposed price controls on basic necessities such as bread and milk in order to keep their cost affordable to society's more needy members. Again, this seemingly compassionate policy created a nightmare for the underclass. Since price controls were set below market-clearing prices, producers of the goods lacked incentive to increase production, some went bankrupt, and others gave up and moved to the cities. Shortages ensued which in turn offered windfall opportunities for unscrupulous government officials and black-marketeers. In situations of scarcity it was rarely the poor and politically voiceless who gained access to needed goods; rather this was the privilege of the rich and powerful. They consumed what they needed and sold what they didn't to the poor and the black market, where prices were far higher than they would have been without price controls.

The failures of the statist approach have become so obvious in the last several years that even before the fall of the Berlin Wall, which signaled the death of socialism, various LDCs were beginning to implement market-oriented reform. Since 1989 this trend has accelerated.

The Not-So-Bitter Pill

No one doubts that the transition from statist to market-friendly economies will take years and will produce social dislocations and hardships. Structural adjustments designed to achieve the transition such as pruning government bureaucracies, privatizing inefficient state-owned companies, rationalizing the exchange rate, decontrolling prices, cutting social spending, are bitter medicines. But they may not be as bitter for the poor as is often assumed. Social services and social spending that are being cut back typically benefited the middle and upper classes, not the poor, and it is these relatively better-off citizens who feel their absence the most. This is not to say, of course, that the poor too do not experience the pains of structural adjustment. Yet accompanying the question of who suffers is a further important question about the causes of such suffering. Some observers of the anguish in LDCs now undergoing austerity programs have failed to distinguish between suffering caused by the adjustment measures themselves, suffering caused by the misguided statist policies that made adjustment necessary in the first place, and suffering caused by the delay or abandonment of the reform measures. . . .

Governments in the LDCs need not adopt a radically laissez-faire attitude during the transition to the market. The point is to remove government's involvement from the economic activities it does poorly and at the expense of private actors, and to shift its energies into the tasks which government must perform if market reforms are to work. These include rebuilding infrastructure, clearly defining and defending property and contract rights, and funding preventative health care and primary education.

The industrialized countries can help too. First, they can bring the Uruguay Round of GATT [General Agreement on Tariffs and Trade] talks to a successful close [the round was successfully renegotiated in December 1993] and begin the process of reducing tariff barriers and dismantling protectionist arrangements such as the Multi-Fibre Agreement and the European Community's coordinated agricultural policy. These policies discriminate against exports of food and textiles from the underdeveloped countries, hurting the poor and making it difficult for LDCs to shift toward an export-oriented development strategy.

Relieve Debt and Increase Aid

Second, the rich countries can offer debt relief to the LDC governments most tenaciously implementing structural adjustment measures. Debt relief should be used as a reward for those countries making the most progress in moving toward the market. Progress can be measured, for example, by a country's success in reducing the public deficit, privatizing para-state enterprises, opening up to foreign investment, rationalizing the exchange rate, decreasing military spending and legalizing informal enterprise.

Third, the North can significantly increase foreign aid specifically earmarked for support of quasigovernmental or nongovernmental institutions established to mitigate the social costs of adjustment. As a result of Bolivia's successful Emergency Social Fund, social-adjustment funds are becoming more common in LDCs undertaking the transition to the market. These funds in essence function as philanthropic foundations. They make grants to local governments and community associations, NGOs [nongovernmental organizations], church groups and other private actors who design and implement projects aimed at meeting the special circumstances attending structural adjustment. With such economic adjustment, societies need to increase private health care services in light of government cutbacks, to retrain workers, to provide credit and training to microentrepreneurs, and to make allowances for low-wage emergency employment, most likely in construction projects, to the poorest of the poor. When Western aid money is channeled directly to funds that provide for such circumstances, less is wasted on administrative overhead, less is siphoned off by corrupt government officials, and more gets into the hands of local associations in touch with real needs.

Harnessing the Private Sector

In short, Third World governments must reconceive their social responsibilities and redesign their policies to show a healthy respect for the energies of the private sector. They must also redirect public funds to provide aid—without stifling bureaucracy and regulation—to the mediating structures of civil society: local nongovernmental organizations, community groups, church-led development projects and so on. Less government is needed in many areas of public life; more, better and more efficient government is needed in other areas. It is imperative that governments shift from their urban bias and carefully target their social welfare support to the poorest members of society, who usually are rural residents. Only in this way can the twin goals of poverty alleviation and structural adjustment (trimming public budgets) be served. Chile has led the way in such efforts and demonstrated that "marketization" of the economy and poverty alleviation can proceed simultaneously. . . .

The choice by LDCs to implement such a two-pronged strategy of market reforms and highly targeted poverty alleviation will be much easier to achieve in the context of a growing world economy and decreasing protectionism on the part of the industrialized countries. It will also be encouraged by timely, carefully targeted and generous Western aid aimed at underwriting social adjustment funds that work to mitigate the worst woes of austerity and help sustain public support for the painful but necessary reforms. The economic lessons learned from the past 40-some years of development experience are clear. What remains to be seen is whether the LDCs have the political will to implement those lessons, and whether the West has the will to adopt the complementary policies that can make the capitalist revolution of the late 20th century one that produces economic growth which benefits the world's poor.

"[Economic reforms are] key instruments in the North's effort to roll back the gains that had been made by the South."

Market Reforms Are Designed to Prevent Southern Economic Development

Walden Bello, Shea Cunningham, and Bill Rau

Since 1980, many Third World nations have submitted to "structural adjustments" designed by the International Monetary Fund and the World Bank to increase their exports and spur economic growth, explain Walden Bello, Shea Cunningham, and Bill Rau in the following viewpoint. But the biggest export from South to North was capital, the authors contend, resulting in economic stagnation and widespread poverty. Bello is principal analyst at the Institute of Food and Development Policy (Food First). Cunningham is a research assistant at Food First. Rau is a board member of the Africa Policy Information Center at the African-American Institute in New York City.

As you read, consider the following questions:

1. What have been the environmental effects of the structural adjustments, according to Bello, Cunningham, and Rau?
2. Why do reforms try to eliminate states' involvement in their economies, according to the authors?

Walden Bello, Shea Cunningham, and Bill Rau, "Creating a Wasteland," *Food First Action Alert*, Winter 1993. Reprinted by permission of Food First/Institute for Food and Development Policy, 398 60th St., Oakland, CA 94618.

On the eve of the 21st century, most of the South is in a state of economic collapse.

Yet, in 1994, the International Monetary Fund (IMF) and the World Bank, which are greatly responsible for the plight of the South, celebrate their 50th year of existence.

For the more than 70 countries that were subjected to 566 IMF and World Bank stabilization and structural adjustment programs (SAPs) since 1980, there is certainly nothing to celebrate.

These countries were told that the "structural reforms" promoted by the SAPs were essential for sustaining growth and economic stability. Most were skeptical, suspicious, or downright opposed to these programs. But faced with the threat of a cutoff of external funds needed to service the mounting debts incurred from western private banks that had gone on a lending binge in the 1970's, these countries had no choice but to implement the painful measures demanded by the Bank and IMF. These usually included:

- Cutbacks in government expenditures, especially in social spending;
- Cutbacks in or containment of wages;
- Privatization of state enterprises and deregulation of the economy;
- Elimination or reduction of protection for the domestic market and less restrictions on the operations of foreign investors; and
- Devaluation of the currency.

Adjustment: Rationale and Reality

More than fourteen years after the World Bank issued its first structural adjustment loan, most countries are still waiting for the market to "work its magic," to borrow a phrase from Ronald Reagan. In fact, structural adjustment has failed—miserably—in accomplishing what World Bank and IMF technocrats said it would do: promoting growth, stabilizing the external accounts, and reducing poverty.

Institutionalizing Economic Stagnation Comparing countries that underwent adjustment with countries that did not, IMF economist Mohsin Khan reported the uncomfortable finding that "the growth rate is significantly reduced in program countries relative to the change in non-program countries." Says Massachusetts Institute of Technology Professor Rudiger Dornbusch: "[E]ven with major adjustment efforts in place, countries do not fall back on their feet running; they fall into a hole." That is, economies under adjustment are stuck in a low-level trap, in which low investment, increased unemployment, reduced social spending, reduced consumption, and low output interact to create a vicious cycle of stagnation and decline, rather than a virtuous circle of growth, rising employment, and rising investment, as originally envisaged in World Bank theory.

Guaranteeing Debt Repayments Despite global adjustment, the Third World's debt burden rose from $785 billion at the beginning of the debt crisis to $1.3 trillion in 1992. Thirty-six of sub-Saharan Africa's 47 countries have been subjected to SAPs by the IMF and World Bank, yet the total external debt of the continent is now 110 per cent of its gross national product.

Dan Wasserman ©1987 *The Boston Globe*. Distributed by the Los Angeles Times Syndicate. Reprinted with permission.

Structural adjustment loans from the World Bank and the IMF were given to indebted countries to enable the latter to make their immediate interest payments to the western commercial banks. Having done this, the Bank and the IMF then went on to apply draconian adjustment policies that would assure a steady supply of repayments in the medium and long term. By having Third World economies focus on production for export, foreign exchange would be gained which could be channeled into servicing dollar-denominated foreign debt.

The policy was immensely successful for first world banks, effecting as it did an astounding net transfer of financial resources from the Third World to the commercial banks that amounted to $178 billion between 1984 and 1990. So massive was the decapitalization of the South that a former executive director of the World Bank exclaimed: "Not since the conquistadores plundered Latin America has the world experienced a flow in the direction we see today."

Intensifying Poverty

If structural adjustment has brought neither growth nor debt relief, it has certainly intensified poverty. In Latin America, according to Inter-American Development Bank president Enrique Iglesias, adjustment programs had the effect of "largely cancelling out the progress of the 1960's and 1970's." The numbers of people living in poverty rose from 130 million in 1980 to 180 million at the beginning of the 1990's. Structural adjustment also worsened what was already a very skewed distribution of income, with the result that today, the top 20 per cent of the continent's population earn 20 times that earned by the poorest 20 per cent.

In Africa adjustment has been a central link in a vicious circle whose other elements are civil war, drought, and the steep decline in the international price of the region's agricultural and raw material exports. The number of people living below the poverty line now stands at 200 million of the region's 690 million people, and even the least pessimistic projection of the World Bank sees the number of poor rising by 50 per cent to reach 300 million by the year 2000. So devastated is Africa that Lester Thurow has commented, with cynical humor tinged with racism: "If God gave it [Africa] to you and made you its economic dictator, the only smart move would be to give it back to him." And so evident is the role of SAPs in the creation of this blighted landscape that the World Bank chief economist for Africa has admitted: "We did not think that the human costs of these programs could be so great, and the economic gains so slow in coming."

Adjusting the Environment IMF and Bank-supported adjustment policies have been among the major contributors to environmental destruction in the Third World. By pushing countries to increase their foreign exchange to service their foreign debt, structural adjustment programs have forced them to overexploit their exportable resources. In Ghana, regarded as a "star pupil" by the IMF and the World Bank, the government has moved to intensify commercial forestry, with World Bank support. Timber production more than doubled between 1984 and 1987, accelerating the destruction of the country's already much-reduced forest cover, which is now 25 per cent of its original size. The country is expected to soon make the transition from being a net exporter to being a net importer of wood. Indeed, economist Fantu Cheru predicts that Ghana could well be totally stripped of trees by the year 2000.

Impoverishment, claims the World Bank, is one of the prime causes of environmental degradation because "land hungry farmers resort to cultivating erosion-prone hillsides and moving into tropical forest areas where crop yields on cleared fields usually drop after just a few years."

The Debt-Relief Imperative

The social and ecological consequences [of the World Bank and International Monetary Fund's lending policies] have been devastating. These consequences are, furthermore, well-documented. They are perhaps best summed up in a single Unicef (United Nations Children's Fund) figure: an extra half-million children die every year as a direct result of the debt crisis.

Neither the Bank nor the Fund has tried to press home to the creditors, their major shareholders, the obvious point that substantial debt relief would be the best—indeed the only—initial step to prevent the total economic and social collapse of sub-Saharan Africa in particular.

Greatly reduced debt would imply greatly reduced interest payments which would, in turn, mean far less pressure to stress exports. Without debt and the structural adjustment programs it entails, without the need to invest so heavily in the export sector, Africa could put its resources into building infrastructure, into feeding, educating and caring for its own populations.

Susan George, *Toward Freedom*, February 1993.

What the World Bank fails to acknowledge is that its structural adjustment programs have been among the prime causes of impoverishment, and thus a central cause of this ecological degradation. In the Philippines, for instance, a World Resources Institute study claims that the sharp economic contraction triggered by Bank-imposed adjustment in the 1980's forced poor rural people to move into and superexploit open access forests, watersheds, and artisanal fisheries.

Rollback: The Strategic Objective

But if structural adjustment programs have had such a poor record, why do the World Bank and the IMF continue to impose them on much of the South?

This question is valid, only if one assumes that the Bank and IMF's intention is to assist Third World economies to develop.

Then, the failure of SAPs can be laid to such things as bad conceptualization or poor implementation. However, it is becoming increasingly clear that, whatever may be the subjective intentions of the technocrats implementing them, structural adjustment programs were never meant to reduce poverty or promote development. Instead, they have functioned as key instruments in the North's effort to roll back the gains that had been made by the South from the 1950's through the 1970's.

These decades were marked by high rates of economic growth in the Third World. They also witnessed successful struggles of national liberation, and the coming together of southern states at the global level to demand a "New International Economic Order" (NIEO) that would entail a more equitable distribution of global economic power. This sense of a rising threat from the South—underlined by such events as the U.S. defeat in Vietnam, the OPEC [Organization of Petroleum Exporting Countries] oil embargo of 1973 and 1979, restrictions on multinationals' operations in Mexico and Brazil, and the Iran hostage crisis—contributed to the victory of Ronald Reagan in the U.S. presidential elections of 1980.

Central to the economic achievements of the South was an activist state or public sector. In some countries, the state sector was the engine of the development process. In others, state support was critical to the success of domestic businesses wishing to compete against foreign capital. It was not surprising, therefore, that when Reaganites came to power in Washington with a clear agenda to discipline the subordinate Third World, they saw as a central mission the radical reduction of the economic role of the Third World state, and structural adjustment programs by the World Bank and IMF as the principal means to accomplish this.

Not surprisingly, few southern governments were willing to accept structural adjustment loans when they were first offered. However, they had no choice but to capitulate, since at the onset of the debt crisis in 1982, Washington, notes Latin America specialist John Sheahan, took advantage of "this period of financial strain to insist that debtor countries remove the government from the economy as the price of getting credit." Similarly, a survey of structural adjustment programs in Africa carried out by the United Nations Economic Commission for Africa concluded that the essence of these programs was the "reduction/removal of direct state intervention in the productive and distributive sectors of the economy."

The New South

By the end of the 12-year Reagan-Bush era in 1992, the South had been transformed: from Argentina to Ghana, state participation in the economy had been drastically curtailed. Government enterprises were passing into private hands in the name of efficiency. Protectionist barriers to Northern imports were being eliminated wholesale. Restrictions on foreign investment had been radically reduced. And, through export-first policies, the internal economy was more tightly integrated into the capitalist world market.

The erosion of Third World economies translated at the international level to the weakening of the formations that the South had traditionally used to attain its collective goal of bringing about a change in the global power equation: the Non-Aligned Movement, the United Nations Conference on Trade and Development (UNCTAD), and the Group of 77 [77 developing countries that vote together in the UN]. The decomposition of the Third World was felt at the United Nations, where the U.S. was emboldened to once again use that body to front the interests of the North, including providing legitimacy for the U.S.-led invasion of Iraq in 1991. Rollback via structural adjustment had succeeded.

Corporate-driven structural adjustment was not, of course, limited to the South. In the U.S., for instance, Reaganomics ensured that inequality and poverty were greater in 1990 than in 1980. (See our book *Dark Victory: The U.S., Structural Adjustment, and Global Poverty*, 1994, for an extended discussion of adjustment in the U.S.) It was, however, the Third World that was made to shoulder the main burdens of adjustment.

In the 1950's and 1960's, the peoples of the South were optimistic that the future belonged to them, the 80 per cent of the world's population that had long been treated as second or third class citizens of the world under colonialism. The illusions were gone by the beginning of the 1990's. As the South stood on the threshold of the 21st century, the South Commission [a loose affiliation of Latin American and African countries to improve international trade] captured the essence of its contemporary condition: "It may not be an exaggeration to say that the establishment of a system of international economic relations in which the South's second-class status would be institutionalized is an immediate danger."

"Development as we understand it today . . . is only possible with a massive use of technology."

Modern Technology Can Increase the South's Standard of Living

José Goldemberg

Studies of future energy use, José Goldemberg reports in the following viewpoint, predict that by the year 2020 Third World nations will have a standard of living that is still a third to a fourth that of the developed nations. Part of the reason for this, Goldemberg claims, can be seen in the South's steadily rising energy consumption rate—a direct result, he maintains, of the outdated technology employed in the Third World. The South must acquire more energy-efficient technologies from the North if it is ever to approximate the North's standard of living, the author concludes. Goldemberg, professor of physical sciences at the University of São Paulo, Brazil, was the Brazilian minister of education. He has written extensively on energy efficiency and technology.

As you read, consider the following questions:

1. What is "technological leapfrogging," in Goldemberg's analysis?
2. What environmental considerations does Goldemberg say are pushing developing countries to adopt newer technologies?

José Goldemberg, "Energy, Technology, Development," *Ambio*, vol. 21, no. 1, February 1992. (The original article is fully annotated.) Reprinted by permission of the Royal Swedish Academy of Sciences.

Development as we understand it today, i.e., access to durable consumer goods such as automobiles, refrigerators, radio, television, etc. is only possible with a massive use of technology. In the distant past some states such as Athens and Rome achieved a high degree of well being without a great use of technology; such well being however was only made possible by the use of slavery and exploitation of colonies. Even in these states only part of the population had full access to the benefits of wealth and security.

Although technology has many facets ranging from the production of mechanical power to the printing of books, energy is an essential ingredient in all of them. It is for this reason that the increase in energy consumption is closely associated with stages of the development of man. . . .

Starting with very low energy consumption of 8 M [thousands] Joules [unit of energy] per day which characterized the primitive man, energy consumption grew to almost 1000 MJ per day. This growth was only made possible by the increased use of coal as a source of heat and power, opening the way to the use of locomotives as an essential instrument for the spreading of civilization and progress in the 19th Century.

This became even more obvious after the advent of the use of electricity and internal explosion engines at the end of the last century which led to the massive use of petroleum and its derivatives.

The Energy-Production Linkage

The close association between progress as measured by Gross Domestic Product (GDP) and energy consumption (E) has led to the idea that there was an inextricable relationship between them. This linkage has never been seriously questioned and conventional wisdom was that GDP and energy consumption growth could not be decoupled.

The consequences of such views are alarming enough: there is an enormous gap, more than a factor of ten, between the GDP of industrialized countries—where 25% of the world population lives—and the less-developed countries (LDCs) where the remaining 75% live.

Approximately the same gap exists in the energy consumption of these countries. Consumption per capita averaged 199 GJ [billion joules] in industrialized countries and only 17 GJ in developing countries in 1980 (excluding non-commercial energy sources).

Even if one includes such sources—used very inefficiently such as fuelwood, charcoal, bagasse and agricultural residues—consumption per capita is only 32 GJ in less-developed countries.

Therefore if the population of all less-developed countries was to achieve instantly the energy consumption per capita of industrialized countries enormous amounts of energy would be needed;

[roughly 3 times as much energy]. Of course this will not happen overnight but it could happen in a few decades.

Projections of Energy Consumption

The projections of world energy consumption into the future made in the last few decades before 1980 reflected the expectations of a sustained growth of approximately 3% per year which means that the total energy consumed would quadruple in less than 50 years.

In that period two leading studies were conducted to predict future energy consumption: WEC [World Energy Conference] and IIASA [International Institute for Applied Systems Analysis].

The WEC study was carried out by the Energy Research Group at the Cavendish Laboratory, Cambridge, England, for the Conservation Commission of the World Energy Conference. This is a global analysis that looked to the year 2020. An important feature of WEC analysis for developing countries is that it took non-commercial energy into account.

Wasting Development Energy

Developing nation economies now require 40% more energy than industrial ones to produce the same value of goods and services. Part of the difference is due to the fact that these countries still are building energy-intensive infrastructure and related industries—but often using outdated technologies that squander energy. These gross inefficiencies—whether in wood stoves, cement plants, light bulbs, or trucks—offer innumerable opportunities to limit energy consumption and expenditures while expanding the services they provide. For instance, the U.S. Office of Technology Assessment estimates that nearly half of over-all electricity use in the South can be cut cost effectively.

To compete in increasingly integrated world markets, while still meeting their own domestic needs, developing nations will have to reap the economic savings that improved energy efficiency offers.

Nicholas Lenssen, *USA Today*, March 1994.

The IIASA study (carried out between 1973 and 1979 by analysts at the International Institute for Applied Systems Analysis, Vienna) made global projections to the year 2030 by aggregating projections for seven regions of the world. The primary emphasis in the study was on commercial energy.

The basic approach in these two studies consisted of two steps:
- estimating future energy demand on the basis of assumptions about future demographic and economic trends, histor-

ical correlations between such trends and energy demand;
- matching this demand to a mix of energy supplies.

This mix is chosen so that it is compatible with estimates of the energy resource base and, in the case of new energy supply technologies, with judgements about how much energy can be produced by these supply technologies at various future dates.

The WEC and IIASA studies had one long-run objective in common: to shift from oil to more abundant energy resources such as natural gas, coal and nuclear energy while preserving significant energy growth. Nuclear energy in particular was supposed to grow in the IIASA scenario 10 to 15-fold by 2020 (one new nuclear plant of 1 GigaWatt-electric capacity every 2 to 4 days in the next 40 years).

According to these studies consumption per capita in LDCs could reach 35 or 38 GJ per year as compared to 17 GJ in 1980 which corresponds to a relatively modest increase of 2% per year.

A Containment of Development

They ought to be compared to the 199 GJ per capita annual consumption in industrialized countries in 1980. Excluding energy used in industrialized countries for heating during winter (which represents approximately 30% of the total energy consumption and is not required in most parts of the developing world), the projections of WEC and IIASA indicate an average level of amenities in developing countries 3 to 4 times lower than in industrialized countries. It is clear therefore that these scenarios represent a containment of the development expectations for LDCs.

Are there any better prospects for developing countries compatible with a better level of life and with due regard to environmental considerations? The answer was given by J. Goldemberg, T.B. Johansson, A.K.N. Reddy and R.H. Williams in their study entitled *Energy for a Sustainable World* (ESW).

Energy for a Sustainable World

In ESW, technical possibilities of modern and energy efficient technologies in meeting the needs of the world population in the year 2020 were explored. The study, which does not propose any change of lifestyles or societal changes, takes a cool-headed technical approach and concludes that the widespread use of technology could permit people in the developing world to attain a level of amenities comparable to those in Western Europe in the middle of the 1970s, with an annual energy consumption of 199 to 101 GJ. Taken together total energy consumption in the year 2020 could remain approximately the same as consumption in 1980 with a much higher level of comfort for the great majority of the world's population.

The large improvements in living standards characterizing the ESW scenario can be achieved with this small increase in per capita energy use, for two reasons:

a) *the shift from traditional, inefficiently used noncommercial fuels, to modern energy carriers* (electricity, liquid and gaseous fuels, processed solid fuels, etc.). The importance of modern carriers is plain. In Western Europe, where noncommercial fuel use is low, per capita final energy use for purposes other than space heating was only 73 GJ per capita in 1975, about 2.5 times the total per capita consumption of developing countries, although per capita GDP was 10 times as large;

b) *the adoption of new and more energy-efficient technologies.* Some of the assumed technologies by ESW illustrate how large increases in amenities can be achieved without increasing energy consumption to Western Europe levels. For example, the same level of lighting provided by five 75 Watt incandescent bulbs operating four hours a day, can be delivered by compact fluorescent bulbs that draw only one-fourth as much electricity. . . .

Energy Intensity and Development

Long-term studies of the evolution of the *energy intensity*, i.e. ratio of energy consumption by unit of gross domestic product . . . for a number of countries indicate that this ratio increases in the initial phases of development when the heavy industrial infrastructure is put in place, reaches a peak and then decreases steadily. Only commercial energy consumption is considered in this figure. Long-period series of energy intensity for different countries are complex to analyze because in addition to technology other factors such as geography, population and history play a role in determining present features.

What the data indicates, however, is that latecomers in the development process follow the same pattern as the previous ones with less accentuated peaks; they do not have to reach high values of the E/GDP ratio even in their initial stages of industrialization because they can benefit from the modern methods of manufacturing and more efficient systems of transportation already developed.

In other words the *coupling* of energy and GDP growth, which were considered iron-locked to each other in the past, is not a general feature of modern economies. These trends started clearly before the oil crisis of 1973 and the increase of oil prices only accelerated the pace of structural changes in the industrialized countries. The reasons, as pointed out by P.F. Drucker, A.M. Strout and R.H. Williams et al., are:

- a saturation of consumer goods consumption; in industrialized societies economic activity has been moving in the direction of services and not heavy industry;

- a revolution in materials indicating clearly a shift in the direction of using less energy-intensive materials;
- a greater attention to efficient energy use.

In contrast . . . the energy intensity in LDCs is increasing. The adoption of outdated technologies foisted on them by the industrialized countries seems to be part of the reason for such trends. . . .

Technological Leapfrogging

From the previous discussion it is clear that one way out for developing countries from the dilemmas posed by environmental and economic concerns, is to *leapfrog* the technological path followed by industrialized countries in the past. This means incorporating energy-efficient technologies in their process of development.

Technology therefore could make development possible for the whole of mankind in the next 50 years if it were not for a new problem which is the *greenhouse effect* provoked by the emission of CO_2 from the combustion of fossil fuels, emissions of other gases such as chlorofluorocarbons (CFCs) and deforestation. Even with the reduced consumption of fossil fuels projected by ESW the amount of CO_2 and other greenhouse gases in the atmosphere is increasing mainly in the LDCs.

The consequences of the resulting warming can be quite alarming, e.g., a significant rise of sea levels, changes in agricultural patterns, migration of forested areas, etc.

Such and other environmental considerations are bound to accelerate and enhance the importance of *energy conservation* (an acronym for efficient energy use) which will play a very important role in the future. The political leadership in the OECD [Organization for Economic Cooperation and Development] countries—pressured by public opinion—will probably adopt public policies designed to cut CO_2 emissions by imposing new taxes on emissions or introducing new mandatory regulations such as the efficiency standards imposed by the US Congress in 1975 which had remarkable success in increasing the fuel performance of American cars by more than 50%.

Cutting CO_2 emissions and recapturing part of the CO_2 already in the atmosphere would probably be the best strategy to avoid or postpone the greenhouse effect.

Technology Is the Answer

Again, technology might be able to avoid an impending disaster. A shift from exhaustible fossil fuels to the inexhaustible solar energy can only be accomplished through the use of the wind energy, photovoltaics, solar-thermal and biomass burning (which is a renewable energy source). A good example of that is the Brazilian Alcohol Program which produces approximately

250,000 barrels of ethanol per day (ethyl alcohol) from sugarcane, replacing approximately 200,000 barrels of gasoline per day without contributing to CO_2 emissions (the CO_2 emitted when alcohol is burned in cars is recaptured from the atmosphere in the following harvest). Another possibility is an increased use of biomass for the production of energy, using advanced technologies such as gas turbines. Together with a reduction in deforestation plus an aggressive program of reforestation which is possible with modern knowledge it seems possible to offset present-day CO_2 emissions.

If it is used wisely by industrialized countries and incorporated early into the process of development in developing countries, technology has the potential to permit development and at the same time help preserve the global environment.

"*The schemes devised by . . . [development]
experts have so far led to a litany of ecological
and cultural disasters.*"

Modern Technology
Transfer Hurts the South

The Ecologist

Modern technology transfer to Third World countries is premised
on the Northern notion that Southern peoples are backwards and
ignorant, charge the editors of the *Ecologist* magazine. In fact,
they argue, indigenous, or vernacular, Southern knowledge and
technology are more useful than Northern varieties because they
are tailored to the people's needs and to local environments.
Efforts to introduce local farmers to modern technologies have
failed due to the North's cultural arrogance and unwillingness to
study indigenous ecology, the *Ecologist* editors declare. The North
continues to push its environmentally unsound technology, they
claim, in order to create new markets for its wares to support its
luxurious standard of living. The *Ecologist* is a United Kingdom-
based bimonthly magazine covering ecological efforts and issues
worldwide.

As you read, consider the following questions:

1. What are the advantages of intercropping, according to the
   editors?
2. How did Northern development planning disrupt the
   Nigerian farming community described by the editors?

Excerpted from "Technology Transfer," *The Ecologist*, vol. 22, no. 4, July/August 1992.
Reprinted by permission of *The Ecologist*, MIT Press/ Journals, 55 Hayward St., Cambridge,
MA 02142.

Central to the logic of technology transfer [from the developed to the developing nations] is the presupposition of the recipient's ignorance. "Ignorance," according to the World Bank, "is an important cause of environmental damage and a serious impediment to finding solutions. . . . Frequently, especially in developing countries, decisions are made in the absence of environmental information. Collecting basic data can be expensive, but the rewards are usually high." And again: "Poverty, uncertainty and ignorance are the allies of environmental degradation. . . . Better-educated people can more readily adopt environmentally sound but complicated techniques such as integrated pest management."

It is predictable that the World Bank should have chosen an agricultural example—pest management—to illustrate their point. The peasant farmer, "especially in developing countries," has always been represented by experts as an archetype of ignorance, "backward" and bound by tradition. In the words of E. Alvord, an agricultural missionary to Rhodesia in the 1920s and 1930s, "we have in my opinion little or nothing to learn from native agriculture," which he characterized as "wasteful, slovenly, ineffective and ruinous to the future interests of Rhodesia," while the natives themselves were "heathens who were grossly immoral and incredibly steeped in superstition."

The language used today by World Bank policy-writers is every bit as racist, if not as crude, as that used by Alvord, and it reinforces similar attitudes further down the hierarchy: for example, Zambian extension agents, working on a World Bank project in the 1980s, described local farmers as "ignorant peasants, too lazy to farm." The word "ignorant" is pregnant with contempt. It epitomizes an attitude that is consciously or subconsciously held by all those who consider that Western technology is a *sine qua non* of environmental stability and human comfort; those who assume, without question, that a small, noisy, polluting refrigerator must inevitably be better than a large, cool larder, that a two-litre motor car must inevitably be more efficient than a two-pedal bicycle, or that an expensive tractor-drawn plough must inevitably be superior to the nimble mattock [a wedge-shaped digging tool].

The assumption, implicit in the World Bank's allegations of "ignorance", that scientific research and technological advance cannot exist outside the research laboratories and computer networks of the developed world is inherent to the logic of technology transfer. Yet until quite recently, even in Europe, almost all scientific research and technological advance took place in the field or on the shop floor. Waterproof suits made from fish-gut and watertight bowls made from grass were not developed in research laboratories; nor were the junks of China, or the kayaks of the Aleut: nor even the traditional "wootz" steel of India, which in the 1840s was judged to be better than anything produced in Britain. The technological advances of the English "agricultural revolution" were originally developed, not by theorists such as Arthur Young who propagated them in the 18th century, but some two or three hundred years earlier by a succession of nameless farmers. This tradition of vernacular science is still very much alive, though its disdain for publicity and the written word have led many academic scientists to doubt its value and even its existence.

The Trojan Horse of Technology

Drawing by P.J. Polyp. Reprinted by permission of the *New Internationalist*.

Human beings are for the most part curious, experimental and concerned for their own well-being. It should therefore come as no surprise to us that groups of people who have lived in an area for generations should evolve systems of agriculture and ways of living that are congenial, effective and sustainable—unless they are prevented by someone else from doing so. This process of native scientific selection and discovery is not always as slow as we have been led to believe. Winin Pereira has described how when the *dandavan* tree, from Australia, was introduced to an area north of Bombay, in the first year that it came into flower the local Warli tribals discovered that its seeds could be used to stupefy and catch fish; and subsequently started using it as a medicine as well. The following year a paper describing experiments by two scientists on the effects of the seed on two species of fish confined to a laboratory aquarium was published in *Environment and Ecology*. Not only did the tribals beat the scientists—their research needed no expensive equipment, no submission of reports and budgets, no academic accolade and was tested on the fish that needed to be caught, in their natural environment. This was research carried out by and for the commons [community]—rather than in the enclosed and jealous world of the academic institution.

The intimate knowledge of the properties of plants is reflected elsewhere in the widespread practice of intercropping. Whereas Northern agriculture finds it easier to cope with one crop at a time—and frequently with one crop all the time—in many parts of the tropics farmers have found it advantageous to grow two or more crops together in one field. In West Africa, 80 per cent of all farmland is intercropped, with up to 60 crop species being grown on any one farm. N.S. Jodha notes a tradition in India "that every farmer should plant nine crops in at least one of his plots. This ritual practice known as *nava dhanyam* (nine grains) is guided by a belief that it is the duty of every farmer to preserve the germplasm which nature has provided."

There are many advantages associated with intercropping. Often there is simply a net gain in yield over growing a single crop on the same area of land. Certain combinations of plants complement each other, by providing shade or windbreaks, and by exploiting nutrients at different levels of the soil. They can also protect each other from pest attacks. Intercropping also minimizes the risks of farming. The more crops and cropping schedules used, the less the likelihood of total crop failure; and staggering different crops means that there will be something to eat in the uncertain period before the main harvest. Also, the work load is spread evenly throughout the year rather than concentrated in a few critical periods. This can be the crucial limiting factor to the amount of food that a farm produces. Paul Richards argues that West Africans are turning increasingly to intercropping techniques, as a response both to land shortages and to labour shortages caused by out-migration. In this respect, "it might be better to view intercropping . . . not as a set of 'traditional' techniques, but as evidence of progress towards an agricultural revolution." Certainly the fact that one observer counted no less than 147 distinct intercrop combinations in three villages in northern Nigeria suggests that much experimentation is taking place. . . .

A Litany of Disasters

For those who rely on the commons [land and resources held in common], defending this body of vernacular knowledge is fundamental to defending the commons. For them, the experience of technology transfer is not that it solves problems so

81

much as that it creates them.

Technology transfer has led to an influx of experts and other outsiders determined to impose their "solutions" on the commons. Since the 19th century, when the scientific academies blossomed and universities acquired departments of agriculture, physics and chemistry, the credit for innovation and the license to innovate have been progressively lifted out of the public domain and placed in the hands of the professional scientist. New breeds of expert have appeared—the architect, the soil engineer, the planning officer, the conservationist, the health and safety officer, the agricultural extension officer—educated in the classroom and the laboratory, entitled with paper qualifications, and entrusted with the enforcement of a growing body of legislation that has been formulated in those same institutions.

No one has suffered more from this invasion of experts than those who have been most consistently stigmatized as ignorant, the poor of the Third World. In the words of Bill Rau, "The widespread failure of agricultural and rural development projects in Africa is largely due to the failure of planners to work with and reflect the complexity and diversity of rural and urban realities." Or indeed to understand them. "The dreams and myths of development 'experts' have been repeatedly altered or rejected by peasants, artisans and the urban poor because the projects were irrelevant, impractical or directly threatening to their well-being."

The schemes devised by these experts have so far led to a litany of ecological and cultural disasters—and there is no reason to suppose that they will not continue to do so. Most frequently the problems are caused not by one or two basic miscalculations, but by a fundamental failure to comprehend the complexities of the local ecology and culture.

A Failed Attempt to "Modernize"

The Kano River Irrigation Project, for example, is an attempt to modernize a local farming community in northern Nigeria. In 1911, E.M. Morel wrote, "There is little that we can teach the Kano farmer . . . they have acquired the necessary precise knowledge as to the time to prepare the land for sowing; when and how to sow; how long to let the land be fallow; what soils suit certain crops; what varieties of the same crop will succeed in some localities and what varieties in others . . . how to ensure rotation; when to arrange with Fulani herdsmen to pasture their cattle upon the land." Sixty years later the Nigerian government and agencies such as USAID [United States Agency for International Development] and FAO [United Nations Food and Agriculture Organization] thought differently. A project was initiated to replace the local *shadoof* bucket-irrigation system with water supplied by the new Tiga dam, which was completed in 1975. The main object was to supply wheat to make western-style bread for sale in the cities.

Technology as Trojan Horse

From President Harry Truman's pledge to provide scientific and technical aid, to the hopes of some countries in recent years to leapfrog the outdated industrial nations with the help of biotechnics [biotechnology] and information technology, the "tools of progress" were regarded as the guarantors of successful development. Indeed, if ever there was a single doctrine uniting North and South it was this: more technology is always better than less.

The popularity of this doctrine derives from the tragic fallacy that modern technologies possess the innocence of tools. . . . In reality, of course, a model of civilization follows hot on the heels of modern technology. Like the entry of the Trojan horse in the ancient myth, the introduction of technology in the Third World paved the way for a conquest of society from within. . . .

For the "technical development" of a country demands putting into effect that multitude of requirements which have to be fulfilled to set the interconnected systems whirring. And this generally amounts to taking apart traditional society step by step in order to reassemble it according to functional requirements.

Wolfgang Sachs, *New Internationalist*, June 1992.

Although the area had been identified as being suitable for wheat, after the first five years of the project yields were only about 15 per cent of the amount predicted. Farmers were pressurized to give up intercropping guinea corn with millet, because the harvest date interfered with the wheat crop, and were encouraged instead to grow maize, which is more demanding on the soil and more dependent on fertilizer. Soil fertility dropped as intercropping declined, and erosion increased because of the work involved levelling the land. The project drastically altered the people's way of life. The cooperative arrangement between the farmers and the nomadic Fulani herders, mentioned approvingly by Morel, was stopped by project organizers who considered the cattle disruptive, and consequently *fura*, a vital food for both groups made out of milk and millet, could no longer be made. Poultry was banned from domestic households and there was a decline in foodstuffs such as sorghum, dates, locust beans (a weaning food), vegetables and other crops dependent upon the defunct *shadoof* irrigation. The increase in men's income and the growing integration into the market economy resulted in a power imbalance between men and women, which, according to P. Stamp, led women to remove themselves "as much as possible from the household economy, creating a separate women's world into which to place their energies and generate independent resources, however meagre, with which to endow their daughters." Despite these problems and repercussions, the Kano River Project is regarded as more successful than others. A similar project in neighbouring Bakolori encountered determined resistance from peasants, culminating in 1980 in the massacre of at least 23 and probably over 100 farmers by the Nigerian police.

The Kano story is just one of a now familiar stream of disappointments and failures that does not seem to be drying up. A report published in May 1992 by the United Kingdom National Audit Office found that of 17 recent aid projects funded by the Overseas Development Administration, (some in conjunction with the World Bank), the ability of more than half to survive after the project teams left was in doubt, and two were already written off as complete failures. In one drainage scheme in Pakistan, designed to alleviate the salinization of cotton fields in the Sind caused by the British-built irrigation systems, only 3 out of the projected 79 drainage sumps were working properly, and in these 3 cases "the water table had fallen below the optimum level and crop yields had reduced.". . .

Grudging Acknowledgement of Tradition

[One] line of defence adopted by the agents of development [in the wake of such disasters] . . . involves a grudging acknowledgement of past failures and of the value of vernacular knowledge and technologies. The World Bank, alongside its denunciation of "ignorance", now concedes that "the belief that traditional knowledge of the environment is simple and static is changing rapidly. More and more development projects are taking advantage of local knowledge about how to manage the environment. . . . Development projects that do not take existing practices into account often fail." These admissions, however, are coupled with a generalized assumption that vernacular systems are [still] inadequate. . . . For example, the National Research Council (NRC) of the US National Academy of Sciences has issued a report entitled *Alternative Agriculture*, half of which is given over to eleven farm casestudies. As Jack Kloppenburg reports, "the conclusions reached in the report relate almost entirely to the need for the application of more *scientific* effort to the development of alternative agriculture, and the report's recommendations focus on how this strategy might best be accomplished. Farmers are regarded as the recipients of technology, advice and information. The authors of the NRC report simply do not conceive of any potential for farmer-generated knowledge except in connection with or translation through 'science'."

Similarly, "integrated pest management" is now being promoted by the World Bank and other agencies as a means of reducing the damage done by pesticide use. "Integrated pest management" has, of course, been practised for centuries by farmers whose inventories include techniques such as mixed cropping, fallowing, selection of resistant varieties, decoy crops, pest-deterrent plants, predator-attracting plants, natural pesticides, burning, flooding and manual labour. The integrated pest management proposed by the World Bank, however, differs in three respects. Firstly, it uses toxic chemicals in "small, carefully-timed applications". Secondly it keeps the farmer dependent upon chemical companies, for whom he or she must earn or borrow money to pay for the input. And thirdly, the farmer is no longer in control, but must bow to the opinion of "experts", who will be hovering round the farm, checking that the applications are small and carefully timed. The farmer is integrated into the scheme—but only as one of a number of factors in a pest-management process determined largely by outside experts.

The Technological Trojan Horse

Forced in this manner into a marriage of convenience with development, "alternative agriculture", "integrated pest management" and similar "appropriate" techniques become complicit in the further enclosure [or fencing off] of vernacular science. Indeed, as the conventional technological solutions, such as large dams, become discredited, other more acceptable technologies must be found to take on the role of Trojan horse. One agronomist, David Norman, explains frankly how mixed cropping improvements are used by [field workers] to get a foot in the door and gain the confidence of farmers:

> Once the farmer has adopted an innovation that does not conflict too much with his present traditional outlook, e.g. improvement of his returns from mixed cropping, it will then be easier for the [field] worker to suggest more radical changes, e.g. sole [one crop] cropping, if evidence obtained under improved technological conditions indicates that this is desirable as far as farmers are concerned.

This is not to imply that appropriate technologies can never be successfully exchanged, but rather that, as David Burch has pointed out, there is no permanent place for appropriate technology in a society that is committed to the standard models of technological growth. The pressures of a market fuelled by the consumption patterns of a wealthy minority are too great. "What is produced within a country is not determined by some objective assessment of needs. . . . Patterns of income distribution biased towards the middle- and upper-classes produce a structure of effective demand for products that can only be produced by capital-intensive technologies."

The current nod in the direction of vernacular science should be regarded in this light. As long as a wealthy minority of people concentrated in the North and within Southern élites continue to exert an effective demand throughout the world for exotic foodstuffs, Western-style clothing and other luxuries, and as long as they rely upon an ever-expanding market for produce such as fertilizers, pesticides, machinery and wheat, we can expect a further enclosure of vernacular science, a continuing succession of hare-brained schemes to drag the "ignorant peasant" into the 21st century, and the relentless growth of an environmentally unsound industrial economy. When cultures develop alongside each other on an even footing, they can and do benefit by borrowing ideas from each other. But this process is in no way linked to the systematic colonization of knowledge that is taking place under cover of the term "transference of technology."

*"The realization dawned in Latin America that
. . . unfettered markets were the key to economic
well-being."*

Free Trade Promotes
Third World Development

Everett Ellis Briggs

In the following viewpoint, Everett Ellis Briggs addresses the
Indiana Summit on Hemispheric Trade, arguing that the 1993
North American Free Trade Agreement between Mexico, the
United States, and Canada should be extended to include the
countries of Latin America. Latin American countries are growing economically because of their adoption of free trade principles, Briggs contends. Accordingly, these countries are interested in establishing closer trading relations with the developed
world, he explains, cautioning that the United States can either
seize this trading opportunity or lose it to Europe. Briggs has
been United States ambassador to Honduras, Panama, and
Portugal and is president of the Council of the Americas, a pro-
private enterprise, pro-trade organization of U.S. corporations
with investments in Latin America.

As you read, consider the following questions:

1. What was the motivation behind the United States' previous
   development strategies for the developing world, according to
   Briggs?
2. Why does the author believe that trade-based development is
   an improvement over the more economically inward-looking
   strategy of state-run import substitution?

Excerpted from Everett Ellis Briggs's remarks at the Council of the Americas Indiana
Summit, December 6, 1994. Reprinted with permission of the author.

From the titles of the several sessions of this important gathering [the December 1994 Indiana Summit on Hemispheric Trade], and from what we have heard so far, it seems evident that all of us—most of us, anyway—share a common vision of where our hemisphere should be headed, as we approach the 21st century: full partners in trade; an association of free and prosperous democracies.

These are the aims of the Council of the Americas, a business organization founded in 1963 by David Rockefeller and a group of like-minded American business leaders, in reaction to President Kennedy's Alliance for Progress. The Council from its inception has been dedicated to free trade, private enterprise and to the promotion of business ties throughout the hemisphere.

The emphasis in the Alliance for Progress was on government promotion of development through what was euphemistically called "cooperation." Under this formula the less developed [countries] agreed to cooperate with the United States by accepting our handouts—in the form of economic assistance—and accepting, too (at least in theory) our lead in cold war foreign policy. The prevailing wisdom at the time prescribed state intervention [in their economies] and import-substitution [where essential industries were imported to attain national self-sufficiency] as the quickest way to economic progress. Our own AID [Agency for International Development] programs were fashioned to support this approach. In the process the economies of many countries became highly distorted and a number of AID recipients became permanent pensioners of the United States.

By the end of the cold war, many painful lessons had been learned—at least in Latin America, if not in academia at home (where intellectuals to this day often remain frozen in their adolescent, socialist fixations). Like welfare programs here, so-called cooperation, in most instances, didn't bring the expected benefits, except to the burgeoning bureaucracies it spawned. State-managed economies were failures, and to the extent U.S. aid prolonged the agony, it doubtlessly did more harm than good.

Trade: The Key to Economic Growth

Gradually, led by Chile—prompted by the debacle of Salvadore Allende—the realization dawned in Latin America that socialism was a fraud, while unfettered markets were the key to economic well-being, to meeting the social needs of the populace, and to sustaining democracy.

Our country for years had resisted the Latins' entreaties for "trade, not aid." And rightly so, for a while anyway, since from the Latin American standpoint this would have meant simply swapping one type of one-way "cooperation" for another, given the high protective tariffs, subsidies and crippling regulations devised by mercantilist elites in league with corrupt strongmen throughout much of the region.

But as we all know, we now find ourselves in a dramatically changed setting—one of breathtaking opportunities.

For the fourth consecutive year, Latin America's GDP [gross domestic product] has grown by almost 4 percent—a rate which soon will exceed that of East Asia.

U.S. exports to Latin America are increasing at three times the global rate—soaring by 14 percent a year between 1985 and 1992, with manufactured goods accounting for the greatest share. In 1995, our exports to Latin America may well surpass those to Western Europe, just as our exports to Mexico nearly exceed those to Japan. The Western Hemisphere, in fact, is fast becoming our biggest market, with a total population soon to reach 800 million and a GDP of $13 trillion.

A Shift in Development Strategies

What has happened, of course, is that there has been a major shift in economic development strategies by Latin American countries over the past decade—from failed, inward-looking, import-substitution stagnation to efficient, outward-looking, export-oriented growth. As trade liberalization has proceeded, the average effective tariffs of Latin American countries have fallen from 26 to 13 percent. The new GATT [General Agreement on Tariffs and Trade] regime will lower these still further.

Governments do not trade; private sector businessmen do. Trade liberalization and the elimination of tariffs, quotas and bureaucratic interference in general enlarge the area of human freedom. Business decisions are prompted by market forces, not politics, ideology, or special interests. Corruption, which feeds on overregulation, is curtailed.

Freedom of association and the ability to conduct business affairs openly should, in fact, be regarded as basic human rights.

The Council of the Americas is dedicated to advancing this proposition. It has long championed two sets of goals:

- Promoting economic integration in the hemisphere with the aim of creating a hemisphere-wide free trade and investment area by the year 2000; and
- Encouraging economic restructuring, from closed, low productivity, import-substitution oriented economies to open, high productivity, globally competitive export-oriented economies.

NAFTA: A Tool for Trade Expansion

The most significant step toward achieving these goals was the NAFTA [North American Free Trade Agreement]—one of the most important trade policy achievements of the past two decades, of

89

the same order of importance for hemispheric relations as the GATT Uruguay Round [the 1986 trade accords, renegotiated in 1993] is for global trade. NAFTA's real significance is its potential for expansion. NAFTA's underlying principles—grounded in over four decades of international trade law and practice, are ideally suited for this purpose. They are readily adaptable to encompass the diversity and independence of this hemisphere's community of nations. What is needed now is action by the three NAFTA members to agree on an accession code based on NAFTA standards, and then invite others to join. Chile, by general agreement, is first in line, and ready.

Trade: A Win, Win, Win Situation

Mexico is today the number one supplier of refrigerators to the United States. . . .

Mexican producers of refrigerators did not establish their plants in order to compete head to head with the huge producers of refrigerators in the United States, but rather they chose a market niche. The market niche for small refrigerators for offices, for hotels, for small apartments in big cities, for university campuses, etc. And by becoming a specialist in that market of small refrigerators, they gained a tremendous margin of competitiveness because being smaller in relative terms than the U.S. producers, they have a great deal of flexibility to adapt to the market changes and to the market requirements. . . .

This is why I have said publicly that NAFTA is a win, win, win situation is not only rhetoric, the point here is that NAFTA can make Mexico more competitive and by making us more competitive it will be a possibly sound gain, and not an ill-found gain. Because the competitiveness that NAFTA will bring about in the region will allow us to get a bigger share of world markets and therefore will create jobs on both sides of the border.

Jaime Jose Serra Puche, *Vital Speeches of the Day*, April 15, 1993.

Chile is clearly the regional leader in long-term macroeconomic stabilization. Its outstanding record of sustained economic growth is unsurpassed. Furthermore, Chile has, as part of its comprehensive, market-based, economic reform program, one of the most transparent and nondiscriminatory trade regimes in the region. Its trade is globally diversified and expanding rapidly, emphasizing that trade is a key component in rapid growth policies designed to expand incomes across the society—and to address social needs in general. For those worried about labor and environmental practices, Chile's appear to be NAFTA-consistent. . . .

Latin American governments in the past often deliberately excluded United States participation in regional trading arrangements. Most now say they would welcome it. If the United States and its NAFTA partners should fail to offer them a means to climb aboard the NAFTA bandwagon, the Latin Americans will have no choice but to associate themselves with others.

Losing Latin American Trade to Europe

This will not be hard given the imperative of trade in the modern world. A case in point: in November 1994 MERCOSUR [a South American free trade group] Foreign Ministers met with Jacques Delors of the European Union to discuss the creation of a free trade zone between the two economic blocs. . . . The EU heads of state discussed this prospect at their quarterly meeting in Germany on December 10, 1994. The timing of this meeting with that of the Summit [of the Americas in Miami, Florida] may not be entirely coincidental.

What is needed is to simplify the accession process by making it as transparent as possible. Chile, as I said, has a privileged place and stands first in line. This is to some extent symbolic, both for Chile and for NAFTA, since Asia, not NAFTA, has become Chile's top trading partner. But Chile's accession sets the precedent for the rest of the continent; and the fact that Chile is itself a global trader is important to NAFTA's eventual prospects.

Advantages of NAFTA

In many respects, trade liberalization under NAFTA has gone far beyond what the GATT Uruguay Round accomplished on a global basis. NAFTA complements and extends GATT actions. NAFTA is the leader, providing valuable guideposts for the future evolution of the trading system both in the hemisphere and globally. Opening NAFTA to new members will make the advantage of trade liberalization more evident to all.

And one of those we should care about is itself already a world-class global trader—the Colossus of the South—Brazil.

Reestablishing the Union of Giants

Brazil and the United States: for years we were close allies, the two big giants who enjoyed a genuinely special relationship as partners, not rivals. The relationship soured in the Carter years, and has yet to be restored.

Brazil, estranged from the United States, seems to have developed a different vision from ours. Its spokesmen talk (in what sounds like European Community-speak) of broadening and deepening MERCOSUR, by attracting other existing South American groupings and hardening MERCOSUR's shell—against outsiders—creating a South American common market with

91

guess who in charge. Brazilians have talked of creating a SAFTA to balance our NAFTA, and maybe when some sort of balance is reached, they might be ready to discuss integration with us.

But Brazil, like the United States, is not monolithic, and there may be other views. Many Sao Paulo, Brazil, business leaders seem to be attracted to the notion of a hemisphere-wide free trade area, sooner rather than later.

"[Economic] theory suggests that all countries gain from international trade. This has obviously not happened."

Free Trade Impoverishes Third World Nations

John Madeley

International trade could theoretically benefit the developing nations, argues John Madeley in the following viewpoint, but the record clearly shows that trade between Northern and Southern countries has benefitted the former at the expense of the latter. The reason for this inequity, Madeley explains, is that in addition to having the advantage in manufacturing, the industrialized nations have also set self-serving restrictions on international trade. Madeley is a writer and consultant on world development and environmental issues.

As you read, consider the following questions:

1. How much higher was the North's gross national product than the South's in 1930, according to the author? How much higher was it sixty years later? What, according to Madeley, do these figures prove?
2. What alternative to the current system of trade does Madeley mention?

International trade has the potential to help materially poor countries out of poverty. Poorer nations have seen richer nations increase their wealth by trading heavily with each other. For a resource-poor country the chance of getting a larger slice of world trade offers a chance to earn more in richer markets, and to gain more resources to fight poverty, and even the chance of moving from a peasant economy to a diversified economy that can meet the growing clamour for jobs. Although the returns from international trade to raw commodity-producing countries are low, they are nonetheless judged to be of importance for development efforts. This helps to explain why developing countries stay in a system which seems hostile to them.

A Trade Profile

In 1990, developing countries of the Southern hemisphere (including petroleum exporters) earned US$951 billion from their export of goods and services; merchandise trade accounted for $738 billion and services for $213 billion of this total. The earnings accounted for just under 40 per cent of the gross national product (GNP) of the developing world. Primary commodities earned $299 billion of trade in goods, and manufactured products $439 billion—the commodities accounted for only 40.5 per cent of merchandise trade compared with 83 per cent in 1966. This is chiefly because of steep price falls, rather than diversification.

Four Asian countries—Hong Kong, Korea, Taiwan and Singapore—account for over a third of the developing world's overall exports, and for most of the growth in the export of manufactures. By contrast, the 69 countries belonging to the African, Caribbean and Pacific (ACP) group of countries (consisting of almost half the countries of the developing world, and nearly all the very poorest countries) accounted for $38.7 billion, less than 5 per cent of developing countries' exports as a whole.

During the 1980s the Third World's earnings from merchandise trade fell steeply in real terms. Earnings increased in monetary terms from $582.7 billion in 1980 to $691.5 billion in 1989, which means that after price inflation was taken into account, they fell substantially. For Africa especially, but also for Latin America, the figures indicate a disastrous situation. They mean that resource-poor countries had less in real terms for development and other purposes. For Africa as a whole the fall was severe, even in money terms—from $94.7 billion in 1980 to $55.1 billion, in 1989. In 1980, the ACP group earned $66.32 billion from the export of goods; by 1989 this had fallen to $38.73 billion. Schemes to compensate for falls in trade earnings—like the ones operated under the Lomé Convention [on ongoing technical and economic cooperation], between the European Community and the ACP group—have proved inadequate; in the meantime, development aid has stagnated. . . .

Trade Theory

The existence of natural, physical resources is an important reason for trade. Zambia has the copper that is needed by Britain's vehicle industries—there is very little copper under British soil. As each motor car contains more than a kilogram of copper, without copper there would be no British-made vehicles. International trade therefore enables countries to make goods they could not make otherwise, and enables people to enjoy a wider range of goods and services than would be available to them if they relied purely on the resources of their own country. In short, trade can raise living standards.

Having a resource endowment gives a country an economic advantage over others who lack such endowments. Furthermore, when a country concentrates on making a certain product, its people become skilled in its production—they develop another type of comparative advantage.

The theory of comparative advantage is one of a very few theories that economists generally agree about, although in recent years the consensus has begun to crack. While it explains the great bulk of world trade, historical factors—especially nineteenth-century colonialism—are also a powerful influence. The theory, according to A. Seldon and F.G. Pennance, states that output and the increase from specialization and exchange 'will be maximized when each country or region specializes in the production of those goods and services in which its comparative advantage is largest'. For a variety of reasons, a particular country may be able to produce something cheaper and better than others. Country A may be able to produce its own watches, but Country B can make them cheaper and of the same quality—it has a comparative advantage over A when it comes to watch making. It may pay Country A to buy watches from B, and for A to concentrate on making those goods in which it has an advantage over B—and then for A and B to exchange goods. . . .

Trade Reality

One problem with the theory of comparative advantage is that it assumes full employment of resources—that everyone is working and that natural resources are fully utilized. If there is unemployment, then putting resources to work even if they have no comparative advantage may be more important to policymakers than economic theory. More seriously, the theory suggests that all countries gain from international trade. This has obviously not happened; some have clearly gained a great deal more than others. Swiss economist Paul Bairoch has estimated that in 1750, GNP per head of people in North and South was about the same; in 1930 it was four times higher in the North; 60 years later it was around eight times higher. Under the theory of comparative advantage, such imbalances were not supposed to happen. For one thing, wages in the North would have become so high that manufacturers would have all moved their factories to the South to take advantage of cheaper labour. At the very least they would open their new factories or locate their new services in the South. But this has not happened to any substantial degree.

"IT'S QUITE SIMPLE. YOU DIG IT OUT, WE REFINE IT AND YOU NEVER SEE IT AGAIN."

From *Politics for Life*, the Green Party manifesto. Reprinted with permission.

A World Bank survey of foreign direct investment (FDI) found that 'during the 15 years from 1970 to 1985, inflows of FDI to developing countries as a whole grew at the same pace as those going to industrialized countries'. The behaviour of financiers and businesses in the North with money to invest appears, at first sight, difficult to understand. As average wages in Britain are around £250 a week and, for example, in Sri Lanka wages average less than £25 a week, why do businesses not put all their money in Sri Lanka and reap the higher profits that come from the lower wages?

There are numerous probable reasons. A firm making clothing could set up a new factory in Britain and be able to export products to other industrialized countries without barriers. If they set up in Sri Lanka, they may be able to export only a limited amount, because of international trade restrictions. Businessmen and investors like political stability; they may feel that their investment is safer in Britain than in Sri Lanka. There may also be administrative problems; it is easier to set up a factory in your own country where you know the rules, rather than in a Third World country where administrative hurdles and unknown factors may have to be surmounted. Whatever the reasons, the theory of comparative advantage has not led to a flow of venture capital that would equalize wages and living standards between countries. But it has also failed to raise living standards in the South for deeply entrenched historical reasons.

The History of Modern Trade

The present pattern of international trade was largely established in the colonial era of the nineteenth century. The British economist John Stuart Mill said that 'colonies should not be thought of as civilizations or countries at all, but as agricultural establishments whose sole purpose was to supply the larger community to which they belong'. The world was thus divided into a small number of countries in the Northern hemisphere that industrialized and enjoyed cheap agricultural produce, and a much larger number of countries in the South that provided the cheap produce and bought some, but not many, of the comparatively expensive manufactured goods. This pattern has changed little today.

The theory of comparative advantage falls down heavily in the twentieth century because it only works if trade is between countries which are roughly equal. Western nations, however, have continued to export manufactured goods, while countries in the South have continued to export chiefly primary products and produce. North-South trade is not taking place between equals, but between a rich block and a poor block, with the gap between the two growing ever wider. . . .

One of the problems for commodity-producing countries is that they face a 'perfect' market for their goods. Information about the product, and of its price at any given time, is said to be 'perfect' in the sense that there is general and universal knowledge about them. The price of coffee beans, for example, is known and applied throughout the world. As there is often over-supply of primary produce, the prices are often low; at present the world has a glut of most of the major agricultural products that are traded on world markets. When people become richer in the North they do not generally buy more coffee and tea; demand for these products is therefore hardly expanding.

Development-Through-Trade Means Low Wages

When we first began to think about economic development, import substitution [the creation of essential industries to achieve national self-sufficiency] was the common strategy for third-world industrialization. For today's theorists, import substitution involves unacceptable protectionist practices, since its success depends on the protection of nascent enterprise from foreign competition. This means in fact the subsidizing of inefficient, or, at least, less efficient industries. But it did create some pressure for higher wages so that there would be greater effective [local] demand for local manufactures. With export-led development this pressure, ineffective as it was, is entirely gone. There is active international competition for the *lowest* wages, and ideas such as community loyalty are regarded as relics of pre-industrial societies.

This very competition provides a strong incentive—or should we say a strong temptation—to governments to discourage such activities as union organizing to the point where real human rights problems arise, and indeed have already arisen in many places. Union organizing is not tolerated. If necessary, death squads will be employed to deter union organizing. Given the way the international labor market works today, this is almost "necessary." If wages are allowed to rise, the industry will move elsewhere.

Jordan Bishop, *Commonweal*, June 17, 1994.

Companies that make manufactured goods, by contrast, enjoy an 'imperfect' market. It is one of the ironies of international trade that 'perfect' is usually bad for producers, and 'imperfect' good. Manufacturers can claim special features for their goods and fix prices accordingly; the market is not 'perfect', so there is inevitably imperfect knowledge. A manufacturer making radios can claim that this or that gadget is new or different and worthy of a higher price. If potential customers believe it, they pay the price. And, as living standards rise, so the demand for radios, watches, etc. also rises.

Industrialized countries have generated enough money from

their manufacture of goods to develop services such as transport fleets, banking and insurance, which again are in growing demand. So these countries are in a much stronger trading position than countries whose economies are based on primary produce. And, in practice, over the last 40 years or more, the price of manufactured goods has increased faster than the price of primary goods.

About half of the foreign earnings from merchandise of non–oil-producing developing countries comes from the sale of one or more primary commodities, usually agricultural, but also from minerals such as copper. Over the past 30 years the prices of the great majority of these commodities have been low and unstable. Attempts to develop international commodity agreements have come to little, while attempts to diversify into producing manufactured goods for export have run into problems, both domestic and external.

Protectionist barriers imposed by Western countries make it difficult for the developing world to branch out into manufactured goods. The West employs not only tariffs, which raise the price of imports, but also a growing range of non-tariff barriers. The 1991 *World Development Report* says that the use of protective measures, such as quotas, subsidies, and voluntary export restraints 'has risen alarmingly since the 1960s'. . . .

'Delinking' from World Trade

With industrialized nations showing little willingness to change the system, developing countries may be unwise to rely on the goodwill of the West for a new international trade. A better option would be to harness the potential of their own resources. Some economists and politicians have argued that the South would be better off 'delinking' from the 'logic of the global system', in the words of one of the most powerful advocates, Egyptian economist Samir Amin. Such a strategy does not mean 'autarky'—the cutting of all South-North trading links. Rather it involves what Amin calls 'submitting external trading relations to the logic of domestic development priorities', with more concentration on national and regional development. He calls it 'polycentrism', and it would, believes Amin, help to neutralize the effects of international trade on a developing country's internal choices.

In Amin's view the present international trading system confines Africa to an 'agro-mineral specialization based upon a destructive, extensive exploitation of land'. He also points out that technological developments in Western countries mean that the West buys fewer of the Third World raw materials and that 'a process of passive delinking is taking place'.

Especially if the terms of trade do not improve in the early years of the 1990s for the developing world, there is likely to be increased interest in delinking, polycentric ideas. It is clearly important that governments do not let international trade become too dominant in their development policy. The words of John Maynard Keynes, 'let goods be homespun whenever it is reasonably and conveniently possible', are a warning against over-emphasis on trade. Both urban and rural communities are likely to be healthier if they have an economic base that provides a high proportion of their needs. Local economics that are too dependent on either exports or imports may be too dependent on outside factors beyond their control—which could in turn threaten their survival.

"Free trade advances environmental goals, not least by fostering the economic growth necessary for environmental protection."

Free Trade Benefits the Environment

Fred L. Smith Jr.

Fred L. Smith Jr. argues in the following viewpoint that the economic development of the South through trade will lead to a cleaner environment because only through economic development can struggling nations afford to turn their attention from matters of immediate survival to investment in more efficient and environmentally friendly technologies. Smith is president of the Competitive Enterprise Institute in Washington, D.C., an organization that promotes environmental protection through the private ownership of natural resources.

As you read, consider the following questions:

1. What is the long-term trend in air quality as countries industrialize, according to Smith?
2. Why, according to Smith, is it counterproductive, even hypocritical, for the United States to impose its environmental standards on developing countries in its trade relations with them?

Excerpted from "Environmental Quality, Economic Growth, and International Trade" by Fred L. Smith Jr., published by the Competitive Enterprise Institute, Washington, D.C. Reprinted with permission.

Environmentalists are not happy with capitalism. They typically view capitalism as guilty of exploiting the finite resources of the Earth in a vain attempt to maintain a non-sustainable standard of living. To some of course, it is not just the perceived inadequacy of free markets to address environmental issues, but the institution of private property itself that drives environmental destruction. There is a belief that such [environmental] values can not receive adequate attention in a commercial world.

At the core of the global environmental debate is the concept of sustainable development. This term is a vague, almost platitudinous concept—who, after all, favors non-sustainable economic growth? Sustainability requires that, as resources are consumed, new resources must be discovered or developed, demands must be shifted to more plentiful resources, or new knowledge must permit us to meet such needs from the smaller resource base. That is, as resources are depleted, they must be renewed or used more efficiently. Can market forces achieve this result? Even in the face of the historical record, much of the environmental establishment answers "no."

Indeed, to the leadership of the environmental movement, today's environmental problems reflect the failure of the market to consider ecological values adequately. This view sees markets as shortsighted, concerned only with quick profits. Thus, markets undervalue biodiversity and other ecological concerns not readily captured in market prices, and ignore negative externalities, such as pollution. Because markets fail in these critical environmental areas, these individuals argue, political intervention is necessary. That intervention should be careful, thoughtful, even scientific, but the logic is clear: Those areas of the economy having environmental impacts must be politically controlled. However, since *every* economic decision has some environmental effect, the market failure paradigm leads to an effort to regulate every economic activity. . . .

Economic Growth Equals Environmental Quality

To many environmentalists, economic growth necessarily leads to environmental hardship. Therefore, economic growth must be restrained if nature is to be preserved. . . .

A more rational examination of the relationship between economic growth and environmental quality finds an initial decline in environmental quality with the onset of industrialization, followed by significant ecological improvement as economic growth continues. (However, if the environment is measured in human terms—that is, the quality of the *human environment*—it is not clear that there is ever a decline in the first place.) A study of 42 countries over a period of 12 years conducted by Princeton University's Gene Grossman and Alan Krueger found that "although economic growth causes a deterioration of air quality at first, it typically brings cleaner air quality when a country reaches a certain level—the point at which Gross National Product is about equal to that of Malaysia or Mexico." As economic prosperity increases, so does the technological capability to provide for increased production at greater efficiency and less environmental impact per unit of output. . . .

Economist Marian Radetzki points out that economic growth creates wealth, thereby satisfying the primary needs that often come before a concern over environmental quality. This point should be obvious. Concern for the environment is highly "income elastic." An individual's first concerns are for food, water and shelter. Countries that struggle to feed their people have less regard for the environment. They can't afford it. The United States enjoys one of the largest economies and highest standards of living in the world. It is no coincidence that we also have an enormous public concern for the environment. Poverty is no friend of the environment.

Economic Growth and the Environment

Mexico and the United States are committed to a cooperative program that will encourage sustained economic growth and environmental protection in both countries. . . . The two are complementary and must be pursued together.

The Government of Mexico knows it faces major environmental problems that threaten the health and well-being of millions of Mexicans. In recent years, Mexico has taken significant steps to address its environmental problems. . . . But the Mexicans also need economic growth to generate resources to transform this commitment into an effective program of regulation, enforcement, and public support. Mexico has over one-third of the U.S. population, but its economy is only 1/25th the size of ours.

The Bush Administration, *International Environmental Affairs*, Summer 1991.

In an address to the March 1992 meeting of the Convention on International Trade in Endangered Species (CITES), Mostafa Tolba, executive director of the U.N. Environment Program, complained that "the rich are more interested in making the Third World into a natural history museum than they are in filling the bellies of its people." Moreover, it should be clear that the necessary economic growth is unlikely to occur in a non-market economy.

The failure to recognize that private property is the keystone for effective environmental protection is endemic in the environmental movement. Imagine, however, that Britain had been dominated by environmentalists during the colonization of America. Would they not have reacted in horror to the rapidity with which the colonists cleared away the old-growth forests that blanketed North America? Certainly, the old-growth forests were "destroyed," but the lands cleared and wood acquired were put to constructive purposes. This made the U.S. wealthier, and now America can boast that it experiences net forest growth on an annual basis. In retrospect, should the colonies have been condemned for their "non-sustainable" policies—or were these policies "sustainable" after all? Are we to deny Brazil or Indonesia this same right to transform natural resources into wealth? Such trade-offs lie at the heart of this important issue.

The Importance of Free Trade

William Reilly, administrator of the U.S. Environmental Protection Agency (EPA) under President Bush, stated that "poverty has left Mexico bereft of the resources it needs to protect the environment and the environment will get no better absent free trade." Yet, despite compelling evidence that free trade advances environmental goals, not least by fostering the economic growth necessary for environmental protection, most of the environmental establishment views trade with suspicion. The costs of a growing anti-trade trend could be tremendous to both the economy and the ecology. Green [environmentalist] trade barriers could severely compromise both the economic and environmental benefits provided by specialization.

Protectionism already costs U.S. consumers approximately $80 billion annually, according to the Institute for International Economics. This is a large burden for Americans to bear, and is a frightening figure for most of the developing world. Nonetheless, the "greening of protectionism" is now well under way and is likely to get much worse in future years. "Green trade" demands are beginning to buttress "fair trade" demands, and are equally detrimental to the consumer.

The basic case for eco-protectionism is that open trade would permit, and actually encourage, industries to avoid the strict, but presumably necessary, environmental policies enacted in the United States. Thus, to save the tropical rainforests, environmentalists have opposed imports of Brazilian orange concentrate grown on lands farther from any rainforest than New York is from Florida. Similar efforts were made to restrict the importation of dolphin-tainted tuna.

In light of the recent protectionist trend, GATT [the General Agreement on Tariffs and Trade] issued a warning against "unilateral trade measures (used) to offset the competitive effects of different environment standards" and stated that there is "a serious risk of environmental issues being exploited by trade protectionist interests." As a result, several instances of U.S. environmental protectionism have been brought before GATT tribunals. GATT has consistently ruled that no country can block the imports from another country due to unequal environmental standards, much to the chagrin of environmental activists. Since the United States has one of the most restrictive systems of environmental, health and safety regulations in the world, more conflicts are inevitable.

Questionable Fears

Free trade opponents also fear that the lower environmental standards prevalent in the Third World will lure industry there, creating massive pollution in areas where there is little, or no, environmental movement. Whether such fears are well founded is unclear. As previously noted, the economic growth associated with such relocations is more likely to improve—not worsen—local concern for environmental quality. Moreover, developed nations like America have the luxury of focusing on minute cancer risks and the like, having conquered the environmental health problems that continue to plague much of the Third World—contaminated food and water. In much of the world, a modest increase in carbon monoxide or SO_2 [sulphur dioxide, which may arguably cause "acid rain"] emissions would be outweighed by the creation of an industrial base that could fund water purification and sanitation systems.

Adding weight to the position that such fears are unfounded is the fact that avoiding environmental costs is not in and of itself a major factor in the economics of plant location. At present, pollution control costs for most industries are less than 4 to 5 percent of all production costs. Those select industries that are highly sensitive to such costs and facing extremely strict regulations—for example, furniture manufacturers once located in Los Angeles—have already relocated. Most U.S. industries with high pollution abatement costs also have high capital costs that are only likely to increase in the Third World due to the lesser availability of technological resources. When one adds the costs of political instability and an untrained labor force, further international relocation becomes even less likely.

Defenders of free trade argue that the maquiladora phenomenon—the large presence of factories near the U.S.-Mexican border—does not reflect a major effort to escape U.S. regulations, but rather the relative economic freedom granted Mexican firms operating in this area as opposed to elsewhere. As a result, this region has developed more rapidly than any other region in the world. As William Reilly pointed out, "Trade, not aid, will drive economic progress in the developing world in the years ahead." As I have discussed, this is to the long-term benefit of the environment. . . .

Trade Restrictions Are Counterproductive

Environmentalists like to claim that green protectionism is necessary to ensure the health and safety of American citizens. For example, environmentalists warn that foreign nations might use pesticides banned in the United States, and possibly export the "tainted" produce back into the United States. This is the basis for the so-called "Circle of Poison" theory advanced by many environmental groups. Trade restrictions, therefore, would be essential to ensure that firms did not circumvent U.S. laws. Of course, this assumes that American risk-management policies have any relation to human health. Yet as EPA's own reports indicate, this often is not the case. Many substances banned in the United States, from Alar [a ripening agent sprayed on apples] to DDT [a pesticide], have no negative impact on human health in the trace amounts that they are encountered in the environment.

Moreover, because "wealthier is healthier," policies that reduce national wealth are also detrimental to public health. Thus, measures that restrict trade will lower the health of the nations affected. In Third World countries this impact can be very severe as even small gains in per capita wealth can have major health benefits. Thus, risk regulations that might be rational in the United States—that is, regulations with costs offset by benefits—might still be irrational—indeed fatal—in poorer nations.

Roberto Sanchez, an environmental specialist at the Colegio de la Frontera Norte, a research institute in Tijuana, emphasized that Mexico is experiencing a period of great changes, environmental and otherwise. However, he cautioned that these changes would only occur "if the American environmentalists give up some of their romantic notions and let (Mexico) find its own way." Furthermore, he noted, the environmentalists may "want to save the planet, but it is not the same planet on their side of the border as it is on (Mexico's). They can afford to defend the environment for its own sake. Our people must use the environment to survive." On the one hand the United States uses its economic might to demand that other countries adapt our environmental values under penalty of trade restrictions, while on the other hand American politicians preach the need for trade liberalization. By insisting on the implementation of their policies, environmentalists impede both economic growth and the development of better solutions.

"*Firms operating in free markets . . . tend to promote virulent strains of environmentally destructive growth.*"

Free Trade Causes Environmental Degradation

Robin Broad and John Cavanagh

In the following viewpoint, Robin Broad and John Cavanagh argue that environmental degradation in developing countries is not the fault of the poor who depend on the environment for their livelihoods but of the local elites who, together with foreign firms, profit by the monopolization and liquidation of their nations' natural resources. Market-based solutions that ignore this difference in resource access and usage will only exacerbate environmental problems, they conclude. Broad is a professor at the School of International Service at the American University. Cavanagh is a fellow at the Institute for Policy Studies at the Transnational Institute.

As you read, consider the following questions:

1. What example do Broad and Cavanagh cite to support their contention that the poor care about their environment?
2. What three reasons do the authors give in support of their belief that market-based solutions to environmental degradation are specious?

Excerpted from "Beyond the Myths of Rio" by Robin Broad and John Cavanagh, *World Policy Journal*, vol. 10, no. 1, Spring 1993. Reprinted by permission of the New School for Social Research, New York.

By the end of the 1992 Earth Summit [in Rio de Janeiro, Brazil], many participants and journalists were articulating a simple equation to explain the complex relationship between environment and development: poverty causes environmental degradation. They portrayed rich countries and wealthy people as environmentalists pressing for curbs on tropical deforestation to combat global climate change. They saw developing countries and poor people as fixated on survival and basic development issues—and if exploitation of natural resources contributed to those goals, so be it.

We have posed this rich-poor, North-South dichotomy to a number of people from organizations of small-scale farmers, fishers, and miners in developing countries. Their responses are instructive: poor people in poor countries may not have heard of global warming or ozone depletion, but their local ecological crises have often forced them to act in defense of the environment.

Peasants Protecting the Environment

Consider but one example. On a hot, dusty day in July 1987, several dozen poor peasants in the southern Philippines sat down in the middle of the narrow dirt road that runs from logging camps in the mountains above, through their town, to the sawmills of the town below. Holding hand-lettered signs that read "LOGGERS STOP!" they proceeded to make "citizens' arrests" of logging trucks. For nearly two weeks, they slept, ate, and held mass on that road until they had blockaded more than 30 logging trucks.

These people sat down to save their lands. As one explained, without the trees whose roots serve as sponges to store water and anchor soil, typhoon rains rush down the bare slopes and wash away precious topsoil. "Without trees," she told us, "there is no food, and without food, no life."

The point here is not simply that they acted; they persevered against government lethargy, corruption, and connivance with the powerful commercial logging interests in the area. The local military brutally dispersed this initial picket; yet, over a year later, the residents of this town moved their protest to the provincial capital. Still stymied by government inaction against the loggers, a number journeyed to the capital city of Manila and conducted a hunger strike. They broke their fast only after then-President Corazon Aquino agreed to halt commercial logging in their area and to help the community with a reforestation project. Now they are joining with groups from across the Philippines to demand that commercial logging be banned throughout the country.

This action highlights one weakness in the conventional Rio analysis of the North-South dichotomy: everyone in the South is considered to have the same interests—government, business, and the majority of poorer rural and urban dwellers. It assumes that governments stand above vested interests to represent broadly shared concerns in the pursuit of societal development.

The Exploitation Lobby

The reality, however, is often quite different. A small number of families in Brazil, Honduras, Zaire, Indonesia, and many other countries control economic and political power and use government power for private enrichment. And in natural-resource-rich countries, the quickest route to wealth is frequently through maximum exploitation of land, minerals, forests, and marine resources. In these countries, the overlapping interests and identities of politicians and business people—commercial logging companies owned by congressional representatives, presidential relatives, and retired military officers—make for powerful lobbies in favor of continued exploitation.

In other words, the poor do not cause most environmental problems; the rich do. It is therefore not surprising that governmental representatives from such countries do not consider environmental concerns to be primary. We do not dispute that poor people under desperate conditions often contribute individually to environmental degradation through rapid population growth and migration to fragile ecosystems, or that most countries need more effective voluntary family-planning programs. But to view poverty as the root cause is to miss the dynamic of inequality and powerlessness. For instance, it is the rich loggers whose roads open up the forest to the poorer settlers; the loggers' vast forest holdings contribute to the grossly inequitable land-distribution patterns typical of natural-resource-rich countries. In Brazil, for example, many of those poor shifting agriculturalists who are blamed for Amazonian deforestation have actually been pushed off their small farms in southern Brazil by agri-businessmen who are expanding their soybean plantations for a profitable export market. Most end up in urban slums or the Amazon because of a land-distribution system in Brazil that allows 1 percent of the landowners to own 50 percent of the arable land. For most, there is simply no place else to go.

Motivated by Survival

On the other hand, to understand why it is the poor who are more likely to become environmentalists in developing countries, often facing off against the rich, one has to appreciate that the majority of environmental problems there involve the depletion and degradation of natural resources at the start of the production chain. Forests and fishing grounds, for most people in the South, are sources of livelihood, not places for recreation. This concern is quite different from the air-and-water-pollution and waste-disposal problems that most city-dwellers and Northern citizens think of as ecological challenges.

Throughout the developing world, poor people motivated by survival are fighting back. Poor Filipino farmers are rejecting the green revolution seeds that indebted them to pesticide and fertilizer companies and, instead, are planting traditional rice varieties that do not require chemical inputs. Women in Kenya and Mozambique have organized "greenbelt movements" to reclaim parts of cities for vegetable gardens and to experiment with sustainable agroforestry techniques. Indians, rubber tappers, nut gatherers, and river people from across Brazil have united in an alliance to save the Amazon.

Free Trade Prevents Environmental Protection

In a precedent-setting case that put environmentalists worldwide on alert, a GATT [General Agreement on Tariffs and Trade] dispute panel, acting on a complaint brought by Mexico, overturned provisions of the U.S. Marine Mammal Protection Act authorizing a ban on the importation of tuna caught in purse-seine nets. The ban was implemented to protect endangered dolphins, tens of thousands of which are "incidentally" killed each year in purse-seine tuna-fishing operations. After hearing arguments in a session closed to the public, the three-member panel ruled that the ban represented an extraterritorial application of U.S. environmental standards, and that nations may not differentiate between goods on the basis of how they are processed or manufactured.

What that means, in practice, is that no country can use trade sanctions to enforce international environmental norms. Moreover, countries are barred under GATT from prohibiting the import of goods manufactured in unhealthy or environmentally unsound ways. Consumer campaigns to regulate imports of tropical timber or rainforest beef could be considered trade-illegal. NAFTA [North American Free Trade Agreement] codifies this ruling, placing a clear territorial limitation on environmental action. This logic could easily compromise the Endangered Species Act, the Migratory Bird Act, the Clean Air Act, and a host of other U.S. laws that seek to control imports.

Kristin Dawkins and William Carroll Muffett, *The Progressive*, January 1993.

To these grass-roots environmentalists, the key question is the one posed by Indian ecologist, Vandana Shiva: "Who protects which environment from whom?" Or as one Philippine environmental leader explained: "Democratizing control of resources is the key to sustainable development." Indeed, the emerging environmental movement in the Philippines, as in Malaysia, Indonesia, Brazil, Kenya, and elsewhere, is a struggle for equitable control and management of natural resources.

The success or failure of any new U.S. initiatives to prevent further environmental degradation in the South depends on the U.S. government and citizens' groups' collaborating with organizations of poorer people. For the poor are often not only the catalysts for halting the destruction but also the initiators of sustainable and equitable alternatives.

Is Free-Market Growth the Solution?

Myths beget more myths. If poor people and Southern countries are viewed as too poor to care about the environment, then poverty must be attacked through economic growth and by siphoning off some of the growing financial resources to clean up the environment. According to conventional wisdom in aid and development circles, the path toward such growth is to unleash market forces. This means ending trade restrictions, cutting government subsidies, and privatizing state enterprises—all "market distortions" that, it is argued, also provoke environmental degradation. As the Rio Declaration on Environment and Development, signed by governments at the Earth Summit, says, "States should cooperate to promote a supportive and open international economic system that would lead to economic growth and sustainable development . . . to better address the problems of environmental degradation."

Princeton economists Alan Krueger and Gene Grossman are often-cited promoters of this argument. Their 1992 study concluded that when countries pass the threshold of $4,000–$5,000 in per capita gross domestic product, emissions of three specific air pollutants tend to decrease. In a *New York Times* opinion piece, Grossman suggested that he could generalize from this finding to conclude that "attention to environmental issues is a luxury poor countries cannot afford. Once a country is able to feed its people, it begins to be willing to pay the costs of controlling pollution and cleaning up problems." In other words, as then World Bank chief economist Lawrence Summers explained, "Growth creates both the way and the will to improve the environment."

Confusing the Issues

This argument is specious for a number of reasons. It confuses government and elite interests with those of the poorer majority. Environmental issues, as we have seen, are anything but a luxury for the many who need resources to survive. Further, as Vice President Gore has argued for the United States, economic activity can either help sustain the environment or it can deplete resources, pollute, and destroy the environment. Just as investment in mass transit, energy conservation, and green technology can create U.S. jobs in a more environmentally sound fashion, alternative energy, regenerative agriculture, and sustainable fishing practices can do the same in the developing world.

Firms operating in free markets, however, tend to promote virulent strains of environmentally destructive growth. In an age of global economic integration, the kind of growth that is being encouraged in both the North and South is one where companies and countries compete by cutting costs anywhere they can. Wages and environmental standards are prime areas for such cuts. Consider Mexico's willingness to be lax in environmental enforcement as an enticement to new investment along the U.S.-Mexican border—an area that unregulated corporate expansion has transformed into what the American Medical Association calls "a virtual cesspool and breeding ground for infectious disease." (The U.S. General Accounting Office conducted a random sampling of twelve U.S. companies operating in Mexico and confirmed that all twelve were out of compliance with Mexico's environmental requirements.) In other words, Mexico's strategy of growth is based on competing in global markets through violations of labor and environmental standards.

Bilateral and multilateral agencies, such as the World Bank and International Monetary Fund, counsel countries to promote growth by freeing markets, to maximize exports, and to cut government expenses. These measures are also encouraged by new free-trade and investment agreements that the Bush administration began negotiating with our neighbors to the south, agreements that would lower barriers to corporate investment across national borders. A major task of the Clinton/Gore administration is to make the growing commerce with our southern neighbors socially and environmentally responsible.

Market Strategies Are Incoherent

Finally, market-based growth strategies that do not address the extreme inequalities of wealth and resource ownership across the developing world not only make no environmental sense, they also make no economic sense in the medium to long term. The fact that so few have access to land and other resources and that unregulated global competition keeps wages low means that there are extreme limits on the creation of markets in much of the developing world. And, in the end, if only 10 to 20 percent of a country's population can purchase the goods that country produces, then prospects for broad-based development are dim indeed.

We do not mean to suggest that market incentives cannot play a role in environmental protection. Indeed, neither the North nor the South will ever internalize fully the environmental costs of timber production, tuna fishing, or auto emissions until systems of corporate and national accounts use full-cost pricing or natural-resource accounting wherein prices reflect environmental and other costs that are passed on to society as a whole. For the South, however, these pricing changes are necessary but not sufficient for solving the problem.

The key issue is still who controls the resources. "You cannot have a technical solution without addressing access to resources," explains Chip Fay, former Friends of the Earth representative to Asia. "Investing into the existing resource-allocation system is investing in a structure that is unsustainable." The only way out is to break the connection between the politicians and the resource-controllers, a feat that—once again—requires democratizing control of resources.

Periodical Bibliography

The following articles have been selected to supplement the diverse views presented in this chapter.

Samir Amin — "Don't Adjust—Delink!" *Toward Freedom*, April/May 1993. Available from 209 College St., Burlington, VT 05401.

Marc Breslow — "How Free Trade Fails: How GATT and NAFTA Harm Democracy, Ecology, and the Third World," *Dollars & Sense*, October 1992.

Patricia Daily and S.M. Ghazanfar — "Countertrade: Help or Hindrance to Less-Developed Countries?" *The Journal of Social, Political, and Economic Studies*, Spring 1993.

Hilary F. French — "The World Bank: Now Fifty, but How Fit?" *World Watch*, July/August 1994. Available from 1776 Massachusetts Ave. NW, Washington, DC 20036.

Kempe Ronald Hope Sr. — "The Subterranean Economy and the Role of Private Investment in Developing Countries," *The Journal of Social, Political, and Economic Studies*, Summer 1993.

David Korten — "Global Integration; Global Rule," *In Context*, Fall 1993.

Sanjaya Lall — "Promoting Technology Development: The Role of Technology Transfer and Indigenous Effort," *Third World Quarterly*, vol. 14, no. 1, 1993. Available from PO Box 25, Abingdon, Oxfordshire OX14 3UE, UK.

Nicholas Lenssen — "Energy Efficiency: The Key to International Growth," *USA Today*, March 1994.

Susan Meeker-Lowry — "Hope for the South: The IMF, World Bank, and Third World," *Z Magazine*, October 1994.

Mohan Munasinghe — "Electric Power, Economic Growth in the Third World," *Forum for Applied Research and Public Policy*, Fall 1993. Available from Executive Sciences Institute, 1005 Mississippi Ave., Davenport, IA 52803.

The New Internationalist — "Development: A Guide to the Ruins," special issue, June 1992.

Gavin Williams — "Why Structural Adjustment Is Necessary and Why It Doesn't Work," *Review of African Political Economy*, June 1994.

Is Democracy a Workable Form of Government for the Third World?

The
Third
World

Chapter Preface

After the collapse of communism in the Soviet Union and Eastern Europe between 1989 and 1991, many in the United States and Western Europe predicted the spread of democracy throughout the world. These observers felt confirmed in their optimism by the democratic elections then taking place in many parts of the Third World—especially in Latin America and Asia.

In parts of the developing world, however, democracy has failed to flourish. Some attribute these failures to the unrelenting poverty of many Third World countries. According to political scientist Anthony Pereira, democracy depends on a vibrant civil society—the segment of society organized to articulate the interests of the people to the state. But, he says, "poverty saps the vitality of civil society." In areas of widespread poverty, such as the northeast region of Brazil, Pereira explains, politicians give away food, clothing, jobs, and even cash to obtain the votes of the rural poor. "In such a system," Pereira asserts, "the associations of civil society are captured by political candidates, who use them as vote banks." Because politicians control civil society, people are denied the opportunity to articulate their demands to the state and to press for more democratic forms of political representation, he says.

Others believe that civil society is promoting democracy in the Third World. According to Larry Diamond, senior research fellow at the Hoover Institution, a national policy think tank at Stanford University, in Chile, South Korea, and South Africa, "extensive mobilization of civil society was a crucial source of pressure for democratic change. . . . Citizens pressed their challenge to autocracy not merely as individuals, but as members of student movements, churches, professional organizations, women's groups, trade unions . . . and the like," he says. There are important challenges facing civil society in countries where the government controls many aspects of public life and expression, Diamond admits. But, he maintains, even in these countries "civil society can, and typically must, play a significant role in building and consolidating democracy."

Whether civil society can facilitate democratization in Third World countries is one of the issues debated in the following chapter.

"Today . . . we have trouble imagining a world that is radically better than our own, or a future that is not essentially democratic and capitalist."

Liberal Democracy Is the Only Viable Form of Government

Francis Fukuyama

As mankind approaches the end of the millennium, both authoritarian and socialist forms of government have fallen into disrepute, declares Francis Fukuyama, leaving only one guiding ideology capable of governing human society: liberal democracy, that wedding of representative democracy with free-market capitalism. Many Third World nations have tried other forms of government, Fukuyama asserts, but these regimes failed economically and repressed their people's freedoms. The result, Fukuyama argues, has been civil unrest and the adoption in those countries of liberal democracy to varying degrees. Fukuyama is a resident consultant to the RAND Corporation, a research institution on national security, and the author of several books, including *The End of History and the Last Man*, from which this viewpoint is excerpted.

As you read, consider the following questions:

1. What region's economic success proved the superiority of capitalism over socialist central planning, according to the author?
2. What region of the Third World does Fukuyama say has not learned the necessity of economic liberalism?

On both the communist Left and the authoritarian Right there has been a bankruptcy of serious ideas capable of sustaining the internal political cohesion of strong governments, whether based on "monolithic" parties, military juntas, or personalistic dictatorships. The absence of legitimate authority has meant that when an authoritarian government met with failure in some area of policy, there was no higher principle to which the regime could appeal. Some have compared legitimacy to a kind of cash reserve. All governments, democratic and authoritarian, have their ups and downs; but only legitimate governments have this reserve to draw on in times of crisis.

The weakness of authoritarian states of the Right lay in their failure to control civil society. Coming to power with a certain mandate to restore order or to impose "economic discipline," many found themselves no more successful than their democratic predecessors in stimulating steady economic growth or in creating a sense of social order. And those that were successful were hoisted on their own petard. For the societies on top of which they sat began to outgrow them as they became better educated, more prosperous, and middle class. As memory of the specific emergency that had justified strong government faded, those societies became less and less ready to tolerate military rule.

The End of Totalitarianism

Totalitarian governments of the Left sought to avoid these problems by subordinating the whole of civil society to their control, including what their citizens were allowed to think. But such a system in its pure form could be maintained only through a terror that threatened the system's own rulers. Once that terror was relaxed, a long process of degeneration set in, during which the state lost control of certain key aspects of civil society. Most important was its loss of control over the belief system. And since the socialist formula for economic growth was defective, the state could not prevent its citizens from taking note of this fact and drawing their own conclusions.

Moreover, few totalitarian regimes could replicate themselves through one or more succession crises. In the absence of commonly accepted rules of succession, it would always be a temptation for some ambitious contender for power to throw the whole system into question by calls for fundamental reform in the struggle against his rivals. The reform card is a powerful trump because dissatisfaction with Stalinist systems is high everywhere. Thus Khrushchev used anti-Stalinism against Lavrenty P. Beria and Georgy M. Malenkov, Gorbachev used it against his Brezhnev-era competitors, and Zhao Ziyang used it against the hard-line Li Peng. The question of whether the individuals or groups contending for power were real democrats was in a sense irrelevant, since the succession process tended to undermine the old regime's credibility by exposing its inevitable abuses. New social and political forces, more sincerely committed to liberal ideas, were unleashed and soon escaped the control of those who planned the first limited reforms.

The weakness of strong states has meant that many former authoritarianisms have now given way to democracy, while the former post-totalitarian states have become simple authoritarianisms, if not democracies. . . .

Bob Englehart for the *Hartford Courant*. Used with permission.

In addition to the crisis of political authoritarianism, there has been a quieter but no less significant revolution going on in the field of economics. The development that was both manifestation and cause of this revolution was the phenomenal economic growth of East Asia since World War II. This success story was not limited to early modernizers like Japan, but eventually came to include virtually all countries in Asia willing to adopt market principles and integrate themselves fully into the global, capitalist economic system. Their performance suggested that poor countries without resources other than their own hardworking populations could take advantage of the openness of the international economic system and create unimagined amounts of new wealth, rapidly closing the gap with the more established capitalist powers of Europe and North America.

The East Asian economic miracle was carefully observed around the world, nowhere more than in the communist bloc. Communism's terminal crisis began in some sense when the Chinese leadership recognized that they were being left behind by the rest of capitalist Asia, and saw that socialist central planning had condemned China to backwardness and poverty. The ensuing Chinese liberalizing reforms led to a doubling of grain production in five years and provided a new demonstration of the power of market principles. The Asian lesson was later absorbed by economists in the Soviet Union, who knew the terrible waste and inefficiency that central planning had brought about in their own country. The Eastern Europeans had less need to be taught; they understood better than other communists that their failure to reach the living standards of their fellow Europeans in the West was due to the socialist system imposed on them after the war by the Soviets.

The Southern Response

But students of the East Asian economic miracle were not restricted to the communist bloc. A remarkable transformation has taken place in the economic thinking of Latin Americans as well. In the 1950s, when the Argentine economist Raul Prebisch headed the United Nations Economic Committee for Latin America, it was fashionable to attribute the underdevelopment not only of Latin America but of the Third World more generally to the global capitalist system. It was argued that early developers in Europe and America had in effect structured the world economy in their favor and condemned those who came later to dependent positions as providers of raw materials. By the early 1990s, that understanding had changed entirely: President Carlos Salinas de Gortari in Mexico, President Carlos Menem in Argentina, and President Fernando Collor de Mello in Brazil, all sought to implement far-reaching programs of economic liberalization after coming to power, accepting the need for market competition and openness to the world economy. Chile put liberal economic principles into practice earlier in the 1980s under Pinochet, with the result that its economy was the healthiest of any in the Southern Cone as it emerged from dictatorship under the leadership of President Patricio Alwyn. These new, democratically elected leaders started from the premise that underdevelopment was not due to the inherent inequities of capitalism, but rather to the insufficient degree of capitalism that had been practiced in their countries in the past. Privatization and free trade have become the new watchwords in place of nationalization and import substitution. The Marxist orthodoxy of Latin American intellectuals has come under increasing challenge from writers like Hernando de Soto, Mario Vargas Llosa, and Carlos Rangel, who have begun to find a significant audience for liberal, market-oriented economic ideas.

As mankind approaches the end of the millennium, the twin crises of authoritarianism and socialist central planning have left only one competitor standing in the ring as an ideology of potentially universal validity: liberal democracy, the doctrine of individual freedom and popular sovereignty. Two hundred years after they first animated the French and American revolutions, the principles of liberty and equality have proven not just durable but resurgent.

Liberalism and democracy, while closely related, are separate concepts. Political liberalism can be defined simply as a rule of law that recognizes certain individual rights or freedoms from government control. While there can be a wide variety of definitions of fundamental rights, we will use the one contained in Lord Bryce's classic work on democracy, which limits them to three: civil rights, "the exemption from control of the citizen in respect of his person and property"; religious rights, "exemption from control in the expression of religious opinions and the practice of worship"; and what he calls political rights, "exemption from control in matters which do not so plainly affect the welfare of the whole community as to render control necessary," including the fundamental right of press freedom. It has been a common practice for socialist countries to press for the recognition of various second- and third-generation economic rights, such as the right to employment, housing, or health care. The problem with such an expanded list is that the achievement of these rights is not clearly compatible with other rights like those of property or free economic exchange. In our definition we will stick to Bryce's shorter and more traditional list of rights, which is compatible with those contained in the American Bill of Rights.

A Special Kind of Liberalism

Democracy, on the other hand, is the right held universally by all citizens to have a share of political power, that is, the right of all citizens to vote and participate in politics. The right to participate in political power can be thought of as yet another liberal right—indeed, the most important one—and it is for this reason that liberalism has been closely associated historically with democracy.

In judging which countries are democratic, we will use a strictly formal definition of democracy. A country is democratic if it grants its people the right to choose their own government through periodic, secret-ballot, multi-party elections, on the basis of universal and equal adult suffrage. It is true that formal democracy alone does not always guarantee equal participation and rights. Democratic procedures can be manipulated by elites, and do not always accurately reflect the will or true self-interests of the people. But once we move away from a formal definition, we open up the possibility of infinite abuse of the democratic principle. In this century, the greatest enemies of democracy have attacked "formal" democracy in the name of "substantive" democracy. This was the justification used by Lenin and the Bolshevik party to close down the Russian Constituent Assembly and proclaim a party dictatorship, which was to achieve substantive democracy "in the name of the people." Formal democracy, on the other hand, provides real institutional safeguards against dictatorship, and is much more likely to produce "substantive" democracy in the end.

Democracy's Universal Validity

Democratic government has broken out of its original beachhead in Western Europe and North America, and has made significant inroads in other parts of the world that do not share the political, religious, and cultural traditions of those areas. . . . The success of democracy in a wide variety of places and among many different peoples would suggest that the principles of liberty and equality on which they are based are not accidents or the results of ethnocentric prejudice, but are in fact discoveries about the nature of man as man, whose truth does not diminish but grows more evident as one's point of view becomes more cosmopolitan.

Francis Fukuyama, *The End of History and the Last Man*, 1992.

While liberalism and democracy usually go together, they can be separated in theory. It is possible for a country to be liberal without being particularly democratic, as was eighteenth-century Britain. A broad list of rights, including the franchise, was fully protected for a narrow social elite, but denied to others. It is also possible for a country to be democratic without being liberal, that is, without protecting the rights of individuals and minorities. A good example of this is the contemporary Islamic Republic of Iran, which has held regular elections that were reasonably fair by Third World standards, making the country more democratic than it was in the time of the Shah. Islamic Iran, however, is not a liberal state; there are no guarantees of free speech, assembly, and, above all, of religion. The most elementary rights of Iranian citizens are not protected by the rule of law, a situation that is worse for Iran's ethnic and religious minorities.

Economic Liberalism

In its economic manifestation, liberalism is the recognition of the right of free economic activity and economic exchange based on private property and markets. Since the term "capitalism" has acquired so many pejorative connotations over the years, it has recently become a fashion to speak of "free-market economics" instead; both are acceptable alternative terms for economic liberalism. It is evident that there are many possible interpretations of this rather broad definition of economic liberalism, ranging from the United States of Ronald Reagan and the Britain of Margaret Thatcher to the social democracies of Scandinavia and the relatively statist regimes in Mexico and India. All contemporary capitalist states have large public sectors, while most socialist states have permitted a degree of private economic activity. There has been considerable controversy over the point at which the public sector becomes large enough to disqualify a state as liberal. Rather than try to set a precise percentage, it is probably more useful to look at what attitude the state takes *in principle* to the legitimacy of private property and enterprise. Those that protect such economic rights we will consider liberal; those that are opposed or base themselves on other principles (such as "economic justice") will not qualify.

The present crisis of authoritarianism has not necessarily led to the emergence of liberal democratic regimes, nor are all the new democracies which have emerged secure. The newly democratic countries of Eastern Europe face wrenching transformations of their economies, while the new democracies in Latin America are hobbled by a terrible legacy of prior economic mismanagement. Many of the fast developers in East Asia, while economically liberal, have not accepted the challenge of political liberalization. The liberal revolution has left certain areas like the Middle East relatively untouched. It is altogether possible to imagine states like Peru or the Philippines relapsing into some kind of dictatorship under the weight of the crushing problems they face.

But the fact that there will be setbacks and disappointments in the process of democratization, or that not every market economy will prosper, should not distract us from the larger pattern that is emerging in world history. The apparent number of choices that countries face in determining how they will organize themselves politically and economically has been *diminishing* over time. Of the different types of regimes that have emerged in the course of human history, from monarchies and aristocracies, to religious theocracies, to the fascist and communist dictatorships of this century, the only form of government that has survived intact to the end of the twentieth century has been liberal democracy.

The Victory of an Idea

What is emerging victorious, in other words, is not so much liberal practice, as the liberal *idea*. That is to say, for a very large part of the world, there is now no ideology with pretensions to universality that is in a position to challenge liberal democracy, and no universal principle of legitimacy other than the sovereignty of the people. Monarchism in its various forms had been largely defeated by the beginning of this century. Fascism and communism, liberal democracy's main competitors up till now, have both discredited themselves. If the Soviet Union's successor states fail to democratize, if Peru or the Philippines relapse into some form of authoritarianism, democracy will most likely have yielded to a colonel or bureaucrat who claims to speak in the name of the Russian, Peruvian, or Philippine people alone. Even non-democrats will have to speak the language of democracy in order to justify their deviation from the single universal standard.

It is true that Islam constitutes a systematic and coherent ideology, just like liberalism and communism, with its own code of morality and doctrine of political and social justice. The appeal of Islam is potentially universal, reaching out to all men as men, and not just to members of a particular ethnic or national group. And Islam has indeed defeated liberal democracy in many parts of the Islamic world, posing a grave threat to liberal practices even in countries where it has not achieved political power directly. The end of the Cold War in Europe was followed immediately by a challenge to the West from Iraq, in which Islam was arguably a factor.

Despite the power demonstrated by Islam in its current revival, however, it remains the case that this religion has virtually no appeal outside those areas that were culturally Islamic to begin with. The days of Islam's cultural conquests, it would seem, are over: it can win back lapsed adherents, but has no resonance for young people in Berlin, Tokyo, or Moscow. And while nearly a billion people are culturally Islamic—one-fifth of the world's population—they cannot challenge liberal democracy on its own territory on the level of ideas. Indeed, the Islamic world would seem more vulnerable to liberal ideas in the long run than the reverse, since such liberalism has attracted numerous and powerful Muslim adherents over the past century and a half. Part of the reason for the current, fundamentalist revival is the strength of the perceived threat from liberal, Western values to traditional Islamic societies.

We who live in stable, long-standing liberal democracies face an unusual situation. In our grandparents' time, many reasonable people could foresee a radiant socialist future in which private property and capitalism had been abolished, and in which politics itself was somehow overcome. Today, by contrast, we have trouble imagining a world that is radically better than our own, or a future that is not essentially democratic and capitalist. Within that framework, of course, many things could be improved: we could house the homeless, guarantee opportunity for minorities and women, improve competitiveness, and create new jobs. We can also imagine future worlds that are significantly worse than what we know now, in which national, racial, or religious intolerance makes a comeback, or in which we are overwhelmed by war or environmental collapse. But we cannot picture to ourselves a world that is *essentially* different from the present one, and at the same time better. Other, less reflective ages also thought of themselves as the best, but we arrive at this conclusion exhausted, as it were, from the pursuit of alternatives we felt *had* to be better than liberal democracy. . . .

The End of History

It is against this background that the remarkable worldwide character of the current liberal revolution takes on special significance. For it constitutes . . . evidence that there is a fundamental process at work that dictates a common evolutionary pattern for *all* human societies—in short, something like a Universal History of mankind in the direction of liberal democracy. The existence of peaks and troughs in this development is undeniable. But to cite the failure of liberal democracy in any given country, or even in an entire region of the world, as evidence of democracy's overall weakness, reveals a striking narrowness of view. . . .

The question of whether there is such a thing as a Universal History of mankind that takes into account the experiences of all times and all peoples is not new; it is in fact a very old one which recent events compel us to raise anew. From the beginning, the most serious and systematic attempts to write Universal Histories saw the central issue in history as the development of Freedom. History was not a blind concatenation of events, but a meaningful whole in which human ideas concerning the nature of a just political and social order developed and played themselves out. And if we are now at a point where we cannot imagine a world substantially different from our own, in which there is no apparent or obvious way in which the future will represent a fundamental improvement over our current order, then we must also take into consideration the possibility that History itself might be at an end.

> *"It is clear that the 'political victory' of the West and the ascendancy of the free market regimes is a historical regression."*

Socialism Is Superior to Liberal Democracy

Jim Petras

The media-proclaimed "victory" of capitalist, or liberal, democracy over communism has caused many socialists to accommodate themselves to capitalism in order to further their political goals, explains Jim Petras in the following viewpoint. These "pragmatists" justify their compromise by arguing that socialism failed, leaving guerrilla warfare and democratic elections as the only avenues for action remaining to the political left, Petras says. But, he argues, this view overlooks the truly democratic and essentially socialist organizations that flourished and continue to flourish among the Latin American people. Organizations like these, he says, may furnish the basis for a renewed socialist political economy to challenge the capitalist one now fragmenting the human community. Petras teaches at the State University of New York at Binghamton and has coauthored the 1995 book *Empire or Republic? American Global Power and Domestic Decay.*

As you read, consider the following questions:

1. What are the three waves of politics in Latin America's recent past, according to the author?
2. What does Petras mean when he says that "to conserve the republic . . . is to be revolutionary"?

Excerpted from Jim Petras, "Notes on the Future of Socialism," *Z Papers*, vol. 3, no. 3, July/September 1994. Reprinted with permission.

Since the mid-1970s Latin America has endured the hardships and inequalities associated with the free market: inequalities have deepened, poverty has increased, natural resources are plundered, public enterprises have been privatized at outrageous prices. The overseas dollar accounts of the wealthy have fattened, the number of billionaires has tripled, U.S., European and Japanese banks have recovered their original loans several times over.

Yet despite the severity of the exploitation, the political response has been relatively weak: sporadic riots and protests, political-social movements struggling to defend the remains of the social and labor legislation of previous eras. . . .

The principal social forces of the Left have experienced a series of traumatic shocks that seriously impaired their capacity to react. In the first instance the violent eruption of military dictatorships and the associated authoritarian political regimes destroyed labor unions, neighborhood organizations and civic groups. Immediately afterwards the Draconian economic shock tactics—the application of the free market policies—virtually dismantled a half century of social legislation and labor rights. Finally the collapse of the Communist regimes and the accompanying disappearance of an ideological and political reference point further divided and disoriented the Left. As a consequence of these "shocks," the discontent and malaise among the populace engendered by the application of neoliberal policies was disconnected from political movements.

Post Traumatic Politics

Today, after two decades of free market policies beginning in the 1970s, there are signs that the end of the neoliberal cycle is approaching. Significant electoral movements are calling into question the supposedly benign effects of free market policies and demanding changes in the social programs and state policy.

Latin America is entering a period of transition from free markets to post-liberalism. The protagonists of the new politics are divided into two sectors. One variant proposes to manage the liberal economy with greater attention to the social costs. The other is calling for systemic changes, structural changes that affect power, property and production.

Two types of political actors are struggling to define the politics of post-liberalism. The first and most visible are the electoral personalities, who seek to negotiate better salaries, increase taxes to finance poverty programs, and re-negotiate the foreign debt in order to free funds to stimulate local industry and increase employment. In a word, they hope to convince the free market establishment to share wealth and power with the popular classes, without touching the changes brought by neoliberal policies.

The second group of actors include the sociopolitical movements composed basically of the urban and rural poor, who want to transform property relations (land and enterprises) and to create new forms of political representation and redistribute income. . . .

Drawing by Anthony Russo. Used with permission.

Each and every center-Left regime will have to confront serious challenges. First the opposition of the United States. The Clinton administration has already indicated its hostility toward any effort designed to reverse the free market model and/or to change the conditions of debt-payment. Treasury Under-Secretary Lawrence

Summers was in Brazil in May 1994 warning the leaders of the Workers Party that any modification of the liberalization process could provoke cuts in the financial flow from overseas banks and lending agencies. The other major challenge to a center-Left regime comes from major investors in Latin America. The CEO's have grown accustomed to functioning with the premise that free market policies will continue, that the labor force will continue to be organizationally weak, poorly paid and dispersed, that the state subsidies promoting exports will continue and that opportunities to exploit public resources will not end. Conditioned by more than a decade in this environment, it is doubtful that big investors are eager to make any agreements with the center-Left to share power and wealth.

If internal and external pressures block reforms proposed by the center-Left, this could open the way for the advance of the sociopolitical movements and strengthen their argument that economic liberalism and social welfare are incompatible. In this context it is possible to imagine the ascendancy of the Left as a result of the frustrated expectations of the popular majorities.

This scenario is not so improbable as it was only a few years back. Below the surface unity between the electoral politicians and the sociopolitical movements, real tensions exist. Not only over the methods of struggle and the nature of the changes, but also over the character of the social actors. Throughout Latin America the social movements are pressuring the organized electoral parties. In Mexico the pragmatic programs of the leaders of the Revolutionary Democratic Party competes with the revolutionary demands of the Zapatista Movement. In Brazil, the realists promoting the electoral campaign of Lula are feeling the pressure from the Landless Workers Movement and the urban and trade union organizations. . . .

Socialist Pragmatism Disarmed

In this emerging post free market world, at times one doesn't know if the pragmatists are the utopians and the revolutionaries are the realists. Basically there are several serious flaws in the pragmatic argument. First, they seriously distort the political experiences of the 1960s and 1970s. . . . The pragmatists have rewritten the past in the service of their current doctrinal preferences. Essentially, they have attempted to reduce the complex and rich mosaic of past popular revolutionary experiences into a conflict between guerrillas and military. Thus the problem of understanding the positive experiences of revolutionary change through popular organizations is evaded. Instead of analyzing the workers' councils in Chile, the experimental schools and democratic patient-doctor committees in the mental institutions of Argentina, the new forms of political representation found in the popular assemblies in the neighborhoods and trade unions in Uruguay and Bolivia, the pragmatic ideologues choose to focus on military confrontations and failures of the guerrilla movements. The experiences of popular representation did not fail, they were defeated by force and violence—they were not utopian yearnings dissociated from everyday experiences. Indeed for the pragmatists to recognize this other reality of the 1960s/70s would certainly raise important alternatives to their current preoccupations with channeling politics among electoral leaders and enlightened elites. The pragmatists, by posing the false dichotomy of the guerrillas/Army of the 1960s/70s, can dismiss the relevance of popular democratic forms of governance to the 1990s. Denying the past, the pragmatists can present contemporary choices as military authoritarianism or electoral politics. . . .

Three Waves of Politics

The best way to conceptualize the political economy of Latin America in the recent past and immediate future is in terms of three waves. Each wave has its beginning, its high tide and ebb. Since the early 1970s, the neoliberal or free market regimes gained ascendancy, implemented their policies, consolidated power and then experienced severe decline. The policies of privatization, deregulation and export specialization led to the emergence of social, economic and political contradictions. In the economic realm, the privatization led to the concentration of wealth and the increased inequalities in society; deregulation facilitated the increasing flow of capital and trade, but also led to the large outflows of capital and the deindustrialization of major regions and sectors; export specialization led to the disarticulation of the domestic economy and the growth of regional inequalities. The combined impacts of these contradictory processes led to the heightening of political contradictions between the marginal, excluded regions and classes and the new rich associated with the neoliberal regime. As these contradictions matured, a process of political decay set in, laying the groundwork for the second wave: the post-neoliberal policy regimes.

The . . . center-Left regimes attempt to harness the neoliberal regime with greater social welfare expenditures and greater state intervention in promoting a diversified economy. The new regimes confront the basic contradiction of attempting to link internationalized capital linked to the world market with the reconstruction of the domestic market and the mobilization of resources for industrial employment. Given the incompatibilities between the logic of externally linked socioeconomic classes and the logic of social redistribution, the second wave of neostructuralism soon confronts structural, budgetary and political constraints. The imminent crisis facilitates the possible opening for the socialist Left. . . .

But one might argue that "socialism" was an abysmal failure, universally recognized as such.

Capitalism Has Not Delivered

Although these may look like bad times for revolutionary politics, from a longer view it is obvious that capitalism has little to offer the Third World. Extreme misery and continuing debt crisis are the order of the day. Even in the center [the developed countries], social life for the masses is taking on more of a Third World aura. The United States, often thought of as the richest country on the planet, is decaying from within. . . .

In the West there are growing popular movements for social justice. Some real innovations in more communal forms have been effected, especially by the most exploited and oppressed sectors of our societies, and these experiments will likely increase as ruling classes implement neoconservative/neoliberal policies that lead to . . . increasing social inequality, unemployment, and homelessness. It is clear that, for growing numbers of people in both center and periphery, capitalism has not delivered the goods, and the argument that socialism is necessary for social well-being has lost none of its validity.

Dave Broad, *Latin American Perspectives*, Spring 1993.

Throughout Eastern Europe and the former Soviet Union, the stark contrast between the present plummeting income levels, out of control crime, and armies of unemployed and penurious retirees and the past welfare state, personal security and stable employment under Communism is provoking a rethinking of the virtues of the "free market" policies promoted by Western governments and their local clients. The rethinking increasingly involves an increased appreciation of the social and economic benefits accrued under Communism. It is time now in the West to make a serious effort to go beyond the cliches of the media celebrating the ideological "victories" of the West and the "demise of Communism." To begin, one must make several distinctions when addressing the historical experience of Communism. First of all it is important to sort out the social welfare gains from the police state regime and to reject the global concept of Stalinism which subsumed the contradictory nature of these societies under a single pejorative phrase. In this regard it is also important to periodicize the Communist experience from the bloody purges of the 1930s to early 1950s, the authoritarian repressive regime of the 1960s and 1970s to emerging pluralist socialist democracies that began to take form in the mid-1980s. It is clear that the democratic social welfare states that briefly appeared prior to the advent of the free market policies, provided a more positive political, economic and social environment for the evolution of these societies than what subsequently has emerged. Finally, sufficient time has passed to offer a tentative evaluation of the free market regimes and it is clear that from most significant socioeconomic and cultural angles, the late Communist period is a more advanced and autonomous polity than at least early liberalism. Theoretically, it is clear that the "political victory" of the West and the ascendancy of the free market regimes is a historical regression. One only needs to look at the bloody ethnic wars, the all pervasive pillage of the economies, the waste of skilled labor and scientists, the decay of public life to note the rapid descent.

The point that needs to be made is that there are many elements of the Communist experience that are historically usable and relevant in posing alternatives to free market policies. One need not shrink from the hysterical reaction (neo-Stalinism) that in all probability will be evoked by the Western media. One surely must be careful in formulating exactly what is being cited or being extrapolated and what is excluded. Clearly one can avoid the trap of accommodating the Western pundits through nostalgic references to the past regime. Most important, there are positive historical experiences which in comparative historical perspective clearly mark out the advantages of social property (even under bureaucratic conditions) to what has emerged under the free market. By calling for a rethinking of Stalinism it is not to defend the previous repressive regime but to point to the positive social experiences that serve as references in the creation of a new political regime: that social property does have favorable consequences over capitalism.

In fact, one could extend the argument. It was the positive social welfare measures of the Communist countries which prodded the Western capitalist countries to sustain welfare programs to meet the ideological competition from the East. It is no coincidence that with the elimination of the Communist welfare alternative, the Western regimes have engaged in large-scale efforts to dismantle their welfare programs. The deeper meaning of the defeat of Communism is the frontal assault on a politically disarmed working class who have been sold a bill of goods: that welfare states don't work, that police-states (Stalinism) and the welfare state are part of the same package, that the whole noncapitalist historical experience was an unmitigated disaster. . . .

Conservatism and Revolution

To be an authentic conservative today is to be a revolutionary. Free market liberalism has everywhere launched a full-scale attack on nations, communities, classes and families. National economies have been decimated as financial resources, capital and ultimately labor have moved to new centers of concentration. Those international centers where the main financial and economic circuits operate have grown and prospered, while the provinces, the working class cities have been depleted of wealth, jobs and social services. The "gird pattern" of national economies has been replaced by giant international spokes: the national market is an adjunct of the economic strategies adopted by the imperial state and the multinational firms. The republic has been subordinated to the empire, the provinces of the periphery have been converted into a collection of impoverished regions dominated by urban metropoles. To conserve the republic against the imperial temptation—the subversive efforts of the free market—is to be revolutionary.

A Socially Destructive System

The international market, the principal driving force of liberalism, has destroyed communities and their social fabric everywhere. In its wake it has spawned the atomized individual. To be revolutionary is to conserve the community against the onslaught of free market modernity. The most destructive force in undermining neighborhoods, family ties, entire communities has been the decision of multinational corporations to move their operations abroad, to other regions, or to shift to financial services. Free market doctrines have undermined all non-market relations without any social restraints. As a result of the loss of manufacturing employment, large urban complexes have been transformed into social wastelands. There is a direct relation between deindustrialization and low paid jobs, unemployment, broken families, teenage pregnancy, high crime rates and the proliferation of drugs. To conserve family and community means to engage in a struggle against free market modernity; conversely, to engage in struggle requires the conservation of community, class and family bonds to construct the social solidarity to engage in political struggle against the transitory relations that corporations develop with workers and communities. The ideal world of the multinational corporations is made up of atomized individuals whose primary ties are dictated by the market. Against the ideology of social or class solidarity, free market ideology promotes consumerism—the substitution of consumer spending for social bonds. Consumerism cultivates relations to things through the market, thus reinforcing the socio-political isolation of the atomized individual.

In the relations between couples, the message of the media increasingly parallels the workplace. The flexibilization of labor allows management to shift workers from one job to another at times and locations most convenient to the corporation. Likewise, the new mode of relations implicit and explicit in the mass media are transitory relations or the flexibilization of personal relations: quick entries, easy departures and plastic smiles. . . .

Challenges on the Horizon

Throughout the world, and in particular Latin America, major challenges to free market doctrines are increasingly on the horizon. Socioeconomic and political conditions are generating a multiplicity of apparent political alternatives—from pragmatic reformers to revolutionary social-political movements. . . . The various traumas that undermined the socialist alternative are no longer the potent factors of a few years back. Contemporary and historical experiences provide lines of inquiry toward the creation of a relevant socialist project. The catastrophic impact of free market policies in the East, the decay of social democracy and the rethinking of the Stalinist experience provide parameters for creating revolutionary or radical new proposals. The new politics, however, must not be built only around economic interests and organization but ethical principles. More fundamentally, the Left can only become a meaningful force if it resists the temptation of free market individualism and returns to conserving class and community bonds and traditions as essential elements to collective action.

> *"[Economic] liberalization, first, then democratization makes a great deal of sense for those who wish to achieve both goals."*

Economic Development Must Precede Democracy

Samuel P. Huntington

Since the mid-1970s the world has been experiencing a shift toward democracy, and another toward free-market economies, argues Samuel P. Huntington in the following viewpoint. But while democracy may be instituted by passing laws, economic reform is not so easy, he contends. Free-market reforms that entail cutting government jobs and social services are painful for most people, he warns. Therefore, economic reform must precede democratization, Huntington explains, if authoritarian states are to remain capable of resisting the public outcry long enough to attain the level of economic development necessary for successful democratization. Huntington is the director of the Olin Institute for Strategic Studies at Harvard University and the author of *The Third Wave*, a book about economic and democratic development in the Third World.

As you read, consider the following questions:

1. How are democratization and economic liberalization different in terms of their political costs and benefits, according to Huntington?
2. What does the author say happens when authoritarian governments democratize before they liberalize? What example does he give?

Excerpted from Samuel P. Huntington, "What Cost Freedom?" *Harvard International Review*, vol. 15, no. 2, Winter 1992/93, ©1993 Harvard Council on International Relations. Reprinted with permission.

During the past twenty years, two great tidal waves of change have swept across the world. One is the shift from authoritarian political systems—military governments, personal dictatorships and communist regimes—to democratic political systems. This wave of democratization began in 1974 in southern European nations such as Portugal, Greece and Spain. It then moved to Latin America in the later 1970s and early 1980s, with shifts to democracy occurring in Ecuador, Peru, Argentina, Brazil, Uruguay, El Salvador, Guatemala, Chile and other Latin American countries such as Mexico, Panama and Paraguay beginning to move in a democratic direction. At present, Cuba is the only Latin American country that has not been touched by this wave. Meanwhile, the democratization wave had moved on to Asia, with transitions away from authoritarian rule occurring in the Philippines, Korea, Taiwan, Pakistan and Bangladesh. In 1989, the communist regimes in East-Central Europe collapsed and were replaced by democratic systems, and now similar changes are occurring in some, if not all, of the former Soviet republics. Apartheid has ended in South Africa, and the major political forces there have negotiated a new democratic constitution. In four other African countries, elections have been held for the first time in years and long-term dictators have been voted out of office. In the Middle East, Turkey made its latest shift to democracy in the early 1980s, and some movement in a democratic direction has occurred in Jordan and Algeria. Overall, more than forty countries have made the transition to democracy since 1974, and many others have moved toward more open politics, even if they have stopped short of true popularly elected governments. Democratization clearly has been a global phenomenon.

The Parallel Economic Movement

The parallel and simultaneous movement toward economic liberalization has also been a global phenomenon. This trend involves efforts to reduce the economic role of the state, to rely more on markets to allocate goods, to privatize state enterprises, to eliminate government regulations, license requirements and subsidies, to reduce tariffs and other trade barriers, to cut government spending, to balance budgets and to curtail inflation. Economic liberalization occurs in various forms and hence it is difficult, if not impossible, to produce a list of countries that can be said to have fully liberalized.

With a few notable exceptions, however, almost every country in the world has been affected by this trend. In the industrialized world, it was epitomized in the goals and policies of the Thatcher and Reagan governments—although the American trend toward deregulation got underway during the Carter Administration. Encouraged by the World Bank and the International Monetary

Fund, most countries in the Third World, including India, Brazil, Argentina and Mexico, have made some movement toward economic liberalization. Among communist countries, China took the lead in introducing major economic reforms at the end of the 1970s. Now all the East-Central European countries and most of the former Soviet republics are moving in a similar direction. Even Vietnam has taken some small steps toward opening up its economy. In the communist world only Cuba and North Korea appear to be relatively unaffected, and signs of change are even now beginning to appear in North Korea.

Economic Growth Brings Democracy

Growth leads to democracy for two reasons. First, as a small slice of the population is enriched, the rest of the citizens agitate for their fair shot at doing better, and such privilege is granted only in democracies. Then, too, rising incomes at first go toward needed goods and investment, then later toward more and more of what economists call "luxury goods," such as higher education. A more educated population tends to demand political and civil rights, and so democratization begins.

Perhaps the best example of this progression is South Korea, where a strong autocratic regime set growth targets and goals for industry. . . . By the mid-1980s, Korea had a strong industrial base, but there were draconian antilabor laws on the books, and labor activists were persecuted. The June 1987 uprising brought calls for democracy, and President Roh Tae Woo, who took over in 1988, started the process by guaranteeing basic labor rights and adopting sweeping reforms. Now President Kim Young Sam—freely elected in 1992—is moving quickly to weed out corruption.

Karen Pennar et al., *Business Week*, June 7, 1993.

The questions I wish to address concern the relation between these waves of political democratization and economic liberalization. . . . How do they resemble or differ from each other? Do they reinforce each other or do they conflict with each other? . . .

Similarities and Differences

What are the similarities and differences between political democratization and economic liberalization? First, they resemble each other in that each limits governmental authority and the power of the state. At least in theory, democratization makes the state apparatus both subordinate and responsible to civil society. Political leaders who want to get into power or to remain in power have to pay attention to the popular will. Liberalization, in turn, reduces the role of the state in the economy. Democratization requires political freedoms from the state—freedom to speak, organize and to protest; liberalization requires economic freedom from the state—freedom to own property, to work, invest, produce and consume without intrusive state regulation. Democratization increases the control of society over the state; liberalization reduces the control of the state over society.

Second, however, is the question of the relation of these trends to the overall global processes of economic development and social modernization that have been at work in the world since the beginning of the Industrial Revolution in the eighteenth century. Alexis de Tocqueville and others have said that democratization is the inevitable trend in modern society. In fact the modern world has seen three major waves of democratization: the first beginning in the early nineteenth century in America and culminating at the close of World War I; the second beginning with the Allied victory in World War II and ending in the early 1960s; and the third beginning in the 1970s. Between these democratization waves, reverse waves back toward authoritarianism occurred in the 1920s and 1930s and again in the 1960s. The reverse waves, however, were weaker than the democratization waves, and the general tendency in the modern world has been toward the expansion of democratic government.

The Economic Trend

Can the same be said with respect to economic liberalization? That appears to be more uncertain. From the late eighteenth to the mid-nineteenth centuries, the overall trend was certainly toward the freeing of economic activity, the weakening of mercantilist state controls and the breakdown of the lingering remnants of feudal or comparable restrictions, such as slavery, on the movement and use of labor, capital, goods and resources. In the late nineteenth century, however, demands arose, in large part as a result of democratization, for expanded state activity to set minimum welfare standards in industrialized societies, to protect elements of the population against exploitation, to cope with downturns of the business cycle, and to insure that the industrial economy would be responsive to the security needs of the nation-state. Wars and the threat of war enhanced the economic power of the state. In addition, throughout the industrializing world, socialist and then communist movements appeared, promoting much greater or even total state control of the economy. By the 1930s, more economic planning, welfare programs, government regulation and nationalization of industry were all seen as the wave of the future in most societies. In the 1960s, all of this began to change. The question necessarily arises: Is this recent shift away from state control and toward economic liberalization simply a temporary interruption, an economic "reverse wave" of a longer term trend toward the growth of state power? Or is it the beginning of a long-term secular decline in state economic activity? Does not the global movement toward democratization generate popular pressures for the state to be more actively engaged in both productive and redistributive activities? It seems plausible to think of democratization as being historically "progressive," but would one say that the contraction of state economic activity or its expansion is historically "progressive"?

Third, a significant difference exists in our knowledge about these two processes. Since Tocqueville, political scientists have studied democratization extensively and produced a vast and variegated amount of literature on the subject. There has been a lot of experience to study, and the past two decades have seen an explosion in democratization studies. As a result, political science has developed a very considerable understanding of the conditions for democratization, the processes by which it occurs and its consequences. Nothing quite similar exists with respect to economic liberalization largely because experience with it since the mid-nineteenth century has been so limited. Until this decade, no command economy had become a market economy, and few, if any, statist economies had become less statist. As a result, economists have had relatively little to say, few theories to offer and fewer lessons to expound about how to move from a state-dominated to a market-dominated economy. This is particularly true with respect to the problems of dismantling totally state-controlled command economies like those that existed in the communist societies. As Paul MacCracken put it, commenting on the problem of moving the East-Central European economies into market economies, "Maybe you can't get there from here." In contrast, political scientists feel reasonably confident that they do know how to get from an authoritarian to a democratic political system.

Different Implementation Obstacles

Fourth, a related factor concerns the differences in the difficulty of making these transitions. At an institutional level, democratization is much easier than economic liberalization. The rudimentary elements of democratization are achieved if reasonably fair, open and inclusive elections are held in which parties and candidates compete relatively equally, the votes are counted honestly and the winners form a government. The consolidation of a new democratic system may require more long-term changes in values and attitudes and the institutionalization of democratic behavior patterns. Yet the election of rulers is the core of democracy, and it can be introduced relatively quickly and easily.

139

In contrast, economic reform, particularly when it involves the dismantling of a command economy, is much more difficult and requires sustained effort over a long period of time. It is much easier to organize elections than to organize markets. While the shift from an authoritarian to a democratic political system can occur quickly, and even relatively painlessly, the shift from a heavily state-controlled economy to a market economy is far more painful and time consuming.

Different Political Costs and Benefits

Fifth, the differences in the institutional problems of introducing elections and markets are compounded by the differences in their political costs and benefits. Democratization may impose costs on those who opposed it or who benefited significantly from the authoritarian regime. A significant majority of "third wave" democratizations, however, were initiated by groups holding power in authoritarian regimes and hence even they saw the costs and risks of democratization to be limited. Overall, democratization tends to produce immediate and widespread benefits for large portions of the population: hence the frequently commented upon phenomenon of the "euphoria" that accompanies almost all democratization movements. Economic liberalization, on the other hand, may produce some immediate benefits for a few groups which are able to take advantage of new opportunities to make money. It is also very likely, however, to impose widespread and often severe economic penalties on much larger groups. Subsidies are ended, taxes are raised, budgets are balanced, workers are discharged, businesses go bankrupt, prices rise, wages fall and production declines. Enormous economic costs must be paid in order to achieve a promised long-term economic nirvana that seems to recede indefinitely into the future. In democratization, the sequence of dominant public attitudes might be described as first euphoria, then disillusionment and finally resignation and acceptance. In the case of economic liberalization, the sequence is first apprehension and fear and then frustration and resentment. Since the major processes of liberalization are still underway the next step is uncertain. One possible final stage could be anger, protest and revolt; the other is passivity and acceptance.

Finally, the level of economic development relates differently to democratization and liberalization. Democratization occurs most frequently and easily in countries that have reached the upper-middle income levels of economic development. Economic and social conditions are then favorable to a broadening of political competition and participation. Economic liberalization, however, is easier in countries at lower levels of economic development. Countries that are still primarily agricultural will have fewer large state-owned industries employing numerous managers and workers, vested bureaucratic interests and substantial groups benefiting from and dependent on subsidies, tariffs and market entry constraints. A society with economic conditions that make democratization easier is thus also likely to have political conditions that make liberalization more difficult and, conversely, a society where political conditions facilitate liberalization is also likely to have economic conditions unfavorable to democratization.

How They Affect Each Other

How does democratization affect liberalization, and liberalization affect democratization? First: economic development promotes democratization. Wealthy countries, with a few exceptions, like the oil rich states, are democratic countries. Poor countries, with a few exceptions, such as India, are non-democratic countries. Transitions to democracy are heavily concentrated among countries at the upper-middle income level of development.

Second, economic liberalization and reform generally promote economic development. This is not always the case: the Soviet Union in the 1930s and East-Central European countries in the 1950s achieved very high rates of economic growth with command economies. In the contemporary world, however, state ownership, controls and regulations have generally hindered economic development. It should also be noted, however, that in some of the countries with the highest rates of economic development, most notably Japan and Korea, the state has played a very important guiding and facilitating role. Yet, still, economic development is more likely to occur with less state economic control than with more.

Third, economic reform requires a strong, authoritative, although not necessarily authoritarian, government. Economic liberalization imposes special hardships on some groups in society and general hardships, such as higher prices, on almost everyone. Political opposition to economic liberalization will be strong, and it will probably be even stronger in more economically developed societies than in more backward societies. Economic liberalization requires either an authoritarian or a democratic government with both the will and the power to put through reforms.

Fourth, the logic of this argument suggests that authoritarian governments are better positioned than democratic governments to promote economic liberalization. . . . They will be more able to resist popular pressures and vested interests opposed to reform. China, under a communist dictatorship, and Chile, under a military dictator, introduced substantial economic reforms and have been rewarded with enviable rates of economic growth.

141

The price was the suppression of liberty which continues today in China and which was intense during the years that General Pinochet governed Chile. Nonetheless, if a country has an authoritarian regime, it would be lucky if its government used its coercive power to promote economic liberalization. Liberalization, first, then democratization makes a great deal of sense for those who wish to achieve both goals. Opening up the political system first, in contrast, is likely to complicate economic reform. In 1989, I was told by top advisers to Gorbachev that they had made a horrible mistake in moving ahead with *glasnost* and a political opening, which had unleashed all sorts of political forces which were then making it very difficult to move toward economic reform. "We should have first concentrated power and pushed economic reform," they argued, "and let the political opening wait. Instead, we did the reverse, and now we no longer have the authority to do what is necessary." In 1991, when President Carlos Salinas of Mexico visited Harvard, he was asked why he, a graduate of Harvard's Kennedy School of Government, was not more forthcoming in promoting democracy in Mexico. His answer was that he needed the immense power he had in the Mexican political system in order to put through the economic reforms needed to bring in foreign investment, privatize state enterprises and generally de-statize the Mexican economy. Once that had happened, he said, political democratization would be in order. . . .

In the US and elsewhere, we hear much criticism of politicians. However, in countries that have had authoritarian governments, it has most often been the leaders of those governments who inaugurated the process of democratization. In other cases, as with General Wojciech Jaruzelski and Lech Walesa in Poland and F.W. de Klerk and Nelson Mandela in South Africa, this process has involved intense negotiation between leaders of the government and of the opposition. Where economic reforms were inaugurated, political leaders like Carlos S. Menem, Boris Yeltsin, Vaclav Klaus, Walesa and Salinas have had the political courage to impose short-term costs on their peoples in order to produce long-term gains for their societies. Democratization and economic reform only occur when political leaders choose to make them occur. As a result, scores of societies around the world have moved from dictatorship to democracy and from state-controlled economies toward open economies. The record of the past several decades should give us hope for the future.

"Political rights can have a major role in providing incentives and information toward the solution of economic privation."

Economic Development Need Not Precede Democracy

Amartya Sen

In the following viewpoint, Amartya Sen challenges the notion that economic development must come before democracy and the attempt to secure political rights. In fact, Sen argues, history shows that democratic polities have been better able to meet the material needs of their people than authoritarian ones because democratic governments must answer to the people for their economic policies, while authoritarian regimes do not. This public accountability, Sen argues, is the principal reason why no substantial famine has ever occurred in a democratic nation. Sen is Lamont University Professor of Economics and Philosophy at Harvard University and the president of the American Economic Association.

As you read, consider the following questions:

1. How does the example of South Korea disprove the argument that economic reform must precede democratization, according to Sen?
2. According to the author, how did the lack of democracy's "informational role" cripple China's economic development plans during the country's Great Leap Forward campaign?

Excerpted from "Freedoms and Needs" by Amartya Sen, *The New Republic*, January 10 & 17, 1994. Reprinted by permission of *The New Republic*, ©1994, The New Republic, Inc.

At the southern edge of Bangladesh and West Bengal in India, bordering on the Bay of Bengal, is the Sundarban, which literally means "beautiful forest." It is the natural habitat of the so-called Royal Bengal Tiger. Few of the tigers are left, but they are now protected by a hunting ban. The Sundarban is famous also for the honey that it produces in large clusters of natural beehives. The people bordering that region, many of whom are desperately poor, go into the forests to collect the honey, but they also have to escape the tigers. In a good year, only about fifty or so honey-gatherers are killed by tigers, but the number can be much higher when things do not go so well.

The tigers are protected, but nothing protects the human beings who make a living in those deep and lovely and perilous woods: this is just one illustration of the force of economic needs in many Third World countries. It is not hard to feel that this force can outweigh other claims, including the claims of liberty and political rights. If poverty drives human beings to take terrible risks, and sometimes to suffer terrible deaths, for a dollar or two of honey, it might well be odd to insist on discussing their liberty and their political rights.

Political Rights as "Luxury"

A concept such as habeas corpus, for example, might not seem very relevant, or even at all communicable, in such a context. Priority must surely be given, or so the argument runs, to fulfilling economic needs, even if it involves compromising political liberties; political rights are a "luxury" that a poor country "cannot afford." This skepticism about the primacy of political rights, including civil rights, is heard very frequently in international discussions. Why bother about the finesse of democracy given the overpowering grossness of material need?

Such a question reflects a deep agnosticism about the urgency of political freedoms, an agnosticism that loomed large at the conference on human rights in Vienna in June 1993, where delegates from several countries argued against a general endorsement of basic political rights across the globe, in particular in the Third World. The focus, it was argued, should be rather on "economic rights" and the satisfaction of elementary economic needs. The declaration that emerged from the Vienna conference was very much a compromise, to which the United States was a leading party; it left many ambiguities in demanding civil and political rights, but it did acknowledge them in a general way, along with economic rights.

The place of political rights also has been under active debate in many other international forums, including various organs of the United Nations, even spilling into the recent meetings of the International Olympic Committee. It has become a particularly urgent question facing sub-Saharan Africa, as democracy begins to regain some of the ground it has lost fairly comprehensively since the 1960s. Indeed, there are few general issues more central to the contemporary, and especially the developing, world.

No Real Contradiction

But is a dichotomous view of economic needs and political rights a sensible way of approaching the problem? Do needs and rights represent a basic contradiction? Do the former really undermine the latter? I would argue that this is altogether the wrong way to understand, first, the force of economic needs and, second, the salience of political rights. The real issues that have to be addressed lie elsewhere, and they involve taking note of extensive interconnections between the enjoyment of political rights and the appreciation of economic needs. Political rights can have a major role in providing incentives and information toward the solution of economic privation. But the connections between rights and needs are not merely instrumental; they are also constitutive. For our conceptualization of economic needs depends on open public debates and discussions, and the guaranteeing of those debates and those discussions requires an insistence on political rights.

The attack on political rights (which include civil rights) on the grounds of the force of economic needs contrasts starkly with a broad current of modern political philosophy that tends to assert, in one form or another, what John Rawls has called "the priority of liberty." That priority takes a particularly sharp form in modern libertarian theory, some formulations of which claim (for example, in Robert Nozick's first book, *Anarchy, State and Utopia*) that extensive classes of rights—varying from personal liberties to property rights—have nearly complete political precedence over the pursuit of social goals, including the removal of deprivation. . . .

 Those who are skeptical of the relevance of political rights to poor countries would not necessarily deny the basic importance of political rights. . . . Instead their arguments turn on the impact of political rights on the fulfillment of economic needs, and they take this impact to be firmly negative and overwhelmingly important.

No Real Conflict

The belief abounds that political rights correlate negatively with economic growth. Indeed, something of a "general theory" of this relationship between political liberty and economic prosperity has been articulated recently by that unlikely theorist Lee Kuan Yew, the former prime minister of Singapore; and the praise of the supposed advantages of "the hard state" in promot-

145

ing economic development goes back a long way in the development literature. Even the sagacious Gunnar Myrdal's extensive skepticism, in *Asian Drama*, of what he called "the soft state" has sometimes been interpreted (rather unfairly to Myrdal) as a celebration of political toughness in the cause of good economics.

Accumulated Resentment

With the exception of South Korea, most of the examples of modernizing authoritarian elites in the Third World were ultimately unable to successfully guide their countries in the transition from underdevelopment. . . .

In both types of command economy [authoritarian and communist], the costs piled up, mainly in the form of deep alienation among workers and other social groups that felt they were being run over by the locomotive of high-speed growth and had no power to stop it. Environmental destruction was partly a product of development from above, since there were no channels for feedback from the grassroots on the ecological impact of various policies.

When the NIC [newly industrialized country] governments, like their counterpart command regimes in eastern Europe, were finally forced to democratize, the legacy of years of accumulated resentment guaranteed that democratic processes would center not on forging a new consensus on economic strategy, but on waging a bitter struggle to redistribute economic and political power. Late democratization, while infinitely better than authoritarian rule, is nevertheless very costly from the perspective of long-term economic development.

Walden Bello, *Toward Freedom*, June/July 1993.

It is true that some relatively authoritarian states (such as Lee's Singapore, South Korea under military rule and more recently China) have had faster rates of economic growth than some less authoritarian states (such as India, Costa Rica and Jamaica). But the overall picture is much more complex than such isolated observations might suggest. Systematic statistical studies give little support to the view of a general conflict between civil rights and economic performance. In fact, scholars such as Partha Dasgupta, Abbas Pourgerami and Surjit Bhalla have offered substantial evidence to suggest that political and civil rights have a *positive* impact on economic progress. Other scholars find divergent patterns, while still others argue, in the words of John Helliwell, that on the basis of the information so far obtained "an optimistic interpretation of the overall results would thus be that democracy, which apparently has a value independent of its economic effects, is estimated to be available at little cost in terms of subsequent lower growth."

There is not much comfort in all these findings for the "Lee Kuan Yew hypothesis" that there exists an essential conflict between political rights and economic performance. The general thesis in praise of the tough state suffers not only from casual empiricism based on a few selected examples, but also from a lack of conceptual discrimination. Political and civil rights come in various types, and authoritarian intrusions take many forms. It would be a mistake, for example, to equate North Korea with South Korea in the infringement of political rights, even though both have violated many such rights; the complete suppression of opposition parties in the North can hardly be taken to be no more repressive than the roughness with which opposition parties have been treated in the South. Some authoritarian regimes, both of the "left" and of the "right," such as Zaire or Sudan or Ethiopia or the Khmer Rouge's Cambodia, have been enormously more hostile to political rights than many other regimes that are also identified, rightly, as authoritarian.

Re-Examining Common Generalizations

Thus, broader empirical coverage as well as greater discrimination and precision are needed to re-examine the common generalizations in favor of the repressive state, and these generalizations do not survive much scrutiny. It is also necessary to examine more rigorously the *causal* process that is supposed to underlie these generalizations about the impact of authoritarianism on prosperity. The processes that led to the economic success of, say, South Korea are now reasonably well understood; a variety of factors played a part, including the use of international markets, an openness to competition, a high level of literacy, successful land reforms and the provision of selective incentives to encourage growth and exports. There is *nothing* to indicate that these economic and social policies were inconsistent with greater democracy, that they had to be sustained by the elements of authoritarianism actually present in South Korea. The danger of taking *post hoc* to be *propter hoc* is as real in the making of such political and strategic judgments as it is in any empirical reasoning.

Thus the fundamental importance of political rights is not refuted by some allegedly negative effect of these rights on economic performance. In fact, the instrumental connections may even give a very positive role to political rights in the context of deprivations of a drastic and elementary kind: whether, and how, a government responds to intense needs and sufferings may well depend on how much pressure is put on it, and whether or

147

not pressure is put on it will depend on the exercise of political rights (such as voting, criticizing, protesting and so on).

Famines as Economic Disasters

Consider the matter of famine. I have tried to argue elsewhere that the avoidance of such economic disasters as famines is made much easier by the existence, and the exercise, of various liberties and political rights, including the liberty of free expression. Indeed, one of the remarkable facts in the terrible history of famine is that no substantial famine has ever occurred in a country with a democratic form of government and a relatively free press. They have occurred in ancient kingdoms and in contemporary authoritarian societies, in primitive tribal communities and in modern technocratic dictatorships, in colonial economies governed by imperialists from the north and in newly independent countries of the south run by despotic national leaders or by intolerant single parties. But famines have never afflicted any country that is independent, that goes to elections regularly, that has opposition parties to voice criticisms, that permits newspapers to report freely and to question the wisdom of government policies without extensive censorship.

Is this historical association between the absence of famine and the presence of political freedom a causal one, or is it simply an accidental connection? The possibility that the connection between democratic political rights and the absence of famine is a "bogus correlation" may seem plausible when one considers the fact that democratic countries are typically rather rich, and thus immune to famine for other reasons. But the absence of famine holds even for those democratic countries that happen to be poor, such as India, Botswana and Zimbabwe. There is also what we might call "intertemporal evidence," which we observe when a country undergoes a transition to democracy. Thus India continued to have famines right up to the time of independence in 1947; the last famine, and one of the largest, was the Bengal famine of 1943, in which it is estimated that between 2 million and 3 million people died. Since independence, however, and the installation of a multiparty democratic system, there has been no substantial famine, even though severe crop failures and food scarcities have occurred often enough (in 1968, 1973, 1979 and 1987).

Kings Never Starve

Why might we expect a general connection between democracy and the nonoccurrence of famines? The answer is not hard to seek. Famines kill millions of people in different countries in the world, but they do not kill the rulers. The kings and the presidents, the bureaucrats and the bosses, the military leaders

148

and the commanders never starve. And if there are no elections, no opposition parties, no forums for uncensored public criticism, then those in authority do not have to suffer the political consequences of their failure to prevent famine. Democracy, by contrast, would spread the penalty of famine to the ruling groups and the political leadership.

There is, moreover, the issue of information. A free press, and more generally the practice of democracy, contributes greatly to bringing out the information that can have an enormous impact on policies for famine prevention, such as facts about the early effects of droughts and floods, and about the nature and the results of unemployment. The most elementary source of basic information about a threatening famine is the news media, especially when there are incentives, which a democratic system provides, for revealing facts that may be embarrassing to the government, facts that an undemocratic regime would tend to censor. Indeed, I would argue that a free press and an active political opposition constitute the best "early warning system" that a country threatened by famine can possess.

The connection between political rights and economic needs can be illustrated in the specific context of famine prevention by considering the massive Chinese famines of 1958-61. Even before the recent economic reforms, China had been much more successful than India in economic development. The average life expectancy, for example, rose in China much more than it did in India, and well before the reforms of 1979 it had already reached something like the high figure—nearly seventy years at birth—that is quoted now. And yet China was unable to prevent famine. It is now estimated that the Chinese famines of 1958-61 killed close to 30 million people—ten times more than even the gigantic 1943 famine in British India.

The so-called "Great Leap Forward," initiated in the late 1950s, was a massive failure, but the Chinese government refused to admit it, and continued dogmatically to pursue much the same disastrous policies for three more years. It is hard to imagine that this could have happened in a country that goes to the polls regularly and has an independent press. During that terrible calamity, the government faced no pressure from newspapers, which were controlled, or from opposition parties, which were not allowed to exist.

Believing Their Own Propaganda

The lack of a free system of news distribution even misled the government itself. It believed its own propaganda and the rosy reports of local party officials competing for credit in Beijing. Indeed, there is evidence that just as the famine was moving toward its peak, the Chinese authorities mistakenly believed that they had 100 million more metric tons of grain than they actually did. Interestingly enough, Mao himself, whose radical beliefs had much to do with the initiation of, and the perseverance with, the Great Leap Forward, identified the informational role of democracy, once the failure was belatedly acknowledged. In 1962, just after the famine had killed so many millions, he made the following observation, to a gathering of 7,000 cadres:

> Without democracy, you have no understanding of what is happening down below; the situation will be unclear; you will be unable to collect sufficient opinions from all sides; there can be no communication between top and bottom; top-level organs of leadership will depend on one-sided and incorrect material to decide issues, thus you will find it difficult to avoid being subjectivist; it will be impossible to achieve unity of understanding and unity of action, and impossible to achieve true centralism.

Mao's defense of democracy here is quite limited. The focus is exclusively on the informational side, ignoring the incentive role of democracy, not to mention any intrinsic importance that it may have. Still, it is significant that Mao himself acknowledged the extent to which disastrous official policies were caused by the lack of the informational links that a more democratic system could have provided.

"Only with sustained, organized pressure from below, in civil society, can political and social equality be advanced."

Third World Civil Society Can Promote Democracy

Larry Diamond

Civil society—that segment of a nation's society that is organized into groups to articulate and further the groups' demands—is a powerful force for democracy in the developing world, argues Larry Diamond, author of the following viewpoint. Because its focus is on state-controlled rights and resources, civil society is in a unique position to criticize government corruption, the author explains. Civil society allows citizens to become politically educated, he says, thereby producing tomorrow's democratic leaders. Diamond is coeditor of the *Journal of Democracy*, the publication of the National Endowment for Democracy (a private organization that supports democracy abroad), and a senior research fellow at the Hoover Institution, a research foundation on national and international policy.

As you read, consider the following questions:

1. Why, according to the author, must civil society remain separate from political society?
2. How does civil society help to bring about economic reform, according to Diamond?

Excerpted from Larry Diamond, "Toward Democratic Consolidation," *Journal of Democracy*, vol. 5, no. 3, July 1994. Reprinted by permission of the Johns Hopkins University Press.

In this third wave of global democratization, no phenomenon has more vividly captured the imagination of democratic scholars, observers, and activists alike than "civil society." What could be more moving than the stories of brave bands of students, writers, artists, pastors, teachers, laborers, and mothers challenging the duplicity, corruption, and brutal domination of authoritarian states? Could any sight be more awe-inspiring to democrats than the one they saw in Manila in 1986, when hundreds of thousands of organized and peaceful citizens surged into the streets to reclaim their stolen election and force Ferdinand Marcos out through nonviolent "people power"?

In fact, however, the overthrow of authoritarian regimes through popularly based and massively mobilized democratic opposition has not been the norm. Most democratic transitions have been protracted and negotiated (if not largely controlled from above by the exiting authoritarians). Yet even in such negotiated and controlled transitions, the stimulus for democratization, and particularly the pressure to complete the process, have typically come from the "resurrection of civil society," the restructuring of public space, and the mobilization of all manner of independent groups and grassroots movements.

If the renewed interest in civil society can trace its theoretical origins to Alexis de Tocqueville [a 19th-century French statesman who wrote extensively on America], it seems emotionally and spiritually indebted to Jean-Jacques Rousseau [an 18th-century political theorist] for its romanticization of "the people" as a force for collective good, rising up to assert the democratic will against a narrow and evil autocracy. Such images of popular mobilization suffuse contemporary thinking about democratic change throughout Asia, Latin America, Eastern Europe, and Africa—and not without reason.

In South Korea, Taiwan, Chile, Poland, China, Czechoslovakia, South Africa, Nigeria, and Benin (to give only a partial list), extensive mobilization of civil society was a crucial source of pressure for democratic change. Citizens pressed their challenge to autocracy not merely as individuals, but as members of student movements, churches, professional associations, women's groups, trade unions, human rights organizations, producer groups, the press, civic associations, and the like. . . .

What Civil Society Is and Is Not

Civil society is conceived here as the *realm of organized social life that is voluntary, self-generating, (largely) self-supporting, autonomous from the state, and bound by a legal order or set of shared rules.* It is distinct from "society" in general in that it involves citizens *acting collectively in a public sphere* to express their interests, passions, and ideas, exchange information, achieve mutual goals, make demands on the state, and hold state officials accountable. Civil society is an intermediary entity, standing between the private sphere and the state. Thus it excludes individual and family life, inward-looking group activity (e.g., for recreation, entertainment, or spirituality), the profit-making enterprise of individual business firms, and political efforts to take control of the state. Actors in civil society need the protection of an institutionalized legal order to guard their autonomy and freedom of action. Thus civil society not only restricts state power but legitimates state authority when that authority is based on the rule of law. When the state itself is lawless and contemptuous of individual and group autonomy, civil society may still exist (albeit in tentative or battered form) if its constituent elements operate by some set of shared rules (which, for example, eschew violence and respect pluralism). This is the irreducible condition of its "civil" dimension.

Civil society encompasses a vast array of organizations, formal and informal. These include groups that are: 1) *economic* (productive and commercial associations and networks); 2) *cultural* (religious, ethnic, communal, and other institutions and associations that defend collective rights, values, faiths, beliefs, and symbols); 3) *informational and educational* (devoted to the production and dissemination—whether for profit or not—of public knowledge, ideas, news, and information); 4) *interest-based* (designed to advance or defend the common functional or material interests of their members, whether workers, veterans, pensioners, professionals, or the like); 5) *developmental* (organizations that combine individual resources to improve the infrastructure, institutions, and quality of life of the community); 6) *issue-oriented* (movements for environmental protection, women's rights, land reform, or consumer protection); and 7) *civic* (seeking in nonpartisan fashion to improve the political system and make it more democratic through human rights monitoring, voter education and mobilization, poll-watching, anticorruption efforts, and so on).

In addition, civil society encompasses "the ideological marketplace" and the flow of information and ideas. This includes not only independent mass media but also institutions belonging to the broader field of autonomous cultural and intellectual activity—universities, think tanks, publishing houses, theaters, film production companies, and artistic networks.

A Primarily Public Function

From the above, it should be clear that civil society is not some mere residual category, synonymous with "society" or with everything that is not the state or the formal political system. Beyond being voluntary, self-generating, autonomous, and rule-abiding, the organizations of civil society are distinct from other social groups in several respects. First, as emphasized above, civil society is concerned with *public* rather than private ends. Second, civil society *relates to the state* in some way but does not aim to win formal power or office in the state [hence different from political parties]. Rather, civil society organizations seek from the state concessions, benefits, policy changes, relief, redress, or accountability. Civic organizations and social movements that try to change the nature of the state may still qualify as parts of civil society, if their efforts stem from concern for the public good and not from a desire to capture state power for the group per se. Thus peaceful movements for democratic transition typically spring from civil society. . . .

The Democratic Functions of Civil Society

The first and most basic democratic function of civil society is to provide "the basis for the limitation of state power, hence for the control of the state by society, and hence for democratic political institutions as the most effective means of exercising that control," according to Samuel P. Huntington. This function has two dimensions: to monitor and restrain the exercise of power by democratic states, and to democratize authoritarian states. Mobilizing civil society is a major means of exposing the abuses and undermining the legitimacy of undemocratic regimes. This is the function, performed so dramatically in so many democratic transitions over the past two decades, that has catapulted civil society to the forefront of thinking about democracy. Yet this thinking revives the eighteenth-century idea of civil society as *in opposition* to the state and has its dangers if taken too far.

Civil society is also a vital instrument for containing the power of democratic governments, checking their potential abuses and violations of the law, and subjecting them to public scrutiny. Indeed, a vibrant civil society is probably more essential for consolidating and maintaining democracy than for initiating it. Few developments are more destructive to the legitimacy of new democracies than blatant and pervasive political corruption, particularly during periods of painful economic restructuring when many groups and individuals are asked to sustain great hardships. New democracies, following long periods of arbitrary and statist rule, lack the legal and bureaucratic means to contain corruption at the outset. Without a free, robust, and inquisitive press and civic groups to press for institutional reform, corruption is likely to flourish.

Second, a rich associational life supplements the role of political parties in stimulating political participation, increasing the political efficacy and skill of democratic citizens, and promoting an appreciation of the obligations as well as the rights of democratic citizenship. For too many Americans (barely half of whom vote in presidential elections), this now seems merely a quaint homily. A century and a half ago, however, the voluntary participation of citizens in all manner of associations outside the state struck Tocqueville as a pillar of democratic culture and economic vitality in the young United States. Voluntary "associations may therefore be considered as large free schools, where all the members of the community go to learn the general theory of association," he wrote.

People Power

While the dramatic events of 1989 in Eastern Europe have given greater credibility to the phenomenon of unarmed insurrections, it is in the Third World where perhaps the most significant examples have taken place. Primarily nonviolent 'people power' movements have overthrown authoritarian regimes in several Third World countries, forced substantial reforms in some and seriously challenged still others. . . . As Gene Sharp describes it:

> When people refuse their cooperation, withhold their help, and persist in their disobedience and defiance, they are denying their opponent the basic human assistance and cooperation which any government hierarchical system requires. If they do this in sufficient numbers for long enough, that government or hierarchical system will no longer have power.

Stephen Zunes, *Third World Quarterly*, vol. 15, no. 3, 1994.

Civil society can also be a crucial arena for the development of other democratic attributes, such as tolerance, moderation, a willingness to compromise, and a respect for opposing viewpoints. These values and norms become most stable when they emerge through experience, and organizational participation in civil society provides important practice in political advocacy and contestation. In addition, many civil organizations (such as Conciencia, a network of women's organizations that began in Argentina and has since spread to 14 other Latin American countries) are working directly in the schools and among groups of adult citizens to develop these elements of democratic culture through interactive programs that demonstrate the dynamics of reaching consensus in a group, the possibility for respectful debate between competing viewpoints, and the means by which people can cooperate to solve the problems of their own communities.

A fourth way in which civil society may serve democracy is by creating channels other than political parties for the articulation, aggregation, and representation of interests. This function is particularly important for providing traditionally excluded groups—such as women and racial or ethnic minorities—access to power that has been denied them in the "upper institutional echelons" of formal politics. Even where (as in South America) women have played, through various movements and organizations, prominent roles in mobilizing against authoritarian rule, democratic politics and governance after the transition have typically reverted to previous exclusionary patterns. In Eastern Europe, there are many signs of deterioration in the political and social status of women after the transition. Only with sustained, organized pressure from below, in civil society, can political and social equality be advanced, and the quality, responsiveness, and legitimacy of democracy thus be deepened.

Civil society provides an especially strong foundation for democracy when it generates opportunities for participation and influence at all levels of governance, not least the local level. For it is at the local level that the historically marginalized are most likely to be able to affect public policy and to develop a sense of efficacy as well as actual political skills. The democratization of local government thus goes hand in hand with the development of civil society as an important condition for the deepening of democracy and the "transition from clientelism to citizenship" in Latin America, as well as elsewhere in the developing and postcommunist worlds.

Creating Constituencies and Training Leaders

Fifth, a richly pluralistic civil society, particularly in a relatively developed economy, will tend to generate a wide range of interests that may cross-cut, and so mitigate, the principal polarities of political conflict. As new class-based organizations and issue-oriented movements arise, they draw together new constituencies that cut across longstanding regional, religious, ethnic, or partisan cleavages. In toppling communist (and other) dictatorships and mobilizing for democracy, these new formations may generate a modern type of citizenship that transcends historic divisions and contains the resurgence of narrow nationalist impulses. To the extent that individuals have multiple interests and join a wide variety of organizations to pursue and advance those interests, they will be more likely to associate with different types of people who have divergent political interests and opinions. These attitudinal cross-pressures will tend to soften the militancy of their own views, generate a more expansive and sophisticated political outlook, and so encourage tolerance for differences and a greater readiness to compromise.

A sixth function of a democratic civil society is recruiting and training new political leaders. In a few cases, this is a deliberate purpose of civic organizations. The Evelio B. Javier Foundation in the Philippines, for instance, offers training programs on a nonpartisan basis to local and state elected officials and candidates, emphasizing not only technical and administrative skills but normative standards of public accountability and transparency. More often, recruitment and training are merely a long-term byproduct of the successful functioning of civil society organizations as their leaders and activists gain skills and self-confidence that qualify them well for service in government and party politics. They learn how to organize and motivate people, debate issues, raise and account for funds, craft budgets, publicize programs, administer staffs, canvass for support, negotiate agreements, and build coalitions. . . .

Seventh, many civic organizations have explicit democracy-building purposes that go beyond leadership training. Nonpartisan election-monitoring efforts have been critical in deterring fraud, enhancing voter confidence, affirming the legitimacy of the result, or in some cases (as in the Philippines in 1986 and Panama in 1989) demonstrating an opposition victory despite government fraud. This function is particularly crucial in founding elections like those which initiated democracy in Chile, Nicaragua, Bulgaria, Zambia, and South Africa. Democracy institutes and think tanks are working in a number of countries to reform the electoral system, democratize political parties, decentralize and open up government, strengthen the legislature, and enhance governmental accountability. And even after the transition, human rights organizations continue to play a vital role in the pursuit of judicial and legal reform, improved prison conditions, and greater institutionalized respect for individual liberties and minority rights.

Spreading the Truth and Establishing Consensus

Eighth, a vigorous civil society widely disseminates information, thus aiding citizens in the collective pursuit and defense of their interests and values. While civil society groups may sometimes prevail temporarily by dint of raw numbers (e.g., in strikes and demonstrations), they generally cannot be effective in contesting government policies or defending their interests unless they are well-informed. This is strikingly true in debates over military and national security policy, where civilians in developing countries have generally been woefully lacking in even the most elementary knowledge. A free press is only one vehicle for providing the public with a wealth of news and alternative perspectives. Independent organizations may also give citizens hard-won information about government activities that does not depend on what government *says* it is doing. This is a vital technique of human rights organizations: by contradicting the official story, they make it more difficult to cover up repression and abuses of power.

The spread of new information and ideas is essential to the achievement of economic reform in a democracy, and this is a ninth function that civil society can play. While economic stabilization policies typically must be implemented quickly, forcefully, and unilaterally by elected executives in crisis situations, more structural economic reforms—privatization, trade and financial liberalization—appear to be more sustainable and far-reaching (or in many postcommunist countries, only feasible) when they are pursued through the democratic process.

Mobilizing Support for Economic Reform

Successful economic reform requires the support of political coalitions in society and the legislature. Such coalitions are not spontaneous; they must be fashioned. Here the problem is not so much the scale, autonomy, and resources of civil society as it is their distribution across interests. Old, established interests that stand to lose from reform tend to be organized into formations like state-sector trade unions and networks that tie the managers of state enterprises or owners of favored industries to ruling party bosses. These are precisely the interests that stand to lose from economic reforms that close down inefficient industries, reduce state intervention, and open the economy to greater domestic and international competition. The newer and more diffuse interests that stand to gain from reform—for example, farmers, small-scale entrepreneurs, and consumers—tend to be weakly organized and poorly informed about how new policies will ultimately affect them. In Asia, Latin America, and Eastern Europe, new actors in civil society—such as economic-policy think tanks, chambers of commerce, and economically literate journalists, commentators, and television producers—are beginning to overcome the barriers to information and organization, mobilizing support for (and neutralizing resistance to) reform policies.

Finally, there is a tenth function of civil society—to which I have already referred—that derives from the success of the above nine. "Freedom of association," Tocqueville mused, may, "after having agitated society for some time, . . . strengthen the state in the end." By enhancing the accountability, responsiveness, inclusiveness, effectiveness, and hence legitimacy of the political system, a vigorous civil society gives citizens respect for the state and positive engagement with it. In the end, this improves the ability of the state to govern, and to command voluntary obedience from its citizens. In addition, a rich associational life can do more than just multiply demands on the state; it may also multiply the capacities of groups to improve their own welfare, independently of the state. Effective grassroots development efforts may thus help to relieve the burden of expectations fixed on the state, and so lower the stakes of politics, especially at the national level. . . .

Democratic Consolidation

Consolidation is the process by which democracy becomes so broadly and profoundly legitimate among its citizens that it is very unlikely to break down. It involves behavioral and institutional changes that normalize democratic politics and narrow its uncertainty. This normalization requires the expansion of citizen access, development of democratic citizenship and culture, broadening of leadership recruitment and training, and other functions that civil society performs. But most of all, and most urgently, it requires political institutionalization.

Despite their impressive capacity to survive years (in some cases, a decade or more) of social strife and economic instability and decline, many new democracies in Latin America, Eastern Europe, Asia, and Africa will probably break down in the medium to long run unless they can reduce their often appalling levels of poverty, inequality, and social injustice and, through market-oriented reforms, lay the basis for sustainable growth. For these and other policy challenges, not only strong parties but effective state institutions are vital. They do not guarantee wise and effective policies, but they at least ensure that government will be able to make and implement policies of some kind, rather than simply flailing about, impotent or deadlocked. . . .

These caveats are sobering, but they do not nullify my principal thesis. Civil society can, and typically must, play a significant role in building and consolidating democracy. Its role is not decisive or even the most important, at least initially. However, the more active, pluralistic, resourceful, institutionalized, and democratic is civil society, and the more effectively it balances the tensions in its relations with the state—between autonomy and cooperation, vigilance and loyalty, skepticism and trust, assertiveness and civility—the more likely it is that democracy will emerge and endure.

"Poverty saps the vitality of civil society, but the lack of democratic participation reinforces poverty."

Third World Civil Society Is Too Weak to Promote Democracy

Anthony W. Pereira

A popular theory today is that the Third World is becoming more democratic, explains Anthony W. Pereira in the following viewpoint, but this political trend is taking place in countries marked by political repression and a growing disparity of wealth. Looking at the northeast sugar-producing region of Brazil, Pereira finds that civil society (the segment of society organizing for labor and political rights), after a brief bloom in the 1950s and another in 1979, has been subordinated by political society and the state, which are unresponsive to the needs of the people. Violence employed by local landlords against protesters keeps civil society weak, Pereira charges, thereby preventing the consolidation of real democracy in countries like Brazil. Pereira is assistant professor of political science at the New School for Social Research in New York City.

As you read, consider the following questions:

1. How did the military contribute to the weakening of civil society in northeast Brazil, according to Pereira?
2. How do clientelistic voting arrangements keep civil society from forming in Pernambuco, in the author's analysis?

Excerpted from Anthony Pereira, "Economic Underdevelopment, Democracy and Civil Society: The North-East Brazilian Case," *Third World Quarterly*, vol. 14, no. 2, 1993. Reprinted with permission.

It has become a platitude in the academic marketplace that the world has recently become more democratic. Yet the world is also increasingly divided between rich and poor. Of the more than 30 countries that have seen some sort of transition away from authoritarianism since 1974, 29 had a 1976 per capita GNP under $3,000. That is, what has been called a global democratic revolution has taken place primarily in developing countries still badly afflicted by poverty and inequality. The purpose of this viewpoint is to explore some recent attempts to theorise about the relationship between economic underdevelopment and democracy, and how democracy can be consolidated, in the developing world. . . .

Democratic Consolidation: The Brazilian Example

Brazil has undergone two major changes of political regime in the post-World War II era. Its fourth republic, a civilian-led democracy with restricted suffrage and an interventionist military, lasted from 1945 to 1964. In 1964 the military and its civilian supporters created a dictatorship, one which retained elections at many levels, and whose most repressive phase was 1968 to 1971. In the mid-1970s, the military regime began to transform itself, resulting in a very gradual and controlled process of democratisation. In 1985 the political elite proclaimed a 'new republic', with an indirectly elected civilian president, and by 1988 a new, democratic constitution had been approved. By 1989 the first direct election for president in 29 years took place, and Brazil was declared by most observers to be a democracy.

The political history of the north-east, Brazil's poorest region, reflects a good deal more continuity than such a brief summary would suggest. The following section is a brief attempt to chart the rise, fall, and partial resurrection of civil society in one fairly representative part of the north-east, the coastal sugar-growing region of the state of Pernambuco, where I have done research.

Civil society in Brazil's north-east, where slavery was widespread until one hundred years ago, has historically been very weak. The resources that sustain voluntary associations of all kinds in a rich country simply do not exist. Furthermore, the exigencies of survival make collective action extremely difficult. Mutual aid among the poor (sharing food, housing, tools, transportation), especially within family and kinship groups, is extremely common and indeed vital for the survival of many. But this mutual aid, which is a form of self-interested exchange whose benefits are restricted to certain households and families, should be distinguished from collective action, in which individuals work for the attainment of a public good. The latter, which is an essential element of civil society, is much more rare in the north-east.

In the coastal sugar-growing area of Pernambuco, it would be fair to say that for rural workers, civil society did not exist until the mid-1950s. In the preceding years, voluntary associations that claimed to speak on behalf of rural labourers, sharecroppers, renters, and smallholders were seen by the dominant class as a problem of public order, to be repressed by the police and private gunmen. This repression was effective until the mid-1950s, when the emergence of industrialists in the capital city of Recife created conflicts within the dominant class between agrarian and urban interests. This in turn allowed organisations of rural labourers, both trade unions and peasant leagues, to spring up, organised by the Church, the Communist Party, and socialist politicians. Pernambuco thus experienced a 'birth of civil society' in the countryside, 20 years after the legislation formally permitting rural unionisation (which was never respected in practice) was passed.

The Repression of Embryonic Civil Society

As in other centres of trade union and Communist Party activity, the military heavily repressed political activity in Pernambuco during and after the 1964 military coup. The previous pluralistic and competitive arrangement for the representation of rural labour's interests was replaced by a hierarchical, centralised, and top-down structure. The military regime prohibited voluntary associations, and allowed only a mandatory and highly controlled unionism in the Pernambuco countryside. For 15 years, the military regime was able to ensure a devastating social peace in the Pernambuco cane fields through repression. In effect, after a brief flowering, civil society in the Pernambuco countryside was once again silenced. Before the coup, it had been suppressed by the private power of the landed class. Under the military regime, it was suppressed by the state.

In 1979, when the union movement in other parts of Brazil was reaffirming its independent character, rural unions in Pernambuco also challenged employers and the state by conducting the first strike since 1963. This represents the rebirth of civil society in Pernambuco, as far as rural labour is concerned. What has happened since that time, however, is salutary. It involves the partial and gradual re-subordination of civil society to political society and the state.

In advanced capitalist countries, civil society is often threatened by the market and economic society—by the dictatorship of production and consumption, the subtle manipulation of advertising, and a commercial culture which subjects every value to the bottom-line calculus of the capitalist enterprise. In underdeveloped regions, the market is much weaker, and high-consumption lifestyles are the privilege of a small upper and middle class. There, civil society is instead overwhelmed by political society.

162

Numerous commentators have remarked that the state in Latin America, compared to its counterpart in North America, is very large and extensively involved in the organisation of society. It is therefore surprising that so far few commentators have worried about the possibility that the return to competitive elections in Latin America will result in the hypertrophy of political society at the expense of civil society. Political parties can become instruments of the control of civil society, rather than vehicles for its self-expression. This is especially likely in underdeveloped areas where civil society is weak. Now that the euphoria accompanying the democratic transitions has died away, perhaps political scientists can begin studying this problem.

The Capture of Civil Society by the State

In Brazil, for example, elections are some of the most expensive in the world. The evidence on this point is anecdotal but persuasive. One scholar calculates that a vote in Brazil costs an average of $35, a high price in a country with a per capita income of $2,200. In the 1989 presidential election, the winning candidate was reported to have raised as much money as did Republican candidate George Bush in the 1988 US election, even though Brazil's economy is one-twentieth the size of the US economy. And in the October 1992 mayoral and city council elections, the average cost of a mayoral campaign in cities of over 1 million people . . . [was] an estimated $1.2 million. If it were possible to calculate the ratio of resources devoted to political campaigns to resources at the disposal of associations in civil society, the figure in Brazil would probably be very lopsided indeed.

In areas of mass poverty such as the north-east, clientelistic voting arrangements [in which support is given to a candidate in the hope of rewards if he wins] and extensive systems of patronage [in which politicians reward those who supported them] remain common. Politicians give away clothes, shoes, building materials, cooking gas, and sometimes cash to obtain the votes of the rural poor. A winning candidate invariably awards hundreds, sometimes thousands of government jobs to his supporters, who do not have to pass exams to enter the civil service. Party coherence is weak, often non-existent. In such a system, the associations of civil society are captured by political candidates, who use them as vote-banks. The direction of influence between political and civil society seems all one way, because the associations in civil society are so dependent on the state for resources. The pressure from below mentioned by some theorists of civil society seems almost non-existent.

In Brazil, clientelism and patronage are reinforced by the excessive weight that the electoral system gives to the north and north-east, where such practices are most deeply entrenched. A congressional deputy from São Paulo, for example, represents 312,100 voters, while one from the northern state of Roraima represents only 10,800. This highly unequal system of representation, devised by the military regime to magnify its support in the agrarian north and north-east, has been preserved despite the transition to democracy.

An Unresponsive State

But the electoral system is not the only means by which political society dominates civil society in the north-east. In the sugar zone, the state presides over the annual contract negotiations between the Pernambuco union federation and the employers. These negotiations are preceded by a strike almost every year. The strike in 1979 that started this process had a spontaneous and political character, and was remarkably effective in galvanising the sugar workers and winning a large wage increase. Since then, however, the negotiations have become bureaucratised and the strike more anemic and less political. The sugar producers do nothing to avert the strike because it helps them in their claims for a higher price for sugar, which is regulated by the Federal government. And local trade union leaders, who do not play a direct role in the annual wage negotiations, feel less and less inclined to mobilise their members. The strike looks more and more like an exercise staged for the benefit of sugar producers, and less and less the expression of demands from below that it was in 1979.

In Brazil as a whole, the effect of 21 years of military rule was to widen the disparities between rich and poor. These disparities have not been reduced during the last seven years of civilian rule. Paul Cammack writes:

> Between 1960 and 1980, the share of national income going to the bottom 50 per cent of the population fell from a poor 17.7 per cent to a disastrous 13.4 per cent; it certainly worsened again in the 1980s. Over the same period, the proportion of land held by the largest owners (the top 5 per cent) increased from 67.9 per cent to 69.3 per cent . . . the central fact of contemporary Brazilian politics . . . [is] that given the material circumstances in which the greater part of the population live, a process of democratization which removes anachronistic and unsustainable obstacles to the participation of all Brazilians as independent citizens will necessarily lead to demands for substantial social and economic reform.

This fact is nowhere more obvious than in the impoverished north-east. The industrialised south-eastern and southern region of the country, with the major cities of São Paulo, Belo Horizonte, Rio de Janeiro, and Porto Alegre, is the most dynamic part of the country and the area most hospitable to democracy. Much of the literature on Brazil gives the mistaken impression that the country is the south writ large. But in the north-east, the obstacles to participation which Cammack mentions are serious.

Economic Dependency and Domination

In the Pernambuco sugar zone, these obstacles include the overwhelming dominance of the sugar mill in the life of the community. This is reflected in the appearance of the sugar zone's towns, where the mill is always the largest structure, dwarfing the next-largest building, the church. Sugar zone communities have the uniform, lifeless appearance of 'company towns', enlivened only by the occasional fairs that travel throughout the region. Physically, the towns reflect the residents' dependence on the sugar mill and its surrounding plantations.

Another obstacle to a democratic civil society is violence against workers on the part of landowners. Workers who challenge employers on matters of compensation and union organisers who confront employers too boldly face the possibility of threats, beatings, and assassination at the hands of landlords' gunmen or members of the local police force. These crimes, a commonplace in the sugar zone, are rarely investigated by the police or judiciary. The enforcement of legal equality, a basic element in the creation of a strong civil society, is missing.

The operation of the state also reflects the weakness of civil society. The Brazilian state has a tendency to rule by decree, without consulting affected groups and associations. The 1985 agrarian reform project is a case in point. This plan envisioned the creation of commissions, made up of representatives of employers and unions, in each state, to decide which lands should be appropriated and redistributed. In Pernambuco, such a commission was set up in early 1986. However, before the commission could do its work, the Federal government issued a state agrarian reform plan in May, 1986 that decreed which lands were demarcated for redistribution. The rural trade unions, convinced that they could have no influence on the plan, withdrew from the commissions in October 1987.

No Policy Influence and No Alternatives

A lack of communication between political parties and civil society seems to be another feature of democracy as it exists in the rural north-east. Even the Workers' Party, which enjoys a reputation for honesty and genuine dialogue with members of various social movements, has been criticised by rural trade unionists in Pernambuco for talking without listening, for wanting the votes of rural workers without listening to their demands.

Finally, a lack of pluralism marks the associational life of the sugar zone. For rural workers, the trade union remains the only place where he or she can obtain some kind of welfare relief, openly discuss politics, and learn about events outside the town. The unions, financed primarily by a mandatory worker check-off administered by the state, stand as the sole potential opposition to the social and political dominance of the local landowners. If the union leadership is bought off by the landowners or disinclined to fight for workers rights, even this potential opposition does not exist. In recent years, some other associations have been formed without much success. Several women's associations, for example, have been formed by women claiming that the trade unions did not adequately represent their interests. However, without the financial sustenance of the state, depending on irregular contributions from international agencies, these associations have gained little influence.

The Challenge of Divided Societies

There is a tendency in civil society theory to assume that all things in civil society are good and all things in the state are bad. In South African civil society there have emerged institutions with strong democratic commitments . . . even if their practices fall short of the promise. But we would be fooling ourselves if we did not acknowledge that civil society is also composed of institutions and associations which are anything but democratic: black ethnic groupings, warlords, gangs, white supremacists and the rough 'popular justice' of necklacing parties [where a flaming tire is placed around the victim's neck] come first to mind. Nor is the banner of the ANC [African National Congress] a guarantee against this or that clique's presenting itself as representative of the people. Indeed, the political language of 'the people' which has played such a large role in oppositional politics in South Africa carries with it the danger of each political grouping's identifying itself with the people and its rivals as enemies of the people.

Robert Fine, *Review of African Political Economy*, March 1994.

This does not constitute an exhaustive discussion of the nature of civil society in the sugar zone. However, the basic point is that there is a reciprocal relationship between underdevelopment and civil society; the lack of liberty in civil society reinforces the poverty produced by economic underdevelopment, and vice versa. Poverty saps the vitality of civil society, but the lack of democratic participation reinforces poverty. The inability of workers to freely pressure employers who cheat them out of their legal wages, for example, reduces their standard of living. It is a truism that simply by enforcing the law in the sugar zone—both labour and criminal law—the state could radically alter the balance of class power. But reflecting as it does the power of the local landed class, the state is unlikely to do this.

Focusing on Civil Society

Poverty in the sugar zone is therefore not the automatic result of impersonal economic forces. It is maintained by millions of petty acts in the intimate sphere of civil society: acts of intimidation, bribery, violence, and persuasion aimed at getting workers to accept the established order. The formal equality of citizenship on which the mechanisms of electoral democracy are based is neutralised by the countless 'micro-despotisms' of civil society and the relative autonomy of the state's repressive apparatus. An improvement in the degree of communication and association permissible in civil society would have the effect of raising worker living standards, just as an increase in worker living standards would increase workers' confidence and assertiveness within civil society.

With this in mind, it is possible to imagine regions with similar economic structures and very different civil societies. Much would depend on how the region was integrated into a national political economy, and the history of the relation between local and national politics. What this section suggests is that the history of the Brazilian north-east has resulted in a civil society resistant to democratic participation, despite the formal end of military rule in 1985.

The relationship between economic development and democracy is not a direct one. . . . This viewpoint therefore advocates the use of the concept of civil society as a yardstick with which to assess the nature of democracies in underdeveloped regions. As social scientists, we have an obligation to develop theories that explain the relationship between economy, civil society, and the state. It is not enough to study only the state or the economy; the intimate and associational spheres also deserve attention.

Civil Society's Weakness in Poverty

Using a sugar-growing region of north-east Brazil as an example, this viewpoint points to the weakness of civil society in poor regions. More specifically, the creation of institutions that enforce legal equality and the right of free association is difficult in a mono-crop region where land and other means of production are highly concentrated and in which a large and nearly destitute labor force struggles to survive. This is perhaps an obvious point, but it is worth saying that it is misleading to take assumptions derived from the study of eastern and central Europe, North America, and other relatively developed regions and apply them to the whole of a country like Brazil. Brazil's reputation as a country with a strong civil society comes from the well-publicized activities of movements in its industrialised south-eastern region, and does not apply to the agrarian north-east.

The case study alluded to in this viewpoint further allows us to conclude that in underdeveloped regions the return to electoral democracy may result in an imbalance between political society (parties, elections, legislatures) and civil society. The former can grow parasitically at the expense of the latter. In moments of crisis and regime transition civil society spontaneously takes the lead, but as politics are 'normalized' more and more energy and resources get transferred into the electoral arena, and candidates use voluntary associations as vehicles rather than vice versa. This results from but further reinforces the predominance of the state *vis-à-vis* society.

It might be thought that the practical implication of these conclusions would be to advocate the strengthening of civil society. This is, in fact, the strategy of international agencies such as the Ford Foundation in Brazil: once entirely concerned with funding state agencies, Ford now channels money to nongovernmental associations representing women, blacks, indigenous people, environmental causes, and so on. In the rural north-east, however, such a strategy has clear limitations. The fact is that the rural poor need the power of the state, which is the only counterweight to the overwhelming power of the landed class in the region. Strengthening the judiciary, the inspection arm of the Ministry of Labour, and creating greater civilian controls over the various police forces are all as important as strengthening social movements if the scope for democratic participation is to be widened.

It is best therefore to think of associations in civil society not as entities always in conflict with the state, but as groups of people struggling to use parts of the state apparatus to promote their own ends. The social crisis in Brazil and other Latin American countries reflects the fact that the state, while still highly bound up with civil society, has lost a great deal of its institutional capacity due to the fiscal crisis of the 1980s and early 1990s. The solution to the crisis should not be, therefore, the neo-liberal one of getting the state out of as many activities as possible, but to selectively rebuild state institutions in order to promote democratisation. This is the agenda of the rural trade unions in north-east Brazil.

Periodical Bibliography

The following articles have been selected to supplement the diverse views presented in this chapter.

Walden Bello	"Only Democracy Insures Healthy, Sustainable Growth," *Toward Freedom*, June/July 1993. Available from 209 College St., Burlington, VT 05401.
Larry Diamond	"Toward Democratic Consolidation," *Journal of Democracy*, July 1994. Available from Johns Hopkins University Press, Journals Div., 2715 N. Charles St., Baltimore, MD 212184-319.
Jonathan Fox	"Latin America's Emerging Local Politics," *Journal of Democracy*, April 1994.
Eric Hanson	"First Build the Economy, Then Democracy Will Come," *Toward Freedom*, June/July 1993.
Prem Shankar Jha	"The Fascist Impulse in Developing Countries: Two Case Studies," *Studies in Conflict and Terrorism*, July/September 1994. Available from Taylor and Francis, 1101 Vermont Ave. NW, Suite 200, Washington, DC 20005.
Nelson Kasfir	"Popular Sovereignty and Popular Participation: Mixed Constitutional Democracy in the Third World," *Third World Quarterly*, vol. 13, no. 4, 1992.
Ian Roxborough	"Neo-Liberalism in Latin America: Limits and Alternatives," *Third World Quarterly*, vol. 13, no. 3, 1992.
Philippe C. Schmitter	"Dangers and Dilemmas of Democracy," *Journal of Democracy*, April 1994.
Hobart A. Spalding	"Marxism in Latin America," *Monthly Review*, February 1994.
Third World Quarterly	Entire issue on Third World democracy, vol. 14, no. 3, 1993.
Third World Quarterly	"Rethinking Socialism," special issue, vol. 13, no. 1, 1992.
Langa Zita	"Towards Unity of the Left," *Against the Current*, July/August 1994.
Stephen Zunes	"Unarmed Insurrections Against Authoritarian Governments in the Third World," *Third World Quarterly*, vol. 15, no. 3, 1994.

What Is the U.S. Role in the Third World?

The
Third
World

Chapter Preface

With the fall of the Soviet Union in 1991, the United States emerged from the Cold War as the world's only superpower. But the end of the forty-year conflict did not result in a more peaceful world. Repeatedly the American government felt called upon to intervene in the affairs of many Third World countries, sending troops to quell civil and interstate war, relieve famine, and restore democracy. Several years of such military and monetary outlay have sparked a lively debate among observers at home and abroad as to what the U.S. role in the Third World should be.

"Over the course of two centuries," declares U.S. secretary of state Warren Christopher, "Americans have found that advancing democratic values and human rights serves our deepest values as well as our practical interests." American efforts to promote the spread of democracy to the Third World, Christopher argues, are the best way to ensure global security since, he says, "states that . . . operate on democratic principles tend to be the world's most peaceful and stable." American efforts have paid off in places like Guatemala, Christopher maintains, where a coup subverting democratic institutions was reversed and "the resolve of the Guatemalan public, backed by the United States . . . resulted in the election of a respected human rights defender as President of Guatemala."

But the United States is not really interested in helping Third World nations to establish democracy, charges political analyst Noam Chomsky. Chomsky argues that U.S. military aid, which the government says is intended to promote democracy, instead supports repressive regimes in many Third World countries. For example, he points out that Colombia, which receives the most U.S. military aid, is the most violent country in Latin America: More than 20,000 people were killed by Colombian forces for political reasons between 1986 and 1994. Such antidemocratic results of American assistance are not limited to Latin America, Chomsky argues. In the East, he says, U.S. dollars prop up the repressive Indonesian regime, which in the early 1980s quashed East Timor's independence effort, killing more than 200,000 people. "Right now," Chomsky explains, "Western oil companies are plundering East Timor's oil . . . [and] terror and repression continue unabated."

In deciding what the proper U.S. role in the Third World should be, it is useful to examine the results that American foreign policy has achieved there already. Those results are among the issues debated in the following chapter.

"Reinforcing democracy and protecting human rights [is] a pillar of our foreign policy."

The United States Supports Human Rights and Democracy in the Developing World

Richard Schifter and Warren Christopher

In Part I of the following viewpoint, Richard Schifter, in an address to the United Nations' Human Rights Commission, maintains that the United States leads the world in the promotion of democracy and human rights around the globe. Schifter heads the U.S. delegation to the Human Rights Commission. In Part II, Warren Christopher, addressing the 1993 World Conference on Human Rights in Vienna, declares that America's promotion of human rights and democracy has succeeded in many parts of the Third World, where free elections are now taking place. Christopher is the U.S. secretary of state.

As you read, consider the following questions:

1. What European examples does Schifter cite to dispute the argument that human rights are culturally relative?
2. According to Christopher, what strategic reason does the United States have for promoting democracy abroad?

From Richard Schifter, "View from the UN: The U.S. Reviews Events Around the World," *U.S. Department of State Dispatch*, April 12, 1993. Warren Christopher, "Democracy and Human Rights," *U.S. Department of State Dispatch*, June 21, 1993.

I

The very first rights spelled out in the United Nations' 1948 Universal Declaration of Human Rights are the rights to life, liberty, and security of person. As we look at the human rights developments of 1992, we must recognize the sad fact that intergroup conflicts, based on ethnic, religious, or even clan differences, have, in many parts of the world, deprived millions of people of these fundamental rights.

We have, rightfully, spent a great deal of time discussing the atrocities which have been recently committed in the former Yugoslavia. But, as is often the case, we tend to follow the media. They cover Yugoslavia. It took some time before they covered Somalia. They seem to have forgotten Afghanistan, and they have yet to discover Rwanda [all areas of ethnic and civil war]. . . .

The U.S. Initiative

The United States has a new, young, and energetic President [Bill Clinton], who strongly believes that words must be followed by action. He has, at the beginning of his term, come before the country to tell the American people that we have serious problems and that their solution requires hard work and sacrifice.

During the course of the political campaign, our President also made clear his commitment to the cause of democracy, human rights, and to multilateralism. The new Administration deeply believes in the ideals set forth in the UN Charter and looks for their realization.

But in the UN system and, more particularly, in the UN Human Rights Commission, too, institutional reform is desperately needed. There is no doubt that, over the years, we have registered accomplishments. But are there not problems in the vast area of human rights which have remained unaffected by our activities? Should it not be a challenge to us to identify those worldwide human rights problems which we have ignored but which we could help solve if we were able to begin to deal with them?

Cultural Relativism

There are those who say that different cultures view human rights differently and that the Universal Declaration represents the views of only one culture. Persons from different cultures undoubtedly see some human rights issues differently. Yet, are there not a great many experiences in life which are common to all humankind? Does the mother in Sarajevo, Bosnia, whose son has been killed in intergroup violence grieve any more than the mother in Kigali, Rwanda? Can a native of Baghdad, Iraq, accept torture more readily than a native of, say, Copenhagen, Denmark? Is a native of Havana, Cuba, culturally better endowed to

173

accept police spying than a native of Madrid, Spain? Is a native of Beijing, China, more willing to accept imprisonment for the mere expression of his views than a native of London, England?

In years past, the question on which I have just touched, namely, that of different views of human rights, was debated in this commission along the East-West divide. After that divide had disappeared, I had occasion to meet one of the persons with whom I had once engaged in verbal jousts in this commission. His first statement to me was: "You knew all along that I did not believe a word I was saying—didn't you?"

Making the World Free

I believe the one overriding lesson the world learned 50 years ago is this: There is no substitute for American leadership. . . .

Without American leadership, freedom fighters in Afghanistan and elsewhere would have faced a far different fate.

Without American prodding, the people of nations like South Africa, the Philippines and Nicaragua would still be waiting for the freedoms they now cherish.

We have also learned that leadership is not cheap. America has paid dearly for our role as leader—both in terms of lives lost and money spent.

But there can be no doubt that results have been worth the cost. The world is a safer, freer and better place because of American leadership.

Bob Dole, *The Washington Times*, June 6, 1994.

So, let us put aside the artificial arguments which have been advanced in this post–Cold War period about North versus South, about Christian culture against non-Christian cultures, and let us agree on the simple fact that we are all members of the human race, that there are goals in the field of human rights that we all wish to attain, and that we should unite in our efforts to reach those goals.

To those who contend that the principles of the Universal Declaration have relevance only to Europe and North America, let me offer a historic reminder. About 700 years ago, many of the basic principles which we now treat as human rights were recognized by the citizens of three communities not far from here: Uri, Schwyz, and Unterwalden—the nucleus of the country which is now known as Switzerland. It is conceivable that members of the court of the Holy Roman Emperor said at that time that, if the rights claimed by these people of courage have any validity at all, they are appropriate only to the Swiss mountains and have no relevance to life elsewhere, most surely not to the rest of Europe. And what may have been said about the relevance of democratic thought and human rights principles to England under Henry VIII, to France under Louis XIV, or to the Soviet Union under Joseph Stalin? . . .

Democracies Are More Profitable

In East Asia, we can find in North Korea the world's most oppressive dictatorship, a society reminiscent of the nightmare vision of George Orwell in his novel *1984* [where the government, known as "Big Brother," has complete control over social life]. Today, North Korea is an economic basket case. The Republic of Korea, by contrast, has evolved both politically and economically. It is now a full-fledged democracy which also enjoys an increasingly higher standard of living.

Throughout the world, we can note that governments which are not controlled by the people and are not called to account by a free press have put into place counterproductive economic policies, or have expended foreign assistance funds improvidently, or have lined the pockets of their leaders with the money which belongs to the people or wasted it on unnecessary military expenditures.

The conclusion we can draw from the foregoing is that economic assistance may, indeed, be needed in many places to spur economic development. But one way of assuring that the assistance will be well used is to improve governance. There are a few countries that may have been able to develop economically under the guidance of a benevolent autocrat. But most autocrats tend to be erratic and greedy, retarding development. Accountability of a leadership produces the best assurance of economic evolution. . . .

Helping Governments to Reform

The UN system, which expends substantial funds on programs and projects of questionable value, should reset its priorities and should focus attention on what it can do to assist countries which seek such assistance, in efforts to ameliorate human rights problems.

That human rights problems can be resolved through political will and the application of resources has been demonstrated time and again. In my own country, the practice of pressing confessions out of persons under arrest was, by and large, brought to an end when our courts simply refused to accept such confessions. In Mexico, President Salinas has, in recent years, demonstrated the political will to change practices in police stations throughout his country. The Mexican Human Rights Commission, under the outstanding and courageous leadership of Judge Jorge Carpizo, who has moved on to the position of Attorney General, has made enormous strides in carrying out the President's mandate. Experiences of this kind can and should be shared with countries whose governments do not wish to see torture practiced but find it difficult to prevent it. We need to explore the role which the Human Rights Center [a UN advisory and reporting body] could play, under an appropriate mandate from the commission, to enable countries to share their experiences in the resolution of human rights problems. As we look to the future, this can, indeed, be one of the most important program goals for this commission.

The War Moved Inside

We also need to recognize that international controversies have now been replaced in large part by intranational disputes. Just as the United Nations has applied itself to international controversies, it can and should apply itself to what is now the most common cause of human rights deprivations: intergroup controversies which result in acts of violence. There are many situations in which outsiders, particularly outsiders coming under the UN flag, might be better able to act as mediators than do persons who come from the country beset with intergroup rivalry. Furthermore, there are educational programs which governments could be encouraged to institute in the schools to overcome hatred and antagonisms based on intergroup differences in race, ethnicity, or religion. Here, too, the Human Rights Center, acting under the commission's leadership, could play a highly significant role.

But, as I noted earlier, the fact that many governments which practice repression as official policy have been replaced does not mean that that phenomenon has vanished from the earth. It is, therefore, necessary for this commission to send a message to these governments that the international community remains deeply concerned about these practices, as well as a message of hope to the citizens of those countries who now are the victims of repression.

Reports . . . on Burma, Cuba, Iran, and Iraq describe systems which differ from each other in detail but which have a common result: that of creating an all-pervasive climate of fear in those countries. No citizen, be he ever so humble and politically disinterested, can escape it. Big Brother is always watching, and even minor deviations from prescribed standards of behavior can be severely punished. Intimidation, denial of economic and educational opportunities, torture, long-term imprisonment, and even summary and arbitrary execution, or execution or imprisonment on trumped-up charges are among the measures these countries resort to to keep their people in check. We must once again draw attention to this state of affairs and urge once again that these forms of repression be brought to an end.

II

I speak to you as the representative of a nation "conceived in liberty." America's identity as a nation derives from our dedication to the proposition "that all Men are created equal and endowed by their Creator with certain unalienable rights." Over the course of two centuries, Americans have found that advancing democratic values and human rights serves our deepest values as well as our practical interests.

That is why the United States stands with the men and women everywhere who are standing up for these principles. And that is why President Clinton has made reinforcing democracy and protecting human rights a pillar of our foreign policy—and a major focus of our foreign assistance programs.

Democracy is the moral and strategic imperative for the 1990s. Democracy will build safeguards for human rights in every nation. Democracy is the best way to advance lasting peace and prosperity in the world.

The U.S. Commitment to Freedom

The cause of freedom is a fundamental commitment for my country. It is also a matter of deep personal conviction for me. I am proud to have headed the U.S. Government's first interagency group on human rights under President Carter. President Carter will be remembered as the first American President to put human rights on the international agenda. He has helped to lift the lives of people in every part of the world. Today, we build upon his achievements—and those of the human rights movement since its inception.

In this post-Cold War era, we are at a new moment. Our agenda for freedom must embrace every prisoner of conscience, every victim of torture, every individual denied basic human rights. It must also encompass the democratic movements that have changed the political map of our globe.

The great new focus of our agenda for freedom is this: expanding, consolidating and defending democratic progress around the world. It is democracy that establishes the civil institutions that replace the power of oppressive regimes. Democracy is the best means not just to gain—but to guarantee—human rights.

In the battle for democracy and human rights, words matter, but what we *do* matters much more. What all of our citizens and governments do in the days ahead will count far more than any discussions held or documents produced here.

I can tell you this: The worldwide movement for democracy and human rights will prevail. My delegation will support the forces of freedom—of tolerance, of respect for the rights of the individual every day in the conduct of our foreign policy throughout the world. The United States will never join those who would undermine the Universal Declaration and the movement toward democracy and human rights.

The Universal Declaration enshrines a timeless truth for all people and all nations: "Respect for human rights and fundamental freedoms *is* the foundation of freedom, justice and peace" on this earth. The Declaration's drafters met the challenge of respecting the world's diversity, while reflecting values that are universal.

Even before the Declaration was adopted, the Cold War had begun to cast a chilling shadow between word and deed. But the framers of the Declaration hoped that each successive generation would strengthen the Declaration through its own struggles. It is for each generation to redeem the promise of the framers' work.

Time and time again since the adoption of the Universal Declaration, human rights activism has unlocked prison cells and carved out pockets of freedom for individuals living under repression. Today, the global movement from despotism to democracy is transforming entire political systems and opening freedom's door to whole societies.

The end of the Cold War is the most uplifting event for human rights since the first World Conference met. Not only were the Vaclav Havels and the Andrei Sakharovs [Czechoslovak and Russian dissidents] set free, in large measure by their own inspiring examples, but hundreds of millions of ordinary men and women were also released from the hold of oppressive governments that controlled their lives. Now, in country after country, they are turning toward democracy to secure their newly won freedoms, guarantee their human rights, and hold their governments accountable. . . .

Peace Through Democracy

The promotion of democracy is the front line of global security. A world of democracies would be a safer world. Such a world would dedicate more to human development and less to human destruction. It would promote what all people have in common rather than what tears them apart. It would be a world of hope, not a world of despair.

In 1993 alone, in addition to a massive turnout for democracy in Russia, we have seen unprecedented free elections in Cambodia, Yemen, Burundi, and Paraguay. The Truth Commission in El Salvador has completed its healing work [of exposing war crimes and trying their perpetrators]. And the people of South Africa have made dramatic progress toward non-racial democracy.

Around the world, people are doing the hard, sometimes painful work of building democracies from the bottom up. They are making democracy work not just on election day, but every day. They are promoting civil societies that respect the rule of law and make governments accountable.

Citizens' groups are pressing for social justice and establishing nongovernmental human rights organizations. Women's groups are advocating equal treatment and fighting the widespread practice of gender-based violence. Workers are forming free trade unions. Independent media are giving pluralism its voice. All are creating counterweights to repression by affirming and asserting fundamental freedoms of expression, association, and movement.

An Enduring Commitment to Democracy

American support for democracy is an enduring commitment. We know that establishing and sustaining democracy is not a linear proposition. The world democratic movement will encounter setbacks along the way. But with constant vigilance and hard work, democracy will succeed.

Look at the recent example given us by the people of Guatemala. In early June 1993, they overcame a coup that had dissolved democratic institutions. They showed that democracy has a new resilience in the Americas, with roots extending deep into civil society. The resolve of the Guatemalan public, backed by the United States and the Organization of American States-led international community, has resulted in the election of a respected human rights defender as President of Guatemala.

To those who say democracy is a Western contrivance, I say, you forgot to tell the people of Cambodia. Ninety percent of them summoned up courage, in the face of real threats, to reclaim their country by voting in May 1993's UN-monitored elections. In what was once a killing field, democracy is taking root.

Democratic aspirations are rising from Central Asia to Central America. No circumstances of birth, of culture, or of geography can limit the yearning of the human spirit and the right to live in freedom and dignity. Martin Luther King, Mohandas Gandhi, Fang Lizhi, Natan Sharansky—all came from different cultures and countries. Yet each shaped the destiny of his own nation and the world by insisting on the observance of the same universal rights.

That *each* of us comes from different cultures absolves *none* of us from our obligation to comply with the Universal Declaration. Torture, rape, racism, anti-Semitism, arbitrary detention, ethnic cleansing, and politically motivated disappearances—none of these is tolerated by any faith, creed, or culture that respects humanity. Nor can they be justified by the demands of

179

economic development or political expediency.

We respect the religious, social, and cultural characteristics that make each country unique. But we cannot let cultural relativism become the last refuge of repression.

A Single Standard of Dignity

The universal principles of the UN Declaration put *all* people first. We reject any attempt by any state to relegate its citizens to a lesser standard of human dignity. There is no contradiction between the universal principles of the UN Declaration and the cultures that enrich our international community. The real chasm lies between the cynical excuses of oppressive regimes and the sincere aspirations of their people.

No nation can claim perfection—not the United States nor any other nation. In 1968, when the U.S. Delegation arrived at the first World Conference on Human Rights, my country was reeling from the assassination of Martin Luther King. The murder of Robert Kennedy soon followed. King and Kennedy were deeply committed to building a more just society for all Americans. Their valiant work and their violent deaths left deep imprints on an entire generation of Americans—among them, a university student named Bill Clinton.

Many young democracies contend with the vast problems of grinding poverty, illiteracy, rapid population growth, and malnutrition. The survival of these democracies may ultimately depend on their ability to show their citizens that democracy can deliver—that the difficult political and economic choices will pay off soon and not just in some distant, radiant future.

Nations that free human potential—that invest in human capital and defend human rights—have a better chance to develop and grow. Nations that enforce the right to seek and obtain employment without discrimination will become more just societies— and more productive economies. And nations that are committed to democratic values create conditions in which the private sector is free to thrive and to provide work for their people.

States that respect human rights and operate on democratic principles tend to be the world's most peaceful and stable. On the other hand, the worst violators of human rights tend to be the world's aggressors and proliferators. These states export threats to global security, whether in the shape of terrorism, massive refugee flows, or environmental pollution. Denying human rights not only lays waste to human lives; it creates instability that travels across borders.

"The pressure on Congress to impose human rights conditions on aid [and] trade. . . . [has been evaded by] every administration from Carter until today."

The United States Does Not Support Human Rights and Democracy in the Developing World

Noam Chomsky

The U.S. government's claim that it supports human rights and democracy in the developing world, argues Noam Chomsky in the following viewpoint, is deceitful. Trade is more important to the United States than human rights, Chomsky maintains. Indeed, he charges, the United States actually promotes repressive Third World regimes because it does not want popularly elected governments interfering with its economic and strategic interests in those countries. Chomsky, an educator and linguist who has taught at the Massachusetts Institute of Technology since 1955, writes extensively on American politics and foreign policy.

As you read, consider the following questions:

1. How did the United States surbordinate human rights to trade in its relations with China, according to Chomsky?
2. What does the author intimate are the two tiers of society in the Third World?

Excerpted from Noam Chomsky, "Democracy Enhancement I," *Z Magazine*, May 1994. Reprinted by permission of the author.

We have passed the five-year mark since the 1989 fall of the Berlin Wall, which marked the definitive end of the Cold War. At last the United States was freed from the burden of defending the world against Russian aggression and could return to its traditional calling: to promote democracy, human rights, and free markets worldwide. Standard doctrine holds further that the promise has been fulfilled. . . . Like earlier angelic powers, we are able to recognize that there are some flaws and errors in the record. But the sophisticated understand that history can teach no lessons about our institutions and the ways they have functioned, surely nothing about what may lie ahead. . . .

At the critical extreme, we do find occasional notice of imperfection. "There's something troubling about the way we select our cases for intervention," Harvard historian Stanley Hoffmann observed in opening a conference at Tufts University. He noted that there has been no "international cry to intervene in ethnic bloodshed in East Timor," the *Boston Globe* reported. The example is instructive.

Let us disregard the phrase "ethnic bloodshed," not quite the term applied to the Soviet invasion of Afghanistan or Iraq's invasion of Kuwait. That aside, some obvious questions come to mind: just who might call for such intervention, and how should it proceed? By bombing Washington and London, the main supporters of Indonesia's aggression and mass slaughter? Suppose that a commentator in pre-Gorbachev Russia had found something troubling about Soviet intervention policy, wondering why Russia did not intervene to prevent the imposition of martial law in Poland or repression in Czechoslovakia and Hungary. Would we even laugh? How could Moscow intervene to bar the policies it actively supported? These questions cannot arise, however, in our case, whatever the facts, given our perfection. No one laughs. . . .

U.S.-Backed Terror in Indonesia

There is no need to review the facts, familiar outside of the doctrinal system, which not only suppressed them with great efficiency as the terrible story unfolded but continues to do so today. Right now, Western oil companies are plundering East Timor's oil under a treaty between Australia and Indonesia, terror and repression continue unabated, and new atrocities have been discovered from the very recent past, among them, the slaughter of many people by Indonesian doctors in hospitals after the November 1991 Dili massacre.

In the United States, public protest has hampered government support for Indonesian atrocities, but not much. Congress cut off funds for military training, but the Clinton administration was undeterred. On the anniversary of the U.S.-backed Indonesian invasion, the State Department announced that "Congress's action did not ban Indonesia's purchase of training with its own funds," so it can proceed despite the ban. Such training has, after all, been quite successful in the past, including the training of officers who took part in the highly praised slaughter of hundreds of thousands of people, mostly landless peasants, as the present government took power in 1965. . . .

The global economy - freeing our markets, freeing our consciences.

Plainly, it would be unfair to deprive the people of the region of such benefits. That is exactly the position taken by advocates of U.S. military training, for example Senator Johnson. His evidence is a quote from the Commander of the U.S. forces in the Pacific, Admiral Larson, who explains that "by studying in our schools," Indonesian army officers "gain an appreciation for our value system, specifically respect for human rights, adherence to democratic principles, and the rule of law." For similar reasons, we must allow arms sales to Indonesia, so that we can continue to have a constructive "dialogue" and maintain our "leverage and influence," so benignly exercised in the past, much as in Latin America, Haiti, the Philippines, and other places where U.S. training has instilled such admirable respect for human rights.

With the support of Senate Democrats, the administration was also able to block human rights conditions on aid to Indonesia. Trade Representative Mickey Kantor announced further that Washington would "suspend" its annual review of Indonesian labor practices. Agreeing with Senator Bennett Johnston, who is impressed by "the steps Indonesia has taken . . . to improve conditions for workers in Indonesia," Kantor commended Indonesia for "bringing its labor law and practice into closer conformity with international standards"—a witticism that is in particularly poor taste, though it must be conceded that Indonesia did take some steps forward, fearing that Congress might override its friends in the White House. "Reforms hastily pushed through by the Indonesian government in recent months include withdrawing the authority of the military to intervene in strikes, allowing workers to form a company union to negotiate labour contracts, and raising the minimum wage in Jakarta by 27 percent" to about $2 a day, the London *Guardian* reports. The new company unions that are magnanimously authorized must, to be sure, join the All-Indonesia Labor Union, the state-run union. To ensure that these promising advances toward international labor standards would not be misunderstood, authorities also arrested 21 labor activists.

"We have done much to change and improve," Indonesia's Foreign Minister said, "so according to us there is no reason to revoke" the trade privileges. Clinton liberals evidently agree.

One effect of the activism of the 1960s was the pressure on Congress to impose human rights conditions on aid, trade, and military sales. Every administration from Carter until today has had to seek ways to evade such constraints. In the 1980s, it became a sick joke, as the Reaganites regularly assured Congress (always happy to be "deceived") that its favorite assassins and torturers were making impressive progress. Clinton is forging no new paths with his Indonesia chicanery.

Looking for Straw in China

Other tasks are proving harder, however, notably China. . . . China is not giving poor Clinton much help in his endeavor to bypass the executive order that he issued imposing human rights conditions—in "fear that Congressional Democrats might otherwise have forced an even more stringent approach" through legislation, Thomas Friedman reports in the *New York Times*, and because Clinton "did not want to appear to be going back on another campaign promise," having "strongly criticized President Bush for 'coddling' China."

The problem arose again as Secretary of State Warren Christopher visited Beijing in March 1994 to express Washington's concerns on human rights, which, the State Department hastened to explain, are quite limited—in fact, limited to finding means to evade Congressional pressures. John Shattuck, U.S. assistant secretary of human rights, clarified to the Chinese leaders that Clinton's requirements for improvement are "very narrow," that pledges of progress may be enough: "What the president is looking for is an indication of direction . . . that is generally forward looking." Please, please, give us some straw, so that we can respond to the needs of our constituency in the corporate sector. The Chinese, however, seem to enjoy watching their partners twist in the wind.

The Undemocratic New World Order

Citing the war against Iraq [who had invaded neighboring Kuwait] as an example of the hypocritical nature of U.S. foreign policy, the former foreign minister of Nicaragua Miguel d'Escoto Brockmann stated, "The whole thing was so ridiculous. Can you imagine this whole surrealism of having the U.S. come out in defense of international law . . . the very country that invaded Panama, invades all over the place and conducted the war here in Nicaragua?". . .

We in the United States should carefully consider this system sold to us as democratic by our leaders and the corporate elite. . . .

What's to be said about a system that invokes the principles of international law when it fits its fancy, but snubs its nose at inconvenient international law invoked by others? What can you call a system which, under a smokescreen of free trade, sets the multinational corporations and the bankers free to starve the poor? Call it what you will, but democratic it is not.

Dennis DeMaio, *People's Weekly World*, March 19, 1994.

As Christopher left for China, the administration announced that it would once again relax the sanctions on high technology transfers, this time by allowing the Hughes Aircraft Company to launch a satellite from China. This "gesture of good will toward Beijing" is one "part of the strategy to engage China rather than to isolate it," Elaine Sciolino reported in the *New York Times*. Asked about this decision while China is under pressure on issues of missile proliferation and human rights, Christopher responded that it "simply sends a signal of even-handed treatment." The "good will gesture," as usual, is directed towards a leading segment of the publicly subsidized "private enterprise" system, much like the "good-will gestures" announced at the Asia-Pacific summit in November 1993, which allowed China to purchase supercomputers, nuclear power generators, and satellites despite their adaptability to weapons and missile proliferation. The Pentagon also sent high officials with Christopher "to discuss ways to upgrade the two countries' military relationship," Sciolino reported, another part of the "strategy."

Christopher did not return empty-handed. At a White House session, Thomas Friedman reports, he "presented a chart . . . showing that on many fronts China was making some progress toward meeting the terms of the President's executive order, but that forward movement had been obscured by the confrontational atmosphere of his visit." On leaving Beijing, he had stated that his discussions with the Chinese leaders were "businesslike and productive." "The differences between China and the U.S. are narrowing somewhat," Christopher informed the press, though he "was hard put to point to examples of specific progress on the vexed human rights issue beyond a memorandum of understanding on trade in prison labour products," the London *Financial Times* commented. China did (once again) agree to restrict exports from prison factories to the United States.

Labor Rights vs. Profits

Such exports have greatly exercised Washington and the press, the sole labor rights issue to have achieved this status. "U.S. Inspections of Jail Exports Likely in China," a front-page story by Thomas Friedman was headlined in the *New York Times* in January 1994. The Chinese "agreed to a demand to allow more visits by American customs inspectors to Chinese prison factories to make sure they are not producing goods for export to the United States," he reported from Beijing. U.S. influence is having further benign effects, "forcing liberalization, factory by factory," including contract, bankruptcy, and other laws that are "critical elements of a market economy," all welcome steps towards a "virtuous circle."

Unmentioned are a few other questions about economic virtue: horrifying labor conditions, for example. Perhaps the case of 81 women burned to death locked into their factory in November 1993, which merited a few lines in the national press in the midst of much euphoria about Clinton's grand vision of a free market future in the Asia-Pacific region. Or 60 workers killed in a fire a few weeks later in another foreign-owned factory. Or the doubling of deaths in industrial accidents in 1993, with over 11,000 just in the first eight months. "Chinese officials and analysts say the accidents stem from abysmal working conditions, which, combined with long hours, inadequate pay, and even physical beatings, are stirring unprecedented labor unrest among China's booming foreign joint ventures," Sheila Tefft reported in the *Christian Science Monitor*. That problem is a real one: "the tensions reveal the great gap between competitive foreign capitalists lured by cheap Chinese labor and workers weaned on socialist job security and the safety net of cradle-to-grave benefits." Workers do not yet understand that in the capitalist utopia we are preparing for them, they are to be "beaten for producing poor quality goods, fired for dozing on the job during long work hours" and other such misdeeds, and locked into their factories to be burned to death. But we understand all of that, so China is not called to account for violations of labor rights; only for exporting prison products to the U.S.

Why the distinction? Simplicity itself. Prison factories are state-owned industry, and exports to the U.S. interfere with profits, unlike locking women into factories, beating workers, and other such means to improve the balance sheet. QED. . . .

Promoting Democracy

Our current vocation, as everyone knows, is promoting democracy. There are many illuminating examples since the fall of the Berlin Wall freed us from the Cold War burden.

The first, and one of the most revealing, is Nicaragua. Recall that just as the Wall fell, the White House and Congress announced with great clarity that unless Nicaraguans voted as we told them, the terrorist war and the embargo that was strangling the country would continue. Washington also voted (alone with Israel) against a UN General Assembly resolution calling on it once again to observe international law and call off these illegal actions; unthinkable of course, so the press continued to observe its vow of silence. When Nicaraguans met their obligations a few months later, joy was unrestrained. At the dissident extreme, Anthony Lewis hailed Washington's "experiment in peace and democracy," which gives "fresh testimony to the power of Jefferson's idea: government with the consent of the governed. . . . To say so seems romantic, but then we live in a romantic age." Across the spectrum there was rejoicing over the latest of the "happy series of democratic surprises," as *Time* magazine expressed the uniform view while outlining the methods used to achieve our Jeffersonian ideals: to "wreck the economy and prosecute a long and deadly proxy war until the exhausted natives overthrow the unwanted government themselves," with a cost to us that is "minimal," leaving the victim "with wrecked bridges, sabotaged power stations, and ruined farms," and providing Washington's candidate with "a winning issue," ending the "impoverishment of the people of Nicaragua."

It would be hard to imagine a more conclusive demonstration of the understanding of "democracy" in the dominant political and intellectual culture. It is inconceivable that the clear and unmistakable meaning of any of this should enter the respectable culture, or probably even history.

That interesting story continues. On March 15, 1994, U.S. assistant Secretary of State Alexander Watson announced that "With the conflicts of the past behind us, the Clinton administration accepts the Sandinistas as a legitimate political force in Nicaragua with all the rights and obligations of any party in a democracy supposing that it uses only peaceful and legitimate methods," as we did through the 1980s, setting the stage for a "fair election," by U.S. standards. The brief Reuters report noted that "the United States financed the Contra rebels against the Soviet-backed Sandinista government." Translating from Newspeak, Washington followed standard procedure, doing everything it could to compel Nicaragua to abandon its despicable efforts to maintain a nonaligned stand [independent of Washington and Moscow] and balanced trade and to turn to the Russians as a last resort, so that Washington's attack could be construed as part of the Cold War conflict raging in our backyard, now to be dispatched to the category of irrelevance for understanding ourselves, or what the future holds.

Washington's willingness to accept the Sandinistas as a legitimate political force, if they mind their manners, cannot claim the prize for moral cowardice and depravity. That is still held by Washington's display of magnanimity towards the Vietnamese, now permitted to enter the civilized world, their many crimes against us put to the side (though not, of course, forgiven) once U.S. business made it clear that the pleasure of torturing our victims must give way to the more important task of enrichment of the wealthy.

The next example of our post–Cold War passion for democracy was the invasion of Panama [a U.S. action entitled "Operation Just Cause"] a month after the Berlin Wall fell, the first exercise of humanitarian intervention in the post–Cold War era. . . .

Democracy in Panama

Operation Just Cause was presented as a "textbook case" of Washington's dedication to democracy—quite accurately, as it turned out. In its January 1994 annual report on human rights, Panama's governmental Human Rights Commission charged that the right to self-determination and sovereignty of the Panamanian people continues to be violated by the "state of occupation by a foreign army," reviewing U.S. army, airforce, and DEA operations in Panama, including a DEA agent's assault on a Panamanian journalist and attacks on Panamanian citizens by U.S. military personnel. The nongovernmental Human Rights Commission, in its accompanying report "Democracy and Human Rights in Panama . . . Four Years Later," added that democracy has meant nothing more than formal voting while government policies "do not attend to the necessities of the most impoverished"—whose numbers have significantly increased since the "liberation." Within a year after the invasion, Latin Americanist Stephen Ropp observes, Washington was well aware "that removing the mantle of United States protection would quickly result in a civilian or military overthrow of [President] Endara and his supporters"— that is, the puppet regime of bankers, businessmen, and narco-traffickers installed by the occupying army. "Drugs and their rewards are more visible today than in General Noriega's time," the *Economist* reported in March 1994, including hard drugs. A senior employee of the Panama Branch of Merrill Lynch was one of those . . . caught in a DEA operation as they were laundering Colombian cocaine cash through Panama's large financial industry, the one real economic success story of the "occupation by a foreign army." "All they were doing is what almost every bank in Panama does," a local investigative reporter commented. All exactly as predicted when the troops landed to restore the mainly white oligarchy to power and ensure U.S. control over the strategically important region and its financial institutions. . . .

Destroying Hope

The great achievement of the massive terror operations of the past years organized by Washington and its local associates has been to destroy hope. The observation generalizes to much of the Third World and also to the growing masses of superfluous people at home, as the Third World model of sharply two-tiered societies is increasingly internationalized. These are major themes of the "New World Order" being constructed by the privileged sectors of global society, with U.S. state and private power in the lead.

"The United States must develop systems to protect itself from nuclear attacks from the Third World."

The United States Must Guard Against a Nuclear-Armed South

Steven R. David

In the following viewpoint, Steven R. David argues that in the wake of the Cold War, the threat of nuclear proliferation in the Third World has increased. Many Third World countries possess or are currently attempting to develop nuclear weapons, David contends. A nuclear-armed South threatens American interests both abroad and at home, David insists, because Third World nations are more likely than Western nations to use such weapons—even against the United States. The United States must therefore keep nuclear weapons out of Southern hands, David proposes, through the support of the Non-Proliferation Treaty and through direct military intervention where necessary. David is a professor of political science at Johns Hopkins University in Baltimore, Maryland.

As you read, consider the following questions:

1. According to the author, why would the Cold War "mutual assured destruction relationship of the superpowers" be difficult to duplicate in a nuclear-armed Third World?
2. What is the lesson that Third World dictators and terrorists learned from the U.S.-Iraqi war in the Persian Gulf, according to David?

Excerpted from Steven R. David, "Why the Third World Still Matters," *International Security*, vol. 17, no. 3, Winter 1992/93. Copyright ©1993 by the President and Fellows of Harvard College and the Massachusetts Institute of Technology. Reprinted by permission of the MIT Press.

The end of the Cold War and the disintegration of the Soviet Union have not ended the importance of the Third World to American interests and worldwide stability, nor have they ushered in a new era of peace. Because war will not become obsolete in the Third World, and because many Third World states are becoming increasingly powerful, the threat that Third World states pose to themselves and non–Third World countries will persist. Preparing to address these threats must be a central component of American foreign policy in the post–Cold War world. . . .

Third World Domestic Instability

Washington needs to be concerned about Third World developments because war is more likely to occur in the Third World than anywhere else. Some of these wars are likely to be fought in areas that are essential for the Western economies (e.g., the Persian Gulf), or with weapons of mass destruction that may inflict terrible damage on the combatants, their neighbors, American allies, or the United States itself. The likelihood of war is so high because Third World states are characterized by domestic instability that leads to internal war and can bring about international war as well. . . .

The belief that states in the Third World are more war-prone stems, first, from their recent history. From 1945 to 1990 there have been over 100 wars (both internal and interstate) in the Third World. Since 1945 nearly 20 million people have lost their lives in wars. Of this number, about 200,000 deaths occurred in Europe during the Greek civil war and Soviet intervention in Hungary. The rest, over 19 million people, died as a result of wars in the Third World. All of the wars and armed conflicts involving the United States have been in the Third World. It is not an exaggeration to say that war since 1945 has been essentially a Third World affair.

Third World conflict is so prevalent because of the characteristics of many Third World states. A key factor is the relative youth of the states. Western Europe and the Third World both confronted similar problems in forging cohesive states. Inculcating a state identity among disparate groups and establishing borders are just some of the fundamental obstacles that had to be overcome. The difference in the Third World is that while it took Western Europe three to four centuries to develop a state, Third World leaders have had only three to four *decades* to accomplish the same task. Even in Latin America, where states have existed for over a century, the time available for state formation has been much less than in Western Europe. It should not, therefore, be surprising that most Third World states lack the cohesion and stability of their West European counterparts.

A second characteristic of the Third World that promotes instability is the legacy of colonialism. Most Third World states are ex-colonies. Outside powers created states where none had existed. Although the degree of correlation with existing ethnic groups varied (high in Southeast Asia, low in Africa and the Middle East), in nearly all cases imposed borders replaced flexible demarcations. . . .

Ed Gamble. Reprinted by special permission of King Features.

Ethnic fragmentation creates problems among states as well as within them. In some cases, colonial borders divided a single ethnic group among many states (e.g., Ogaden Somalis inhabit Somalia, Ethiopia, Kenya, and Djibouti). Since many in the ethnic group owe allegiance to their group over the state, and since some states will each compete to exploit that allegiance to bring members of the group under its jurisdiction, the outcome is often continued tension, at times erupting into war. The denial of statehood to certain ethnic groups (e.g., the Kurds in the Middle East) has also created conflict and instability as these groups seek to rule themselves, while existing states act to suppress their moves towards self-determination. Colonialism's inattention to the needs of ethnic groups, whether a drive towards statehood, secession, or autonomy, has created instability throughout the Third World, and laid the basis for perpetual conflict and outside intervention. . . .

The persistence of internal warfare is especially worrisome since it has been a major cause of the interstate warfare that has been all too common throughout the Third World. Internal disorder provokes international conflict as neighboring states act to prevent instability from spreading to them, as India did when it supported the efforts of Bangladesh to secede from Pakistan in 1971. Leaders will be inclined to go to war to divert attention from domestic difficulties, as occurred when Argentina invaded the Falklands in 1982. Domestic instability might leave a country too weak to suppress sub-national groups who are left free to provoke attacks from bordering states, with such results as the Israeli invasion of Lebanon in 1982. Internal instability can create the impression that a foe has been so weakened that a "window of opportunity" for invasion has been opened, as seen in Somalia's 1977 assault on Ethiopia. . . .

The Third World Threat to American Interests

[One] way in which Third World states can endanger American interests is in their ability to threaten the United States and other countries militarily. Approximately a dozen Third World countries have or are attempting to develop nuclear weapons. This group includes Libya, Iraq, Iran, and North Korea, who are avowed enemies of the United States and its allies. As the near development of nuclear weapons by Iraq demonstrated, international inspection in a country and formal adherence to the Non-Proliferation Treaty is not enough to prevent it from acquiring nuclear arms. The Iraqi episode is further evidence of how little the United States knows about the developing nuclear capabilities of Third World states, including those that are its adversaries. A small number of nuclear weapons directed against the United States or an ally would do catastrophic damage, and an effective defense against nuclear attack has not been devised. Far from allaying U.S. fears, the disintegration of the USSR has exacerbated concerns about nuclear proliferation. Not only has the restraining influence of the USSR on global proliferation been lost, there are also thousands of Soviet nuclear scientists now out of work who may be tempted to offer their services to Third World bidders. Several of the countries who are most likely to take advantage of the expertise of emigrating Soviet scientists, such as Cuba and Syria, are of special concern to the United States because of their support of terrorism and anti-American actions. Moreover, the breakup of the Soviet Union has raised fears that nuclear weapons will be—or may already have been—transferred to Third World countries. . . .

The key question is not whether Third World countries will be able to threaten the United States in the post–Cold War era with such weapons—they will—but rather whether they will be inclined to do so. Those who argue that proliferation should not be a major concern of the United States (most notably, Kenneth Waltz) assume that Third World states will behave essentially like the existing nuclear powers in their use or non-use of nuclear weapons. Since nuclear weapons have induced caution and reduced the margin for miscalculation among the great powers, there is no reason to believe it will be different for the minor powers. Radical and revolutionary states, they say, would not use nuclear weapons recklessly because their leaders would recognize the price of doing so. Even leaders assumed to be irrational (at least by Western standards) are still sensitive to costs. Accidents, unauthorized launchings, or theft of nuclear weapons would not be more likely in the Third World, it is asserted, since the leaders of the countries would have every incentive not to allow their nuclear arms to fall out of their control. Third World conflicts are seen as being no more intense than conflicts elsewhere, and even if an interstate nuclear war broke out, for example between India and Pakistan, or Israel and Iraq, they argue that American interests might be best served by remaining aloof. In sum, this view asserts, Third World states are no more likely to use nuclear weapons than the major powers, and if they do the result would not threaten American interests.

The Likelihood of Nuclear Use

These are all cogent points, but precisely because Third World states are more likely to engage in internal and external warfare, nuclear weapons are more likely to be used and American interests are more likely to be endangered than if such weapons were deployed by more stable states. Internal conflict in the Third World heightens the likelihood of nuclear use in several ways. Widespread domestic turmoil may prevent a state from exercising control over its nuclear weapons despite its best efforts to do so, and nuclear weapons could thus fall into the hands of terrorists, particularly in the Middle East where terrorist groups are so prevalent and powerful. Terrorist groups are likely to have fewer inhibitions about launching nuclear strikes. Nuclear weapons might fall into the hands of insurgents in a civil conflict; because civil wars are often more brutal and destructive than interstate wars, the intensity of feelings could overcome any inhibitions that threats of retaliation would engender. For example, it is doubtful that nuclear deterrence could have been relied upon to keep the peace if a Lebanese faction had gained control of nuclear arms during that country's civil war, or if Peru's Shining Path movement possessed nuclear weapons today.

The greater propensity of many Third World states to engage in interstate war also undermines the arguments of those who dismiss the consequences of nuclear proliferation. For deterrence to work, a state needs to be able to identify its adversary. But in a Third World filled with conflict, this will be problematic for several reasons. First, the number of Third World states acquiring nuclear weapons is likely to increase in the near future. Equally important, in a Third World where the threat of war is always present, many Third World states have multiple enemies. The United States and the Soviet Union had the luxury of being able to focus on each other in establishing their deterrent relationship. The emergence of medium nuclear powers complicated the superpower balance, but did not alter it. But in the Third World there may be many small nuclear powers, most of which face many adversaries. With nuclear weapons able to be launched from sea, air, and even from trucks, it might be difficult if not impossible to determine the origin of a nuclear strike. If Israel is attacked in a Middle East where Iran, Iraq, Libya, Syria, and Saudi Arabia all maintain nuclear weapons, against whom should it retaliate? Countries might also use terrorist groups to launch nuclear strikes in an effort to avoid responsibility and thus retaliation.

The Probability of War

The intensity of the conflict faced by many Third World states also makes nuclear war more likely than among the great powers. It is true that the United States and the Soviet Union have had tense relations, and that the Soviet Union and China even engaged in brief armed clashes in 1969. Nevertheless, these countries have never experienced the degree of hostility that characterizes many Third World countries (e.g., Israel and most of the Arab states, or North and South Korea). Moreover, because the very existence of some Third World states is threatened, their resort to nuclear weapons becomes all the more probable. Israel, for example, was reported to consider the use of nuclear weapons against invading Arab forces during the October 1973 War on at least two occasions. In addition, the problems of preempting another state's nuclear capability did not prevent Israel from attacking Iraq's nuclear reactor in 1981. As more states seek nuclear weapons, attacks of this kind and retaliations, some of which might be nuclear, cannot be ruled out.

Because the threat of war is so high, the possibilities of accidental or unauthorized launchings will also be greater in the Third World than elsewhere. The need to prevent preemption of small nuclear forces could force new nuclear states to adopt a "hair-trigger" response to conventional or nuclear attacks. Such a response combined with primitive radar and command and control capabilities might lead to inadvertent nuclear strikes. In addition, it is likely that Third World regimes would disperse nuclear weapons and move them from place to place to enhance their protection from attack. These steps might also increase the chances that lower-ranking officers could launch nuclear weapons without authority from the government, and that the nuclear weapons themselves would be more vulnerable to subnational or terrorist groups.

Finally, it is true that Third World states might be able to duplicate the mutual assured destruction relationship of the superpowers. But deterrence is essentially a psychological concept in which one side attempts to persuade the other not to do something it is fully capable of doing, by threatening it with unacceptable costs. The culture and psychology of the leadership necessarily play a role in determining when costs outweigh benefits. Risking the destruction of several cities for some political gain would be unthinkable for most leaders, but not necessarily for all. Western concepts of nuclear deterrence may not obtain everywhere.

The American Interest

This spread of nuclear weapons to a Third World beset with internal and international instabilities threatens American interests in many ways. Internal war in an economically critical area (such as the [oil-rich] Persian Gulf) could cause catastrophic damage to the economies of the United States and its allies. Nuclear war within a Third World country could make subsequent nuclear use more likely, while encouraging the proliferation of nuclear weapons to still more countries. The use of nuclear weapons in a domestic conflict might also spread beyond the borders of the country involved, threatening American allies. The environmental effects of nuclear war, even an internal one, cannot be dismissed, especially if many weapons are employed.

The greater likelihood that Third World states will use nuclear weapons against other states is even more threatening to American interests than their use in a domestic conflict. The possession of nuclear arms by an enemy of the United States could deter the United States from acting to defend its interests. It is difficult to believe that the United States would have intervened against Saddam Hussein by placing some half a million troops in a relatively small area if Washington had believed that Iraq had nuclear weapons. Indeed, a major lesson of the U.S.-Iraqi war for would-be Third World hegemons is not to refrain from attacking American interests, but to wait to acquire a nuclear weapons capability before doing so. The United States might also be deterred from taking actions against states engaged in terrorist activities. As Libyan Leader Muammar Qadhafi remarked, "If at the time of the U.S. raid on Tripoli [1986] we had possessed a deterrent-missile that could reach New York, we could have hit it at the same moment." Nuclear war between

Third World states, for example in East Asia, could interrupt international trade, badly hurting the Western economies. Interference with American commerce propelled the United States into war in the past (for example, the War of 1812 and World War I), and could do so again, especially given the far greater damage a nuclear conflict would produce.

The Continuing Danger of Russia's Nuclear Arsenal

Scattered somewhere across Russia's vastness, more than 19,000 nuclear warheads are waiting to be taken apart and destroyed.

The good news: The Russian military doesn't want them anymore. The bad news: Nobody knows where they all are—nobody in the U.S. government, and perhaps nobody in the Russian government, either.

And that makes U.S. officials nervous. . . .

"If you consider how hard [Iraqi leader] Saddam Hussein was working to get two kilograms of enriched uranium . . . [in the former Soviet Union] you see hundreds of thousands of kilograms of material—some fabricated into weapons, some just sitting there, some still being made," said Ashton B. Carter, assistant secretary of defense in charge of non-proliferation efforts. "Never before have we had the disintegration of a nuclear power. That is new and uniquely dangerous."

Already, agents of Iran's radical Islamic regime have reportedly been sighted in Russia and formerly Soviet Kazakhstan, offering large sums of money for nuclear hardware.

Doyle McManus, *Los Angeles Times*, May 8, 1994.

American allies are also threatened by the prospect of nuclear-armed Third World states. Any close friend of the United States, including states in Western Europe (which are geographically closer to likely proliferators), could be threatened with nuclear attack by countries seeking to influence American policy. U.S. resupply of Israel during a Middle Eastern war, for example, might be undermined by threats to strike at America's European allies. More generally, regional conflicts endanger U.S. allies and friends throughout the Third World. South Korea, Taiwan, Israel, India, and Pakistan are all threatened by nuclear-armed adversaries.

Most alarmingly, nuclear weapons might be directed against the United States itself. Motives for attacking the United States are as wide-ranging as the groups and countries of the Third World who hate the United States, its actions, and its policies. At least six Third World states are expected to have intercontinental ballistic missiles by the end of the 1990s, making them capable of instant destruction of American cities. Many others, no doubt, will follow in their footsteps. Moreover, Third World states and other actors without ballistic missiles could still deliver nuclear weapons against the United States by using aircraft, cruise missiles, ships, and conceivably even suitcases. Aside from the obvious catastrophic damage done to American interests should one of these arms actually be detonated, efforts to prevent threatened attacks could result in suspension or compromise of civil liberties. . . .

What the United States Must Do

The United States must . . . be prepared to deny control over nuclear weapons to regimes, groups, and individuals who are likely to threaten American interests. The United States must continue its efforts to enhance international norms against the spread of nuclear weapons such as the Non-Proliferation Treaty, improve international safeguards, and reassure friendly states (at times with treaty guarantees) that they will not need nuclear weapons to ensure their security. Should these efforts fail, the United States needs to be prepared to use military action to preempt the developing nuclear capabilities of countries and groups who are likely to use those weapons against American allies or the United States itself.

Assuming that an anti-proliferation policy will never be foolproof, the United States must develop systems to protect itself from nuclear attacks from the Third World. A defensive system designed to deal with the Third World ballistic missile threat need not be on the scale of the space-based Reagan-Bush Strategic Defense Initiative or even the increasingly ambitious "Global Protection Against Limited Strikes" (GPALS) program. Instead, a more modest ground-based system of far less cost that is consistent with the Antiballistic Missile treaty (or a reasonable modification of it) would be preferable. For non–ballistic missile nuclear threats, the United States needs to improve air and coastal defenses and develop better means to prevent nuclear materials from being smuggled into the country. . . .

The United States must not allow its understandable joy over the ending of the Cold War become an excuse for isolationist complacency. The growing power and instability of some Third World states threatens American interests in ways whose implications are still unknown. The threats may not be as catastrophic as those presented by the former Soviet Union, but they are far more likely to arise. Just as the United States had to confront the challenge presented by the USSR, so too will it have to address the new threats posed by less powerful but potentially more dangerous adversaries.

"The use of American military force to combat the problem of the spread of nuclear weapons spurs proliferation."

The United States and Other Western Nuclear Powers Should Disarm

Mark Schapiro and the Campaign for Peace and Democracy

In November 1993 the Non-Aligned Movement (NAM), a group of 110 developing nations, sponsored a United Nations resolution to criminalize nuclear weapons. In Part I of the following viewpoint, Mark Schapiro reports that while the major nuclear powers—led by the United States—strongly oppose the resolution, representatives of many Western countries agree with the Southern nations that nuclear arms should be outlawed. Schapiro is a New York–based freelance writer. In Part II, the Campaign for Peace and Democracy, a New York–based group advocating international peace and democracy, argues that the United States' militaristic posture will encourage nuclear proliferation in the Third World. According to the campaign, America must delegitimate nuclear arms by dismantling its own nuclear arsenal.

As you read, consider the following questions:

1. Why do the three major nuclear powers oppose a World Court declaration, according to Schapiro?
2. What reasons does the Campaign for Peace and Democracy give for Third World attempts to arm themselves with nuclear weapons?

Mark Schapiro, "Mutiny on the Nuclear Bounty," *The Nation*, December 27, 1993. Reprinted by permission of *The Nation* magazine, ©1993 The Nation Company, L.C. Campaign for Peace and Democracy, "Statement on Iraq and Nuclear Proliferation," *Peace & Democracy News*, Winter 1992/93. Reprinted with permission.

I

In November 1993, the Western nuclear powers stared the cold war in the eye, and flinched. Faced with the prospect of endorsing a United Nations resolution sponsored by the 110 members of the Non-Aligned Movement (N.A.M.) calling on the World Court to declare nuclear weapons illegal, the United States, Britain and France were roused into a frenzy of frantic transcontinental lobbying to stop the initiative before it reached the General Assembly. Their power play insured that the doctrine of mutual assured destruction, the glue that so inextricably bound the cold war antagonists together, would survive even the disappearance of an enemy. Mexico's Geneva-based disarmament counselor, Miguel Marin-Bosch, who was in the middle of the battle, offered a blunt assessment of the scene at the world body during the last two weeks of November. "The nuclear powers," he said, "are scared shitless. Their turn is up. And they are holding on to the only toys that have been the guarantee of their legitimacy." Or, as the Canadian disarmament ambassador, Peggy Mason, described it, "Hysteria is not too strong a word to describe the nuclear weapons states' point of view around here."

Questioning the Legality of Nuclear Weapons

What prompted such strong language from the normally cotton-mouthed speakers of the diplomatic community was a resolution, introduced by the Non-Aligned Movement and supported by a loose coalition of citizen groups—including the International Physicians for the Prevention of Nuclear War, the International Peace Bureau (both winners of the Nobel Peace Prize) and the International Association of Lawyers Against Nuclear Arms—that called for the U.N. General Assembly to seek an advisory opinion from the World Court (officially known as the International Court of Justice) in The Hague, Netherlands, on the legality of the use or threatened use of nuclear weapons.

Such a declaration would be largely symbolic, but it would be a powerful symbol, coming from the premier arbiter of international law. For anyone inclined to discount the power of symbols, consider the reaction from the Western nuclear powers, which launched a sequence of démarches (a polite term for diplomatic arm-twisting visits) to capitals across the non-aligned world—including in Zimbabwe, Chile, the Philippines, Morocco and Colombia—to discourage the N.A.M. from forcing the measure to a vote in the General Assembly after it was introduced in the U.N.'s First Committee, which handles disarmament questions. In the end, "incredible pressure," in the words of one Latin American delegate, forced the N.A.M. (which requires a unanimous vote of its members to act) to retreat. Within N.A.M., a small group of nations with close ties to the nuclear powers succeeded in blocking a consensus to bring the resolution to the floor for a vote. Those countries, each with unique ties to one or more of the three Western nuclear powers, included Ghana (a former British colony), Benin (a former French colony) and Indonesia (with longtime ties to the United States). They, exclaims Marin-Bosch, "are being run by remote control from Paris, London or Washington."

Drawing by Francis Jetter. Reprinted with permission.

Barely a word about the controversy appeared in the American press, but what it amounted to was a near-mutiny by the non-nuclear world—which constitutes about 80 percent of the

global population—against the continued domination of the nuclear powers. The N.A.M. reserves the right to bring the proposal to a vote; whatever the outcome, the controversy reveals
growing fissures within the old cold war structures, especially
NATO [North Atlantic Treaty Organization].

Resistance to Change

Getting a government to reveal its position on a vote it was
not forced to take is not an easy matter. "One of the pleasures of
not having to vote is that you don't have to say how you would
have voted," says Peggy Mason of Canada. There are indications, however, of how certain key NATO countries would have
gone. Mason herself faces a major policy shift on the part of her
government; while the previous Conservative regime clearly opposed the measure, the new Canadian Prime Minister, Jean
Chrétien, issued a letter in September 1993, when he was still
leader of the Liberal opposition, indicating his party's desire for
a complete review of Canada's position on nuclear deterrence
policy—including an endorsement, "in principle," of the World
Court initiative. In Italy, the Foreign Affairs Commission of the
Senate passed a unanimous motion in October 1993 calling on
the government to support the measure if it came to a vote in
the General Assembly, which the government subsequently
agreed to do.

A similar situation occurred in Ireland, which is not a NATO
member but is a member of the European Community. In Dublin
the Joint Foreign Affairs Committee of Parliament voted to request the government's support for the measure; a representative
of the Irish mission to the U.N. confirmed that he very likely
would have been asked to vote yes. The vote promised a show-
down that would have revealed the slow erosion in the bipolar
structure based on nuclear weaponry that has reigned since the
end of World War II—and the resistance to that change by the
three aforementioned "official" nuclear powers. Neither of the
other two, Russia and China, played a significant role in opposing the measure, preferring instead to lie low and not alienate
their allies in the Third World.

The nuclear triumvirate of the United States, Britain and
France argued privately that such a declaration would create an
unfriendly working environment at a time when negotiations
for a comprehensive test ban treaty are poised . . . and would
undermine efforts to strengthen the Non-Proliferation Treaty.
The U.N.'s First Committee did make a near-unanimous endorsement of both these initiatives, and of a measure by Canada
to block further production of fissionable materials to be used
for nuclear weapons—signs that the end of the cold war has
softened the bloc politics in the normally contentious First

Committee. But the real fear of the nuclear powers is that an adverse ruling by the World Court would undermine the status quo, which enshrines who has access to nuclear weapons and who does not.

A Double-Faced Nuclear Power

"We are shooting ourselves in the foot," says a senior Congressional arms expert who has followed the debate closely. "We are refusing to accept as illegal what 98 percent of the world is being asked to accept as illegal—an elite view that we are the only ones who can hold on to nuclear weapons. . . . It makes us look like a double-faced nuclear power, talking one game and playing another. It plays into the hands of the North Koreans' efforts to obtain nuclear weapons, and countries like Ukraine's efforts to hold on to them."

The N.A.M. initiative follows closely on the heels of a similar resolution passed in May 1993 in Geneva by the governing body of the World Health Organization, the World Health Assembly. That resolution, spearheaded by Zambia and Mexico, and opposed by the Western nuclear threesome, passed by a significant majority and calls for the World Court to issue an advisory opinion on the legality of "the use" of nuclear weapons. . . . The N.A.M. resolution would have broadened the request to include "the threat of use of nuclear weapons." A negative judgment by the Court would immediately brand all the nuclear powers equally as pursuing a criminal policy, according to international law. Needless to say, such a prospect was hardly comforting to the big powers, though there is ample precedent for such a finding. The Geneva and Hague Conventions, to which all the nuclear powers are signatories, establish prohibitions against indiscriminate harm to civilians, destruction of neutral countries, severe damage to the environment and the use of poison gas (i.e., radiation)—all of which could be the result of nuclear attack. "You cannot expect France or Britain or the United States to fill up with great warmth if something that is a critical part of their defense is suddenly declared illegal," comments Richard Butler, Australia's ambassador to the U.N. and a leading disarmament advocate.

In the end, the battle to persuade the World Court to consider the legality of nuclear weapons holds considerable import for the post–cold war configuration of power. Within the U.N. itself, it is linked to a growing movement to reform the structure and expand the membership of the Security Council, now dominated by the five nuclear powers with permanent seats. The governments of Singapore, Mexico, Australia and Ireland are at the forefront of an effort to expand the membership of the Security Council to reflect the dramatic growth in U.N. membership—to 184 countries today from 82 before 1960—and the changes in relative economic and military power that have become far more relevant than the cold war standoffs of the past. The question of who holds the keys to the most powerful weapons on earth strikes at the heart of this increasingly obsolete balance of power.

Rethinking the Cold War Power Structure

Marin-Bosch of Mexico comments, "What is at the heart of this debate is that it detonates a rethinking of the whole nuclear business, which in turn forces a rethinking of the whole cold war power structure. . . . Look at France. This whole debate is driving the French crazy. The French government thinks that their legitimacy comes from having nuclear weapons. Take their nukes and their Security Council veto, and what are they? A little more than Italy and less than Germany." The British, no doubt, are aware of this calculus as well—as are Germany and Japan, the most likely candidates for permanent membership in an expanded Security Council.

Meanwhile, of course, even if all the existing nuclear weapons agreements are adhered to, the world will be left with close to 20,000 warheads in the year 2003. Proponents now fear that, having suppressed the General Assembly initiative, the Western nuclear powers will attempt to force the World Health Organization to reverse its commitment to have the case heard. . . . However that case is resolved, the Court initiative seems to have succeeded, at the least, in jump-starting a long-term campaign to change the nature of the debate over nuclear weapons. Michael Christ, coordinator of the International Physicians for the Prevention of Nuclear War's World Court Project, comments, "The N.A.M forced the Western nuclear powers to cash in a lot of their chips on this one. The question of the legality of nuclear weapons was in their face, forcing them into a defensive action to hold on to their nuclear weapons—a highly untenable position in the long run."

[More than four years] after the fall of the Berlin wall the controversy reveals that the cold war perks of power that came with nuclear weapons did not disappear along with it. In the words of ambassador Butler, "There is no post–cold war order. The first step to getting there is the elimination of nuclear weapons."

II

The Campaign for Peace and Democracy believes that the use of American military force to combat the problem of the spread of nuclear weapons spurs proliferation, accelerates non-nuclear arms build-ups, and undermines efforts to establish a world based on democratic decision-making, peaceful conflict resolution, and social equity. The belief that military strikes are the appropriate response to would-be proliferators is a product of a post-Cold War mentality within foreign policy circles in the U.S., a mentality that seems to be using proliferation rather than Communism as the new excuse for militarism.

America's Unnecessary Nuclear Threats

It should be beyond dispute that America and its allies can deal with all future security problems—that they can prevail in any military encounter in Europe or anywhere else—without using nuclear arms. The Persian Gulf war made it clear that we will not initiate the use of nuclear weapons, no matter how serious the military challenge, and that we need not do so.

As long as our nation clings to the idea that implicit threats of first use of nuclear weapons are essential to its security, we will be unwilling to radically restructure our defense policy.

We must face and overcome the central contradiction of our nuclear policy: the world's most powerful country needs to threaten to use nuclear weapons first in order to meet its security needs, but other nations must forgo them in the interests of international security.

Unless we are prepared to say that we need not rely on such threats, we will be unable to persuade countries with more serious security problems—Israel, Pakistan, India—that they can forgo nuclear weapons.

Morton H. Halperin, *The New York Times*, October 1, 1991.

This approach holds that a) with the demise of the Soviet Union, the U.S. is the sole remaining superpower; b) the alternative to "unipolarity" is chaos; therefore c) the U.S. must take up its truncheon as the world's supreme power and prevent the further spread of nuclear weapons (particularly to countries considered unfriendly to American interests). This line of reasoning is in vogue not only within conservative think-tanks, but in the leadership of the Democratic Party as well. When asked to delineate legitimate uses of force in the service of U.S. interests, President Bill Clinton often cites halting states with nuclear programs.

The application of military solutions to nuclear proliferation—a problem which is profoundly political in nature—is particularly disturbing in light of one of the most important lessons to be learned from the settlement of the Cold War. The U.S.-Soviet nuclear stand-off, which impoverished nations and politics for the better part of a century, began to ease only after the political and ideological hostilities of the Cold War rivalry faded.

The same will be true with nuclear states in other parts of the world—that is, their reliance on military might will not end until political insecurities are addressed. Nuclear states in the Third World have acquired or are striving to acquire their own nuclear arsenals to redress their sense of military insecurity, to achieve "big power" status, or to threaten other countries. In addition, many states take note of the fact that the United States and the other Western powers exercise a flagrant double standard where "third party" [those without connections with the nuclear powers] nuclear programs are concerned, having condoned such programs in, for example, Pakistan, South Africa, Israel, and now India, while insisting that Iraq and North Korea must not have one. Nuclear weapons are a military symptom of an underlying political illness.

More concretely, military action against Iraq's or another country's nuclear facilities will not prevent the renewal of those efforts once the coast is clear. The nuclear genie, as we know from the U.S.-Soviet experience, is definitely out of the bottle—no technical or military safeguards will ever permanently prevent the manufacture of nuclear weapons. And the use of military force will simply reinforce the perception that such measures are a legitimate way of resolving conflicts, thereby shoring up the prestige and perceived utility of nuclear weapons themselves.

We are also convinced that U.S. preoccupation with military solutions is promoting rather than discouraging nuclear proliferation by continuing to send large quantities of conventional weapons to regions such as the Middle East. In so doing, the [United States] is ignoring the link between conventional arms races and the spread of nuclear weapons. Growing conventional stockpiles have a poisonous effect in various regions, with the likely outcome that more states will seek nuclear weapons as the ultimate trump card.

Put America's House in Order

The sanest policy toward Iraq's (and all other countries') nuclear programs or stockpiles is to implement vigorous disarmament measures in both the domestic and international spheres, and to embark on a new foreign policy that emphasizes social change, democratization, and collective security. With regard to disarmament, the most important step the U.S. could take would be to put its own house in order: the U.S. should step up the process of dismantling its nuclear arsenal, including strategic, intermediate, and short-range weapons; it should immediately adopt a comprehensive nuclear test ban; it should adopt a policy of "no-first-use" of nuclear weapons; it should work with other countries to end the conventional arms trade; it should promote a global campaign to convert military industries to civilian use; and it should, without exception, pressure the other nuclear powers and aspirants to destroy their stockpiles and terminate their nuclear weapons programs.

The world is faced with an unusual opportunity to construct international institutions and ways of thinking which will allow a sea-change in global politics. The United States needs to move from its current reliance on militarism to sustained international cooperation to address some of the root causes of militarism and nuclear proliferation—sectarian and ethnic conflict, poverty, and inequality.

"The [American] retreat from the two-thirds of the world who . . . are ill housed, ill clad and ill nourished is bound to have [grave] consequences."

The United States Must Aid the Third World

John Cavanagh, Robin Broad, and Peter Weiss

In this economically troubled era the United States must not turn away from the pressing needs of the Third World, a regression that would only speed up environmental damage and political instability in the South, claim John Cavanagh, Robin Broad, and Peter Weiss in the following viewpoint. What is needed, the authors contend, is an entire reform package that would get shrinking American economic aid directly to the indigenous poor who will participate in local economic development. Equally important, the authors assert, is the reform of the World Bank and the International Monetary Fund, whose lending policies have stripped poor countries of much-needed capital, exacerbating poverty and environmental decline. Cavanagh is a fellow at the Institute for Policy Studies and Broad is a professor at American University, both in Washington, D.C. Weiss is an international lawyer.

As you read, consider the following questions:

1. On what grounds do the authors criticize Bill Clinton's handling of the NAFTA debate and trade talks with China?
2. How and why should corporations be regulated as a part of the "global New Deal," according to Cavanagh, Broad, and Weiss?

John Cavanagh, Robin Broad, and Peter Weiss, "The Need for a Global New Deal," *The Nation*, December 27, 1993, adapted from the authors' article in *State of the Union 1994*, edited by Richard Caplan and John Feffer. Reprinted with permission of the publisher, Westview Press, Boulder, Colorado.

For the past four decades, the problem of how to close the ever-widening gap between the earth's rich and poor occupied an important place in the political discourse of the United States and the other industrialized nations. Yet in the turning inward that has afflicted all major economic powers since the end of the cold war, this concern has largely disappeared. It was not a topic in the 1992 presidential campaign and, except in the discussion on the reform of bilateral aid, it has practically disappeared from the Clinton political agenda.

Turning Away from the Needy

The retreat from the two-thirds of the world who, in Franklin Delano Roosevelt's phrase, are ill housed, ill clad and ill nourished is bound to have consequences as grave as the failure to recognize the linked nature of ecological problems. In *The Debt Boomerang*, development specialist Susan George and her colleagues at the Transnational Institute persuasively demonstrated the effects of Third World debt and poverty on the industrialized world: Large debts pressure countries to cut forests for foreign exchange and for agricultural use, adding to global warming and swelling the numbers of environmental refugees; debt and poverty stimulate coca production and marketing; debt-induced austerity programs restrict countries' imports from the industrialized nations, costing jobs there; grinding poverty fuels instability in many countries, and the resulting conflict and war affect us all.

In this cutthroat global economic atmosphere, the Clinton Administration's rallying cry to U.S. companies and workers to outcompete other nations in a relatively "free trade" atmosphere becomes little more than a license for U.S.-based firms to bargain down wages and working conditions, and to slash work forces. This opens a downward spiral of destructive competition among U.S. workers, since companies (many of them U.S.-owned) in Mexico and China are likely to continue to upgrade factories with the latest technological breakthroughs while the governments there continue to keep wages depressed.

The Clinton Administration failed to turn the NAFTA [North American Free Trade Agreement] debate into an opportunity to address the problems of a rich country integrating with a country where labor rights and environmental standards are routinely violated. In his trade talks with China, the President missed another chance to make the same linkages. The U.S. trade deficit with China has edged upward over the past decade as thousands of subsidiaries of foreign firms have moved to that country to take advantage of the extraordinarily low wages and virtually limitless supply of workers. Again, candidate Clinton made a principled promise: He would condition China's continued access to U.S. markets on that nation's human rights and arms sales records. Worker-rights advocates have highlighted the continued use of prison labor in China and the denial of basic worker rights, and their pressure convinced Levi Strauss to announce a phase-out of its apparel subcontracting there. But in May 1993, after a concerted lobbying effort by Weyerhaeuser, General Electric and other Fortune 500 firms that export to China, Clinton renewed China's most-favored-nation status. In the end, the President caved in to a well-financed corporate lobby.

Missed Opportunities

The two other major trade issues of 1993 were the struggle to conclude the General Agreement on Tariffs and Trade and attempts to narrow the U.S. trade deficit with Japan. As with NAFTA, the Clinton Administration passed up the opportunity to insert social and environmental issues into the GATT agenda. On Japan, the President launched a desperate attempt at bilateral negotiations during a July 1993 summit of the leading industrial nations. He trumpeted a last-minute agreement, wherein the Japanese agreed to pursue a "highly significant" reduction in their trade surplus; in Japanese, the phrase was translated as *jubun iminoaru*, which means "sufficiently meaningful." No details were agreed to on how to implement either formulation.

While Clinton's approach toward trade failed to offer fresh departures from the free-trade approach of the Bush Administration, in the area of aid there were some hopeful signs. Early in his tenure, Clinton set up a task force headed by Deputy Secretary of State Clifton Wharton that launched a fundamental rethinking of the Agency for International Development (A.I.D.). Early drafts of the "Wharton Report" demonstrated a shift in the direction of supporting a more sustainable development process, in which participation by community groups was central. Thus was noteworthy, since so many U.S. aid projects have failed simply because the people they were supposed to benefit were never let into the process of design or implementation.

Before long, however, the task force got embroiled in a battle with an interagency working group that Clinton had set up under the more conventional leadership of the National Security Council and the National Economic Council to assess overall U.S. security and economic interests in, and assistance to, the rest of the world. This new working group pressed the structural adjustment, free-market model of development popular with the World Bank and International Monetary Fund (I.M.F.) that pushes governments to spend less, privatize more and gear economies toward the export of everything from coffee to toys. With such contradictory visions, A.I.D. reform slowed down. While the top A.I.D. bureaucrats understand the need for fundamental change, the failure to act quickly and decisively in a new direction killed a great deal of the momentum for change.

As important as shifting the direction of U.S. bilateral aid is U.S. participation in the major multilateral economic institutions, particularly the World Bank and I.M.F. These institutions have been at the forefront of pushing structural adjustment, an approach that has exacerbated poverty and accelerated environmental decline in already poor countries. It is still too soon to judge whether the Clinton Administration will help shift the orientation of the bank, its regional counterparts and the fund, but early indications are that no fundamental rethinking will take place.

Reforming, Not Quitting

What actions should the Administration take? Aid reform and debt reduction are central to initiatives to relieve global inequities in a fashion that reinforces the interests of U.S. citizens and the rest of the world. On the aid front, the Clinton Administration faces two sets of organizations in need of reform: global lending institutions and the U.S. bilateral lending agency. As to the first, economic journalist Walter Russell Mead reminds us that [economist] John Maynard Keynes and President Franklin Delano Roosevelt intended the World Bank and I.M.F. to play key expansionary roles in the world economy. Instead, during the past decade they have become the chief enforcers of draconian austerity in the developing world and have overseen the yearly net financial outflows from poor debtors to creditor banks and institutions.

The Clinton Administration should take the lead to work with other donor and borrower countries to insist not only that equitable and sustainable policies be the foundations of World Bank adjustment programs but also that bank projects incorporate significant public participation in design and implementation through regular consultation with organizations of the poor, women, peasants, workers and others in affected areas. Many citizen groups called for a 1994 Bretton Woods II conference on the fiftieth anniversary of the bank and fund to address these issues and to rebuild institutions based on democratic procedures and voting rights that reflect the world of 1994, not 1944. [Bretton Woods, New Hampshire, is where the World Bank and the I.M.F. were founded by the Allied powers in 1944.] Until the World Bank shifts its approach to development, the U.S. government should make major cuts in contributions. The same criteria should apply to our contributions to other multilateral institutions.

As for the A.I.D. the Administration should separate the reform agenda there from the deliberations of the National Security Council and the National Economic Council. Foreign aid should be delinked from the vestiges of cold war strategic alliances, and military-related assistance should be phased out. In addition, one of the great new challenges of the 1990s is the overdependence of many economies, led by our own, on the manufacture of arms. We suggest serious study of a proposal by international law professor Burns Weston: the establishment of an "international weapons into plowshares agency through which the conversion of national arms industries to socially redemptive production could be facilitated."

Why Foreign Aid?

Foreign aid remains an extension of the American character; we are a compassionate people who find it morally indefensible to accept poverty, sickness, and unfulfilled human potential. In responding to natural and man-made disasters, U.S. assistance—yes, our tax dollars—has saved the lives of millions of children, promoted freedom, and prevented tens of millions of people from starving to death. America's generosity toward fellow nations is quite simply unprecedented in the history of the world. At the same time, that "generous" foreign assistance effort presently constitutes less than one-half of 1 percent of the federal budget.

Richard Bissell, *The World & I*, May 1992.

In order to slow environmental degradation in poorer countries, U.S. aid programs should also stress the need to democratize control of resources so that communities can manage them more sustainably. The goal is clear: getting smaller amounts of aid—grants, not loans—to organizations that are committed to more equitable and participatory development. Viable plans do exist. The Development Group for Alternative Policies, along with fifteen other U.S. citizen groups and in consultation with organizations in the developing world, crafted a "Development Cooperation Act" in 1990. The act spelled out guidelines to insure "consultation with the poor at all stages of the development process" and new mechanisms to get aid directly to women, the landless, subsistence producers, migrants and others who need it most and can use it best. Now is the moment to refine and implement these guidelines.

Small Grants Locally Targeted

In addition to these proposals, there have been actual experiments in getting small amounts of aid directly to citizen organizations. In the Philippines, $25 million in U.S. aid was approved to endow a new Foundation for the Philippine Environment.

Based in Manila, the foundation is run by a board composed primarily of leaders of Philippine organizations that work on sustainable development. The board approves small grants to nongovernmental organizations, communities and training institutions to fund new experiments in natural resource preservation, community management of natural resources and education on the environment. Despite some tensions with the U.S. government, the foundation has begun to approve grants to worthwhile projects.

We can also learn a great deal from other nations, such as the Netherlands, Canada, Australia and Sweden, that have made small amounts of aid money go a long way. The Dutch government targets its aid on poverty alleviation. It disburses up to one-tenth of these outlays through agencies that fund grass-roots development initiatives directed at the poor. Part of this pays for education and training of individuals in citizen organizations in order to increase the participation of people in the development process. Likewise, a share of Canadian and Australian aid supports sustainable development programs that are designed by Canadian and Australian citizen groups in collaboration with nongovernmental groups in the recipient countries. These programs have stressed sound ecological practices, advocacy of human rights and the active involvement of women.

How can we pay for such aid schemes in a period of widespread economic downturn? One innovative solution comes from Jan Tinbergen, the noted Swedish economist, who calls for a large-scale global realignment of resources through an international income tax, as well as taxes on luxury durables, arms and the use of natural resources. Other notable ideas in the tax realm include a worldwide system of checkoffs on tax returns, by which citizens could make voluntary contributions to sustainable development funds, or an international tax of 0.5-1.0 percent a year on individuals' assets above a certain amount, say $500,000.

On the issue of debt, the Clinton Administration should take the lead in setting up an international conference that would reduce commercial Third World debt by at least 50 percent over the next five years and official debt by even more. Debt reduction should be delinked from World Bank and I.M.F. conditions. Instead, debts should be reduced by countries' repaying in local currencies into the kinds of broad-based national development endowments outlined above.

A Global New Deal

While the ability of large private companies to shift jobs, capital, factories and goods across national borders has increased, the power of governments to insure the basic social rights of their people has decreased. As governments find it harder to meet the employment and other needs of citizens, corporations have not been inclined to fill the vacuum. We desperately need to address this adverse shift in power and press our governments to create the necessary checks and incentives to prevent corporate activity from undermining the common good. A global New Deal is needed.

Protecting Workers' Rights

A good place to start is North America, where a broad range of environmental, labor, family farm, religious and consumer groups has begun to piece together "A Just and Sustainable Trade and Development Initiative for North America." The initiative suggests that NAFTA be replaced by a new set of continental rules and measures, including the protection of labor rights and workplace health and safety standards. The labor-related provisions of the U.N.'s Universal Declaration of Human Rights and conventions of the International Labor Organization could serve as the basis for standards to be enforced by each country. Companies that violate internationally recognized worker rights would be subject to trade sanctions. The precise composition of "internationally recognized" worker rights would be negotiated by the three countries [Canada, the United States, and Mexico], but they must include, at a minimum, the rights of free association and collective bargaining; the right to strike; and protections against child labor, slave labor and all forms of discrimination. Complaints about violations of these rights could be filed by any party either with a trinational labor commission or with the administrative agencies or courts of one's own country or of the home country of the company accused of the infraction. When appropriate, penalties could be imposed on individual corporations when they use violations of labor rights to gain unfair advantage in trade.

Over time, the Administration should also work with other countries to create mechanisms to raise wages worldwide as corporations increase productivity. In the context of a new North American agreement, the minimum wages in the traded-goods sectors of the two lower-wage countries should move rapidly toward that of the highest-wage country. The United States must promote high-skill, high-wage strategies around the world if it is to help stimulate enough purchasing power among the world's hundreds of millions of workers to reinject dynamism into the world economy.

As corporations become more global, there is a need for new codes to increase their public accountability. The U.N. negotiations on a code of conduct on transnational corporations, which, among other measures, prohibited bribery of public officials, required corporate disclosure of potential dangers of products and production processes, and banned the export of goods or factories that are deemed unsafe in one country, should be revived. As a first step, the Clinton Administration should encourage its allies to adopt their own versions of the U.S. Foreign Corrupt Practices Act, which has been quite successful in reducing bribery by U.S. corporations.

U.S. workers and consumers elected Bill Clinton . . . because he promised to focus his Administration's energies on the economic woes that had become the electorate's major concern. In his first year, Clinton raised the public's hopes and then largely dashed them because he failed to create a strategy that reflected the expanding linkages that bind the U.S. economy and work force to a shaky world economy. It has been a disappointing performance.

"The history of official foreign aid to India provides
an example of the failure of foreign aid and its
symbiotic relationship with central planning."

U.S. Aid Hurts
the Third World

Shyam J. Kamath

India has received more foreign aid since 1950 than any other
developing nation and yet lags significantly behind these other
countries in most indicators of the quality of life, asserts Shyam
J. Kamath in the following viewpoint. Financial assistance, especially American, has subsidized in India one of the largest, most
inefficient public sectors in the noncommunist world, while ne-
glecting the more productive private sector, Kamath charges.
The answer to India's, and the Third World's, economic underdevelopment is therefore not more foreign assistance, Kamath
concludes, but the invigoration of the private sector through "a
comprehensive reliance on market forces." Kamath is a professor of economics at California State University at Hayward.

As you read, consider the following questions:

1. What evidence does Kamath cite to support his contention
   that American aid has favored centrally directed economic
   growth in developing countries?
2. What example of U.S. aid does the author use to show how
   foreign aid tends to depress domestic production?

Shyam J. Kamath, "Statism, Foreign Aid, and Poverty in India," *Cato Policy Report*,
July/August 1991. Reprinted by permission of the Cato Institute, Washington, D.C.

It has long been an article of faith among development economists and policymakers that foreign aid is a necessary and central component of economic development. However, if one examines the record of Indian economic development since 1947, that view is belied rather conclusively.

India has received more aggregate aid than any other developing nation since the end of World War II. Yet it has had one of the slower rates of growth of all the developing countries and remains one of the poorest countries in the world. Foreign aid has played a significant role in financing central planning and control in India and has fueled the growth of one of the noncommunist world's largest and most inefficient public sectors.

Aid Results in India

In the early 1950s most observers thought that India, with its vast natural and human resources, had the best prospects of any of the developing nations for achieving accelerated and self-sustaining economic development. Now, after nearly half a century of planned economic development, almost 40 percent of Indians live below the official (and rather meager by world standards) poverty line, and per capita income remains about $300 a year. The absolute number of Indians living below the poverty line increased sharply between the late 1950s and the mid-1980s.

India lags behind other developing nations on most indicators of the quality of life. While considerable progress has been made since independence, the 1981 census revealed that life expectancy at birth was 50.5 years and the adult literacy rate was 36 percent; it was estimated that less than 40 percent and 10 percent of the population had access, respectively, to safe drinking water and sanitation facilities.

As a result of India's centrally planned industrialization strategy, more than 60 percent of investment in the industrial sector in the postindependence period has been in the public sector. The private sector has been severely restricted by bans on private investment in major industries; a strict regime of industrial licensing; intrusive quantitative, price, and distribution controls; uneconomical preferences for cottage, village, and small industries; extensive labor-market and employment controls; and comprehensive controls on imports, exports, and foreign investment.

Over 20 million Indians are on the public payroll, and around 70 percent of all organized-sector employment is in the public sector. The government's wage bill is estimated to consume two-thirds of its annual revenues. Confiscatory tax rates combined with ever-escalating controls in the 1960s led to the growth of one of the largest and most thriving underground economies in the world; it is estimated that approximately 50 percent of India's economic activity takes place in the underground sector.

India's jungle of red tape is one of the largest and most complex in the world. For example, permission to open a hotel involves 45 applications that are reviewed by more than 25 different governmental agencies. Bribery and corruption constitute the norm for conducting business.

Foreign "Aid" Does Not Help

Unfortunately, despite the assumption embodied in the term "foreign assistance," there is little evidence that American financial transfers actually aid Third World peoples. Even a Clinton administration task force admitted that "despite decades of foreign assistance, most of Africa and parts of Latin America, Asia and the Middle East are economically worse off today than they were 20 years ago.". . .

No amount of assistance can overcome the stifling statism of so many nations—bloated government bureaucracies, money-losing state enterprises, price and production controls, and perverse monetary, fiscal and credit policies—or counteract the powerful incentives for political and economic elites to exploit the rest of their populations.

Indeed, foreign assistance often makes the problem worse, insulating governments from the natural consequences of their policies, thereby reducing pressure for reform. . . .

Decades of painful experience have proved the benefits of foreign assistance to be largely illusory. The most important reform would be to end foreign assistance to collectivist autocracies and fledgling democracies alike.

Doug Bandow, *Conservative Chronicle*, August 10, 1994.

India's system of centralized five-year planning and comprehensive controls produced only about 1.5 percent annual growth of per capita real income from 1950 through 1985, compared with growth rates of 5.5 to 6.5 percent in the "newly industrializing countries" of Hong Kong, South Korea, Singapore, and Taiwan and 3 to 4 percent in Indonesia, Malaysia, and Thailand. Thus, even though India was unique among those nations in that it was a democracy during that period (except for a brief two-year lapse), its economic performance was quite disappointing.

What sets India apart from other developing Asian nations is its dirigiste [state-controlled economic planning] policy orientation, its lack of openness to trade and investment, and the large amount of foreign aid it has received. India's experience with foreign aid throws clearly into relief the inefficiencies, the politicization, the false hopes, and the obstacles to economic development that arise from nonmarket, governmentally mediated transfers and activities.

The Underlying Vision of Aid

It is ironic that the World Bank, which was set up to help war-devastated and developing economies to grow, is hard pressed to find any nations among its clients that have successfully developed after over 40 years of ever-escalating budgets and ever-increasing levels of multilateral foreign aid.

The history of official foreign aid to India provides an example of the failure of foreign aid and its symbiotic relationship with central planning. The role of foreign aid in India became dominant simultaneously with the adoption of a centrally directed heavy industrialization and "self-reliant" import-substitution planning strategy at the beginning of the Second Five-Year Plan in 1956–57. That planning strategy was explicitly modeled on the Soviet heavy industry planning model, and its chief architects, Professor P. C. Mahalonobis and Prime Minister Jawaharlal Nehru, espoused a socialistic framework of economic policy and development.

Nehru, who was India's prime minister for the first 17 years after independence, said in his 1936 presidential address to the Congress party that there was

> no way of ending the poverty, the vast unemployment, the degradation, and the subjection of the Indian people except through socialism . . . the ending of private property, except in a restricted sense, and the replacement of the private profit system by a higher ideal of cooperative service.

That dirigiste vision of economic development was reflected in the views of policymakers and intellectuals in the donor countries and the foreign aid experts. John P. Lewis, the dean of American foreign aid experts, argued in 1962 that

> there is much less need now for such a defense of the very concept of comprehensive economic planning in countries like India. Today the same kind of planning is officially viewed as an essential concomitant of any national development that merits American assistance, and the United States government is urging such planning upon Latin American, African, and Asian governments that do not yet practice it.

Multilateral aid agencies such as the World Bank espoused a similar unconstrained vision by the early 1950s. For example, the *Fifth Annual Report* of the World Bank said that

> the Bank would prefer to go further, wherever that is feasible, and base its financing on a national development program, provided that it is properly worked out in terms of projects by which the objectives of the program are to be attained.

The preference for comprehensive development plans made

countries such as India, Tanzania, Indonesia, Ethiopia, and Mexico, which had all adopted centrally directed economic development policies, favored recipients of World Bank and concessional international development agency aid. Foreign aid to India was both a result and to some extent the cause of increased government control of the Indian economy and the lives of the people, especially the poorest.

India's Aid Cornucopia and Statism

India has received more foreign aid, in aggregate terms, than any other developing nation since the end of World War II, and that aid has played a major role in enlarging the Indian public sector. During the 1960s and early 1970s, foreign aid accounted for most of the growth in government outlays for development and the central government budget.

Throughout the postindependence period, the private sector and the rest of the world provided the savings needed to finance the ever-growing public sector. Until the 1970s foreign aid remained the primary source of funds for growth, accounting for well over 50 percent of the government's deficit during the Second Five-Year Plan.

To the extent it displaced private saving, foreign aid further retarded self-financing growth, and in fact the lack of domestic saving was one of the many reasons given for nationalization of the major Indian commercial banks in the late 1960s. Thus, foreign aid may have indirectly contributed to the socialization of the economy.

The Role of U.S. Aid

The United States has been the single largest donor of foreign aid to the world and to India since World War II. Between 1945 and 1983 the United States gave away almost $321 billion (in then-year dollars) in overseas foreign assistance, concessional loans, military aid, and humanitarian assistance.

It is significant that the bulk of U.S. aid to India was disbursed from 1955 through 1971, when India was nationalizing its economy and effecting national economic planning aimed at heavy industry and import substitution. As a consequence, the major part of American aid went to the burgeoning Indian public sector. The neglect of the private sector in the provision of aid was diametrically opposed to the U.S. government's desire to win "the hearts and minds" of developing nations for "capitalism and democracy."

A significant component of U.S. aid to India was food aid. Food aid under the Food for Peace Program, the Emergency Food Aid Act of 1951, and the 1954 Agricultural Trade Development and Assistance Act (Public Law 480) was given directly to

220

the Indian government, which in turn distributed the food through its public distribution system.

Good Intentions Gone Awry

The PL 480 program provides a classic example of good intentions gone awry and the pernicious nature of foreign aid. Before the advent of the heavy industry–oriented Second Five-Year Plan, food production in India was growing steadily and very little food was being imported. Foodgrain prices were quite stable before 1956.

The demand for food imports increased under the Second Five-Year Plan. As food shortages began to develop and foreign exchange reserves fell sharply, the Indian government entered into an agreement with the U.S. government for assistance for the import of foodgrains under PL 480. A major effect of PL 480 was to repress the price of wheat and other commodities that were imported under the program. As a result, domestic production of those items declined as farmers reacted to the lower prices. And the price repression and output effects spread to competing cereals and reduced the acreage planted in those cereals as well.

The PL 480 scheme subjected Indian farmers to doubly regressive taxation. Since the government fixed procurement prices for a substantial part of agricultural output at below open-market prices, farmers were deprived of a commensurate portion of their profits. And since the ration shops in the public distribution system were mainly in the urban areas, the system acted as an instrument of income redistribution from the poorer rural areas, where the majority of the population lives, to the richer urban areas.

All of that was done in the name of "helping" a predominantly agricultural country that had a significant amount of uncultivated arable land and the potential to expand its food production, as demonstrated by the fact that India's yield per acre was one of the lowest in the world.

The World Bank and India

India has also received more World Bank aid than any other country in the postwar period. Most of the funds received by India from the World Bank group (the International Bank for Reconstruction and Development, the Agency for International Development, and the International Finance Corporation) have gone to the public sector. Government corporations that have been directly aided by World Bank funds include firms in the power, coal-mining, irrigation, oil, petrochemical, gas, telecommunications, fertilizer, steel, railway, airline, and cement sectors. The World Bank's willingness to support the Indian public sector is evidenced by some $16 billion in aid that has been committed by the bank but remains unutilized because the matching rupee resources cannot be found either by the central government and its undertakings or by the state governments and their undertakings.

A substantial part of the World Bank's (and also the U.S. Agency for International Development's) concessional loans to India has gone for irrigation, area development, infrastructure development, dairy development, rural and urban drinking water supply, population control and nutrition, and agricultural extension and training projects. The effectiveness of such loans can be judged by examining the World Bank's own review of its experience with rural development over the 1965–86 period:

> The most conspicuous project failures were in the large group of area development projects. . . . That form of area development project that came to be known as "integrated rural development". . . performed so poorly as to raise questions about the utility of that approach in many situations.

Limited economic liberalization in the 1985–88 period produced an unprecedented spurt in economic growth, and per capita GNP [gross national product] growth rates averaged between 3.5 and 5 percent. However, the entrenched bureaucracy and special-interest groups were soon able to halt and even reverse the pace of economic reform. Economic growth slowed, and the many years of unchecked government spending, unproductive public-sector investment, and mismanagement of the economy resulted in an economic crisis in 1991. India's budget deficit reached about 9 percent of GDP [gross domestic product], the external debt was over $70 billion, interest payments and amortization of external debt exceeded 30 percent of export earnings, and foreign exchange reserves in early 1991 could cover less than two weeks of imports.

Band-Aid Solutions

The solution to those endemic problems has been the standard band-aid medicine of more aid and "austerity" economics. The interim care-taker government has administered classic, International Monetary Fund–style adjustment therapy to the Indian economy by effecting a deliberate "austerity" contraction—curbing imports, raising taxes, "devaluing" the rupee to boost exports, and limiting privatization in anticipation of the second IMF credit. The objective is to attempt a "quick fix" of the fiscal and external payments crisis and make the borrower more creditworthy.

Unfortunately, those attempts to resuscitate the dying patient reveal a fatal flaw in the conventional wisdom. No amount of cosmetic manipulation of macroeconomic aggregates is going to help as long as the microeconomic and institutional fundamentals remain unchanged. Without replacement of public property rights by enforceable private property rights, establishment of the rule of law, across-the-board scrapping of controls and regulations both internal and external, dismantling of the public sector, and restoration of a voluntary exchange market economy, any efforts to solve the crisis will meet with only temporary success at best. The fundamental limitation of austerity economics is that it is not possible to make a borrowing country more creditworthy by reducing its potential future income through higher taxes. Such policies in themselves will put the chances of even temporary success in doubt by reducing the incentive to produce. No amount of artificial or "real" devaluation is likely to have a lasting effect on trade if the institutional and microeconomic fundamentals are left unaltered.

Foreign Aid's Results

The dirigiste vision of Indian policymakers in the postindependence era led to the central tenet that the public sector must dominate the "commanding heights" of the economy and produce the bulk of the basic goods and infrastructure of the economy. Foreign aid was seen as the crucial means of financing that strategy and was successfully tapped to fuel the growth of the public sector. However, the results of the strategy can be gauged from the dismal failure of the constituent public-sector firms.

Government expenditure as a proportion of GDP grew from around 19 percent in 1960–61 to around 35 percent in 1985–86. The number of central government public-sector companies grew from 5 in 1951 to over 250 by 1985. By 1979 the gross fixed assets of the central public sector (excluding the joint public-private sector, the state public sector, the government-owned railways, and the public utilities) exceeded that of private-sector industry by over 16 percent. The inefficiency of the public-sector undertakings is indicated by the fact that they accounted for 66 percent of total fixed capital and 27 percent of total employment but only 25 percent of industrial output and value added in 1980—despite their near or complete monopoly of oil production and distribution, power generation and distribution, railways, air transportation, coal mining, certain minerals and metals, banking, life and general insurance, and other basic industries.

In 1980–81 the top 157 public-sector companies sustained an overall loss of over $160 million. Meanwhile, the top 100 private-sector companies made an overall profit of $415 million on a total capital employed of $9 billion.

Thus, the public sector in India has been a black hole in the foreign aid constellation, sucking in huge amounts of foreign taxpayers' money and sinking it into inefficient, loss-making public-sector projects.

No amount of additional foreign aid is likely to help India break the vise of underdevelopment. Fundamental changes in policy are required—the dismantling of the overbearing and nihilistic central planning system, restoration of absolute rights to private property and voluntary exchange, and a comprehensive reliance on market forces. A free-trade and investment regime with a freely convertible currency needs to be established as a first step toward economic and political freedom. Halfhearted moves toward liberalization, such as those of the late [prime minister] Rajiv Gandhi, will just not do.

For their part, the Western nations and multilateral aid organizations must wean clients like India from the drug of foreign aid. Their largesse and support have actively encouraged the impoverishment of nations. It is time to stop.

Periodical Bibliography

The following articles have been selected to supplement the diverse views presented in this chapter.

Richard Bissel   "Foreign Aid and the American Interest," *The World & I*, May 1992. Available from 2800 New York Ave. NE, Washington, DC 20002.

Noam Chomsky   "The United States on Human Rights," *Lies of Our Times*, September 1993.

Warren Christopher, Timothy Wirth, and John Shattuck   "America's Commitment to Human Rights," *U.S. Department of State Dispatch*, February 7, 1994.

Andrew Cohen   "The Help That Hurts," *The Progressive*, January 1994.

Barbara Conry   "The Futility of U.S. Intervention in Regional Conflicts," *Cato Policy Analysis*, May 19, 1994. Available from 1000 Massachusetts Ave. NW, Washington, DC 20001.

Henrietta Holsman Fore   "Lean Development and the Privatization of U.S. Foreign Assistance," *The Washington Quarterly*, Winter 1994. Available from MIT Press Journals, 55 Hayward St., Cambridge, MA 02142.

Morton H. Halperin   "Guaranteeing Democracy," *Foreign Policy*, Summer 1993.

Llewellyn D. Howell   "Trade and Human Rights," *USA Today*, May 1994.

William A. Nitze   "Swords into Ploughshares: Agenda for Change in the Developing World," *International Affairs*, January 1993.

Daniel Pipes   "The American Conspiracy to Run the World," *The Washington Post National Weekly Edition*, November 14-20, 1994. Available from 1150 15th St. NW, Washington, DC 20071.

Scott Thompson   "The Role of the Nonaligned Movement," *The World & I*, May 1992.

What Should
Be the Future of
North/South Relations?

The
Third
World

Chapter Preface

During the late nineteenth and early twentieth centuries, European nations colonized much of the Third World in search of raw materials for their factories and markets for their goods, as well as to improve their strategic positions against foreign rivals. During this period of expansion, Africa, India, Indochina, the East Indies, and other regions were largely under foreign control. This trend reversed after World War II, however, as moral and practical opposition to colonialism spread in Europe, and colonies demanded and fought for independence.

Some contemporary commentators argue that, in light of widespread ethnic conflict and societal chaos in many Third World countries, the concept of colonialism—and the related idea of imperialism—should be revived. Political analyst Paul Johnson contends that the "instant decolonization" that occurred following World War II left many Third World countries—especially in Africa—unable to govern themselves. Consequently, he argues, these countries have experienced "civil and tribal conflicts, invasion, corruption and man-made famine." He says of these nations that "their continued existence, and the violence and human degradation they breed, is a threat to the stability of their neighbors as well as an affront to our consciences." Johnson proposes that the developed nations take over and run these turbulent countries "until they are reasonably certain that the return to independence will be successful this time."

Others oppose this resurgent colonialism, arguing that the history of colonialism has been the cause of ethnic and societal unrest in the Third World. According to political science professor Daniel Hellinger, "Even the most cursory glance at a historical atlas shows that the roots of ethnic conflict and civil disorder in most of this world were laid by colonialism." Steven R. David, political science professor at Johns Hopkins University, explains that the inflexible borders imposed by colonialism fostered ethnic conflict and civil unrest because these borders divided ethnic groups and combined others that had little in common. "Colonialism's inattention to the needs of ethnic groups . . . has created instability throughout the Third World, and laid the basis for perpetual conflict," he says. It is this historical reality, argues Zimbabwean political issues writer Yash Tandon, that makes any attempt to resurrect colonialism today a "wrong in itself."

Whether colonialism or imperialism is a viable solution to the conflict plaguing many Third World countries today is one of the issues addressed in the following chapter on the future of North/South relations.

"Large-scale logging is not the only way to get income from these magnificent forests."

The South Must Conserve Its Forests

Eugene Linden

Strapped for cash, the countries of the north coast of South America are selling their unspoiled forests to several Asian logging companies, explains Eugene Linden in the following viewpoint. Conservationists are trying to convince the governments of Suriname and Guyana not to sell their trees but to encourage ecotourism to these areas. He reports that conserving the forests could prove more profitable than stripping them because they might be home to plant species that could be worth much more than the timber royalties if they yield a successful pharmaceutical compound. Linden is a senior writer for *Time* magazine.

As you read, consider the following questions:

1. Where does the author say the logging companies dealing with Suriname and Guyana come from? Why does he consider their countries of origin important?
2. What economic drawbacks does Linden cite in the sale of forests for cash? Why do governments sell them anyway, according to the author?

Eugene Linden, "Chain Saws Invade Eden," *Time*, August 29, 1994. Copyright 1994 Time, Inc. Reprinted by permission.

From high atop a massive bald rock called the Voltzberg, visitors to Suriname can look in awe at the same sight that greeted explorer Sir Walter Raleigh 400 years ago: an emerald forest that seemingly stretches to infinity in all directions. Even though the world has 11 times as many humans as it did in Raleigh's day, the north coast of South America still contains one of the largest unbroken tracts of tropical forest left in the world. Fewer than 50,000 people live in a natural kingdom larger than California that encompasses nearly all of Suriname, Guyana and French Guiana and is buffered by virgin rain forest in Brazil and Venezuela. Some parts of the woodland are so isolated from civilization that monkeys are more curious than fearful when they encounter humans.

That may soon change. The governments of Guyana and Suriname have begun to open huge tracts of forests for logging by timber and trading companies from Korea, Indonesia and Malaysia. Conservationists around the world are horrified at the prospect, aware that in southern Asia the loggers have ravaged forests, leaving a legacy of eroded hills, silt-choked rivers and barren fields. If such exploitation cannot be prevented in sparsely populated countries like Guyana and Suriname, the environmentalists ask, can deforestation be stopped anywhere? For thousands of years, deforestation has presaged the fall of civilizations. Now, for the first time, humanity is facing the consequences of forest destruction on a global scale.

As the international logging juggernaut lurches toward Suriname and Guyana, several conservation groups have chosen to make a stand in this unspoiled part of the world. Some, like Washington-based Conservation International, are trying to show the two governments that large-scale logging is not the only way to get income from these magnificent forests. Another possibility is prospecting for natural medicines produced by the area's trees and flowers. San Francisco's Rainforest Action Network and Britain's World Rainforest Network have taken up the cause of the region's indigenous peoples threatened by logging. Even the World Bank, whose investments have led to deforestation elsewhere in the tropics, has become involved, encouraging Guyana to slow down the pace of logging and look at alternative means of development.

Only circumstance has protected the Guyanas, as the region is called, from the chain saws and bulldozers leveling forests elsewhere. Though colonized centuries ago by the British, Dutch and French, the area became known for its penal camps and slave rebellions and never had enough appeal to draw huge numbers of European settlers. Today the population of Suriname, Guyana and French Guiana totals only 1.3 million people, nearly all of whom live in coastal cities. Up to now the city dwellers have put little pressure on the forests or the few thousand indigenous Amerindians who live in the woodlands. But economic hardship and the lure of logging revenue have begun to make the region's natural treasures more vulnerable.

Suriname has been in political and financial turmoil almost from the time it gained its independence from the Netherlands in 1975. At first the Dutch and other foreign donors gave the new country generous aid, but they cut back sharply in the 1980s when Suriname suffered a series of coups and massacres. The violence culminated in a six-year civil war that led to the fall of the military regime of Lieut. Colonel Desi Bouterse in 1992.

Alternatives to Logging

There are . . . uses of forests in a conserved state. These uses include key ecological functions, e.g. watershed protection, material cycling and energy flow and microclimatic regulation; indirect values, such as recreation and tourism in forest areas; the *option value* of the future use of forest resources, particularly its biodiversity; and *existence value* derived from the desire of people to pay for the very existence of these resources, irrespective of whether they use them or not. . . .

Unfortunately, because they are difficult to measure and not easily expressed in monetary terms, non-market [conservation] values are often ignored. The benefits to be derived from these uses are reduced by the use of the forest for complete timber harvesting or for conversion to alternative uses. The way in which an economically efficient strategy can be achieved is by making those who seek to exploit the use of forest resources in any one form take into account the forgone benefits from the uses in other forms.

Edward Barbier, Joanne Burgess, and Anil Markandya, *Ambio*, April 1991.

Though peace holds at the moment, international donors are reluctant to resume large-scale aid until the government of President Ronald Venetiaan puts its tottering economic house in order. Production is in decline, the unemployment rate tops 20% and per capita annual income is only $500. Rather than risk public unrest, the government provides generous subsidies for fuel, food, water and telephone service. But the budget now exceeds revenues by 150%, and the government has been looking for easy sources of foreign exchange.

So officials were receptive in August 1993 when an Indonesian investment group named N.V. MUSA Indo-Suriname asked to buy the rights to Suriname's trees. Cash-starved regimes are fond of selling timber concessions because they can put money in a treasury at little immediate cost to the government, while other industries can take years to produce results. Timber operations often ultimately drain more money than they yield by burdening a nation's infrastructure and degrading precious natural assets, but it is easy for a sitting government to ignore these costs because they become a problem only for subsequent administrations.

The MUSA group boldly asked for timber rights to more than 15 million acres of Suriname, nearly one-third of the country. The Venetiaan administration avoided a messy political debate by instead granting a smaller concession of 375,000 acres near the Guyana border. MUSA then began logging without specifying how it will abide by Suriname's strict forestry code. Experts claim that the only profitable way to harvest MUSA's particular stretch of rain forest would be to clear-cut the region, leaving behind a wasteland. Other Asian interests have also put in timber bids. The Malaysian investment group Berjaya Group Berhad is trying to secure rights to 7.5 million acres in Suriname.

Neighboring Guyana, also desperate for quick cash, has granted huge concessions to Asian logging consortiums. The former British colony, a victim of years of Marxist economics, is poorer than any other Latin American nation except Haiti and is staggering under a $2 billion foreign debt load, an amount 10 times its gross domestic product. In 1991 the government of President Desmond Hoyte granted a Malaysian-Korean joint venture called Barama Co. Ltd. the rights to log 4.2 million acres in the country's northwest. When voters elected former Marxist Cheddi Jagan as President in 1992, Guyanese conservationists urged him to revoke that concession; instead Jagan toured Southeast Asia at Barama's expense, and his government is considering bids that would put roughly 75% of Guyana's timber under foreign control.

And what will Guyana get in return? Not much, if the agreement with Barama represents a precedent. Barama was granted a five-year tax holiday and will make only modest royalty payments. Within five years, this concession is expected to produce $20 million to $30 million annually for Guyana, but conservationists argue that this is a pittance for sacrificing nearly 10% of the country.

Russ Mittermeier, president of Conservation International, argues that Guyana should consider development alternatives that produce income while leaving the forests in place. He notes that the country might receive royalty income equivalent to what will be generated by the Barama concession should even one species of tree yield a chemical that turns into a successful pharmaceutical compound. Another option is an ecotourism business that would take visitors to Guyana's spectacular natural wonders, including Kaieteur Falls. Unfortunately, outsiders have come up with few other suggestions. Says a World Bank official: "It's incredibly frustrating to think that there are so few alternatives to logging at present."

Both Guyana and Suriname have a coterie of conservationists who are aware that the area possesses something special in this crowded world. Says Brigadier General Joe Singh, chief of staff of Guyana's army and an influential voice in his small nation: "There is a commitment here to make sure that Guyana does not repeat the mistakes of other countries." To see examples of these mistakes, President Jagan need only take another look at the forests of the Asian nations bidding for Guyana's and Suriname's timber. And this time he might ask why consortiums from nations that once contained some of the largest tropical rain forests on earth now must look for wood 11,000 miles from home.

> *"If it is in the interest of the rich that we do not cut down our trees, then they must compensate us for the loss of income."*

The North Must Help the South Conserve Its Forests

Mahathir Mohammed

Writing just prior to the 1992 Earth Summit in Rio de Janeiro, Brazil, Mahathir Mohammed makes a timeless argument in the following viewpoint against the North's efforts to force the South to limit its use of tropical timber. The North wiped out its own forests and created 80 percent of the earth's pollution in the process of developing, Mohammed contends. Hence, if the Northern countries want a clean, well-forested environment, he says, they must compensate Southern nations for lost timber sales, on which they depend for their development. Mohammed is prime minister of Malaysia.

As you read, consider the following questions:

1. What three economic reasons does Mohammed give for the South's inability to comply with the North's environmental demands?
2. Besides paying more for the timber it buys from the South, what does the author recommend the North do to conserve the global environment?

Mahathir Mohammed, "End the North's Eco-Imperialism," *Los Angeles Times*, June 2, 1992. Reprinted by permission of the author.

The Rio conference can be the watershed moment when the North starts to clean up its own back yard and stops making the South the scapegoat for the ecological sins the North committed on the road to prosperity. This opportunity for partnership between North and South should not be wasted.

At Rio, the North should abandon its effort, taken in the name of a "common heritage," to lock up the tropical forests and other natural resources critical for our development. At Rio, the eco-imperialism of the North ought to be put to rest once and for all.

If the global environment is going to be cleaned up, those most responsible for polluting it must bear the burden proportionately.

Who Pollutes?

Eighty percent of the Earth's pollution is due to the industrial activities of the North. In the name of biodiversity and absorption of carbon gases, Northern nations have campaigned against the use of the tropical timber on which our livelihood depends. Yet, for fear of damaging their own economic competitiveness, they can't even agree—thanks mainly to U.S. objections—on a schedule to stabilize their own gas emissions that warm the atmosphere [the United States refused to sign the conference's climate treaty].

The South must, of course, do its part as well. But our burden must be borne in strict proportion to our culpability. By no means can we accept the sacrifice of our development so that the rich and powerful can enjoy ever-improving standards of living. If the rich North expects the poor to foot the bill for a cleaner environment, then Rio will be an exercise in futility. Poor countries cannot develop if they are not allowed to extract their natural wealth.

Quite frankly, the North's current fear of environmental degradation provides the South with economic leverage that did not exist before.

We are fully justified in approaching global environmental issues in this way because, unless we can force stronger international economic support in areas ranging from improved commodity prices to technology transfer, the South will forever remain at the bottom of the heap. Yet, whether we like it or not, the people of the North—having destroyed their own natural heritage—want to declare that whatever is left intact in the developing countries also belongs to them.

The logging of tropical timber is a case in point.

Logging Is Economically Necessary

We in Malaysia are fully aware of the role that tropical forests play in preserving the environment's delicate balance. We are aware of the thousands of species of flora and fauna that are to be found only in our forests. We are aware that trees absorb carbon dioxide and give back the precious oxygen without which we would all drop dead.

But we are also acutely conscious that we are a developing country that needs the wealth afforded by our forests. We do not cut down our trees foolishly, but we need living space, we need space for agriculture and we need the money from sales of our timber.

Meanwhile, back in the Pacific Northwest. . .

If it is in the interest of the rich that we do not cut down our trees, then they must compensate us for the loss of income. Instead, what has the North done? It launched a boycott of our

235

timber, reasoning that if it does not buy, we will stop cutting our timber.

Cost-Free Environmentalism?

In doing so, those behind the boycott are ignoring the hundreds of thousands of people whose lives depend on the timber industry. They ignore the loss of government revenue with which we subsidize and support our people, particularly the poor. In other words, they want to preserve Malaysia's forest at our expense, but at no cost to them.

The harvest of timber can be easily reduced without making us pay for it. If the rich will pay twice the price, logging can be reduced by half. It is that simple.

Once upon a time, this planet was almost completely covered by forests; the deserts that now hold vast reservoirs of petroleum were once swamps and forests.

If we sincerely believe in equity and burden-sharing, why not reforest those vast farms in Europe and America that are subsidized to limit food production? All trees, after all, provide oxygen—not just tropical hardwoods.

If ground water can be drawn up to build exclusive golf courses in the deserts of California and to create lakes surrounded by luxury hotels, why not use the same technique to water the desert and reforest it?

Toward North-South Cooperation

My point is that the whole burden shouldn't be thrust upon the poor South. We should all work together to protect and resuscitate the environment.

The North can close down inefficient farms and polluting industries and reforest the land that is made available. It can move the processing of primary products to developing countries to assist in their development. It can help reforest the deserts in rich as well as poor countries. The North can coordinate the prevention and fighting of forest fires worldwide, which regularly destroy valuable acreage. It can pay more for tropical timber. All of these are positive actions the North could take.

What can the South do? At Rio, Malaysia will propose a comprehensive greening of the world that calls for at least 30% of the Earth's land surface to be forest by the year 2000. Since 27.6% of the land is now forested, in the coming eight years that area need only be increased by 2.4%. It is an eminently reasonable and reachable goal.

For its part, Malaysia will ensure that at least 50% of our land area will be permanently forested.

Under the Malaysian proposal, a global fund financed by national contributions assessed on the basis of population and threshold of carbon dioxide emissions would be created to assure the success of this vast effort at reforestation and new forestation. Such a project would not only solve, at least partially, one of the world's more important environmental problems, it would also exemplify an approach to saving the Earth through cooperative efforts that are fair and just for all, not merely for the North.

"The principal aims must be peace, order, and the maintenance of contracts."

The North Must Maintain Order in the South

Lincoln Allison

Imperialism—the acquisition or rule of one country by another—has been condemned by many commentators on the basis that it violates state sovereignty. In the following viewpoint, Lincoln Allison contends that many Third World elites espouse the concept of national autonomy and portray themselves as anti-imperialists in order to protect their corrupt and inefficient regimes from foreign intervention. Allison rejects the concept of state sovereignty, arguing that it is used to absolve the North of its responsibility to maintain peace and stability in the Third World. He calls for a new form of imperialism that incorporates ethical principles. Allison is a senior lecturer in politics at the University of Warwick in England.

As you read, consider the following questions:

1. What is the purpose the author ascribes to the "linguistic game" he says is played by Third World elites with the term "imperialism"?
2. What concrete goals does Allison suggest for the new imperialism?

Excerpted from "A New Imperialism" by Lincoln Allison. This article appeared in the January 1994 issue and is reprinted with permission from *The World & I*, a publication of The Washington Times Corporation.

"This is the new imperialism, and I don't like it." It was strange to hear Edward Heath, a former Conservative prime minister of Britain, talking in this way. He was, essentially, defending the immunity of Saddam Hussein, with whom he had just been negotiating about British hostages, from any attack by non-Arab troops. It is an interesting political assortment of people who condemn imperialism and fear its revival: Third World intellectuals and "conservative" Soviet generals might be expected to use such language, and one would expect a variety of Western radicals to do so, but a former Conservative prime minister? Seems odd. During the Anglo-Argentine war over the Falkland Islands in 1982, we also had the anomaly of fascist generals of wholly European extraction, representing a country that had exterminated its indigenous peoples, using the language of anticolonialism and anti-imperialism to solicit international support. . . .

Imperialism must be treated as a concept with many dimensions. The imperial people can rule over the object of their activities; they can colonize their land; they can come to own its assets. By extension, they can exert a coercive or manipulative power over nominally independent governments (as Britain did in princely India for two centuries or in much of the Middle East during the interwar period), or they can assume a policing or refereeing role between independent states. Finally, "cultural" imperialism is also possible, the promulgation of one people's norms, values, and meanings to another. Although by far the vaguest sense of domination, it is also, to many people, the most threatening and insidious. . . .

The Failure of Third World States

It is sad, now, to recall the mood of postimperial euphoria in which many Third World states began their existence [following World War II]. They believed in their elaborate plans for economic development that would move their levels of prosperity toward those of the West. Little problem was envisaged in the maintenance of mass support for governing parties and movements and in the belief that governments would meet their peoples' aspirations. Throughout the Third World, ordinary people spoke proudly and possessively of their government and its plans. They were pleased to look westerners in the eye as friendly equals. . . .

Ever since the 1960s, inexorably, year by year, the mood has changed. By now most of the youth of North Africa feel, at least in certain moods, a bitter sense of injustice and a hatred of the developed world. In the 1960s their fathers considered fundamentalist Islam a reactionary folly, and they would have seen Saddam Hussein for the blustering tyrant that he is; in the

1990s they seek solace from the former and admire the latter.

What lies behind this bitterness? In North Africa and the rest of the Third World, the answer is the same: The massive, multi-dimensional failure of states to meet the expectations of their people. They have failed: economically, to grow sufficiently; politically, to sustain or develop honest and accountable forms of government; ethnically, to weld together their diverse tribes and religions. Perhaps this failure was inevitable; perhaps it was not their fault. But it is undeniable. With few exceptions, "developing countries" referred to an aspiration rather than a trend. The original category, "underdeveloped countries," was more accurate. Even India, which has sustained a democracy, is now probably in its worst condition since independence: There are more extremely poor and homeless people on its city streets, communal violence rises daily, and the population climbs toward a billion people. . . .

Intervention: An Ethical Improvement

As the Cold War has faded, the United States and its allies have embarked on a growing series of direct interventions in other states. The invasion of Grenada in 1983 was a miniature prototype, followed by the bombing of Tripoli in 1986, the invasion of Panama in 1989, and the Gulf commitment the following year. The scale and confidence of these actions have grown. One could argue that this change could be taken as an improvement from many Third World perspectives. The politics of the Cold War contained many interventions by the superpowers. Both sides acted through surrogates and puppets and were concerned only to outmaneuver the other. Both sides supported hideous regimes simply because they were "our" villains, authoritarians, perhaps, but not totalitarians in Western parlance. The most legitimate anti-Americanism in the world must be that of the victims of some of the appalling regimes that the United States created or supported. The new world order must, in many respects, be an ethical improvement: When you intervene directly, at your own command, bearing responsibility for your actions, you must do so according to your own values, answering to your own public opinion and international reputation. Thus, there must be a degree of honesty and responsibility about your actions, an ethical accountability quite different from the Cold War manipulations of security forces, the unseen puppetmaster's power, truly the prerogative of the harlot. . . .

Debating Imperialism

It would be odd, historically, to assume that imperialism, in every sense, is a thing of the past. The gap between the resources of the Western world and those of the rest is greater than it ever was. Imperialism has its ups and downs. Between 1780 and 1830 the empires of the day, the European empires in the New World, were largely destroyed. But after 1850 the European powers came back with new empires in Africa and Asia. The British Raj is not going to be reestablished per se, but that is not to say that Western involvement in and control of the Third World is not going to be increased in the next half-century. Nothing is inevitable, and consequences depend on choices; the important debate at this stage is about whether imperialism is a good thing or not. . . .

Disintegrating Societies

After a recent trip to Rwanda, J. Brian Atwood, head of the United States Agency for International Development, wrote in *The Washington Post*: "Disintegrating societies and failed states with their civil conflicts and destabilizing refugee flows have emerged as the greatest menace to global stability. . . . Increasingly, we are confronted by countries without leadership, without order, without governance itself."

Indeed, in August 1994 Atwood sat in on the private briefing for Al Gore and other officials, where the experts listed 25 developing nations in Africa, Asia, Latin America, the Middle East and the former Soviet Union that have collapsed or are in danger of disintegration under the weight of poverty, population growth or internal conflict.

With the end of the Cold War and the sudden end of military and economic aid from the superpowers, the failures of Marxism may be giving way to the grim 19th century vision of Thomas Malthus— that populations growing faster than resources must inevitably be decimated by famine, disease and war.

Saul Friedman, *The Manchester Union Leader*, August 19, 1994.

The alternative to imperialism as a justification of sovereignty is nationalism; as an international system, it consists of the single rule that states are autonomous. One of the most obvious disadvantages of nationalism is that it simply does not fit the world. People do not, generally, sort themselves into discrete, definable nations inhabiting well-defined territories. Even where they do, the units thus created may be of an insupportable size, either militarily or economically. This was a lesson of the interwar consequences of the breakup of the Austro-Hungarian Empire. Where peoples do not, the claim that territories belong to preexisting nations that must protect and express their identities has become perhaps the most pain-creating shibboleth of

241

the modern world. Merely tedious in Norway, unpleasantly repressive in the Republic of Ireland, it becomes divisive and disastrous in Northern Ireland, the Balkans, or Africa. The extent
to which the world is dominated by ethnic and religious struggles that are now both endemic and increasing is an unforeseen
tragedy. Nationalist against loyalist in Northern Ireland, Turk
against Greek in Cyprus, Jew against Arab, Christian against
Muslim in the Middle East, Armenian against Azerbaijani in the
Caucasus, Sikh against Hindu, Muslim against Hindu in India:
The list is endless. Academic textbooks in a dozen fields refer
routinely to nation-states, but in reality there are none. In part
these struggles are the consequence of an acceptance that nationality is the moral basis of political organization. Under the
Ottoman, British, or Austro-Hungarian empires, many of the
people concerned coexisted relatively peacefully.

The Absurdity of Nationalism

The system of sovereign states that has evolved out of the old
empires can be seen as an absurdity. The idea that Malawi, say,
is a state in the same sense as the United States and that both
have sovereignty could never be more than a legal fiction. The
fetishism with which states now recognize each other's independence would have caused great amusement to the political commentators of earlier ages. But there is nothing wrong with a bit
of absurdity. The real disadvantage of the system is the structure
of moral responsibility that it creates. Rich and powerful countries may be rich and powerful in their relations with the poor
and weak, but they exercise no authority; they cannot properly
be said to have duties and responsibilities. For all that vague
sense of a generalized duty to do right that affects Western populations when they see the more extreme evidence of tyranny
and economic incompetence in the Third World, the places
where these things occur have governments that deny the possibility of a responsible outside authority. To put the point as a
rhetorical question, Could a contemporary British, French, or
American empire tolerate the misery and deprivation in its
colonies that is currently tolerated by sovereign states?

In every capital, the existing system of absolutely sovereign
states creates overblown political classes that have enormous
power and a vested interest in the system; they form an immense obstacle to change, despite the economic undermining of
their authority in many cases. Another obstacle is the prevailing
rhetoric of anti-imperialism. This is, perhaps, best explained in
terms of the "emotive theory of ethical terms" developed by the
American philosopher Charles Stevenson in the 1940s, though
George Orwell grasped the same point in an effective, though
unrefined, form in the same period. Imperialism has a negative

dynamic meaning: It is a bad thing, just as racism and fascism are bad things and democracy is a good thing. Words with dynamic meanings become subject to persuasive definitions that use their emotive power in ways that serve the interests of the speaker. Thus, democracy extends to the rule of a single party that is supposed to represent the working class in a broad, historic dimension; violence extends beyond assault to macho or discriminatory attitudes; fascism detaches itself entirely from the content of Gentile's *La Dottrina del Fascismo* and applies to any political position you do not like.

A Linguistic Game

The dangers of this linguistic game are that it can legitimize actions that would not be accepted under any other name. The term racism is degraded: The concept of race explains very little biologically, and historical evidence suggests that the existence and evolution of discrete races has been much exaggerated; in any case, most people feel a repugnance for the idea of judging others by the color of their skin. But the rhetoric of antiracism now justifies giving people jobs on the grounds of race. It also justifies tolerating the independence of Islamic communities in England and France that beat and terrorize their children, arrange their marriages and, in extremis, circumcise girls. To be against these practices, which we would not tolerate in relation to white people, is to be against multiculturalism, and opposition to multiculturalism is a form of racism. There are two philosophies of freedom in conflict in relation to these crimes: One seeks to emancipate persons from laws and powers (including those vested in cultures); the other, to emancipate cultures or nations. If you believe that freedom must always be of persons, the latter view has moral weight only if you accept a form of divisive essentialism in which human beings are Irish, Arab, or Islamic at least as profoundly as they are human beings.

Anti-imperialism is similar to antiracism and operates in similar ways. Thus, some radical writers in England attack those who would seek to interfere with local Islamic cruelties and those who sought to oppose Saddam Hussein in more or less the same terms. That imperialism and racism are essentially the same thing is a sophistry well developed by such writers as Salman Rushdie, in his pre-*Satanic Verses* period, and David Edgar, whose 1973 play *Destiny* brings together in England during the early 1970s a group of people who had met in India during the 1940s, in the last days of empire. Of course, one can turn this on its head and say that to object to the West interfering with Arabs tyrannizing over Arabs because that is an Arab matter is to fail to take seriously the proposition that Arabs are human beings.

Nationalist political classes build the idea of nationality within their borders by building the myth of their own heroic status in overthrowing imperialism. Thus they exaggerate and demonize the workings of imperialism. The most debilitating and harmful consequence of such mythologizing is that, by attributing the massive failings of contemporary states to the legacy of imperialism and the continued influence of imperialism, it directs the frustration and anger many people feel away from those who are really responsible. Instead, their anger is channeled into forms of hostility to outsiders rather than toward constructive projects. As the Egyptian writer Mohammed Sayid Ahmed has put it, "People in the Arab world feel enslaved by a system that leaves them no dignity. They feel manipulated by others. All the conspiracy theories that run through the Middle East come first from the frustration of knowing your own system doesn't work."

A Program for the New Imperialism

These arguments in favor of a new imperialism have not been intended to culminate in a recommendation that empires in the nineteenth-century style be revived. History never repeats itself, and dead institutions cannot be resuscitated. Nor do they recommend the establishment of a new American empire per se. They are meant to suggest the possibility and desirability of a more honest responsibility and authority in the relationship between powerful countries and those that need help, a set of relationships that weakens the power of nationalist elites and requires a responsibility from imperialist investors that goes beyond the short term and the exploitative. The principal aims must be peace, order, and the maintenance of contracts, the conditions of prosperity and human development. The principal practical implications all build on tendencies manifest in the 1980s:

- *Hegemonic arms control.* We must not accept the argument that "if you are entitled to defend yourselves, we are too" and must prevent the development of another Iraqi army. For poor countries to spend 25 or 40 percent of their GNP on arms is utter folly; it still gets them nowhere near a capacity to compete with developed countries. They should seek their protection in treaties with developed countries.
- *Terrorism.* The West should take action in the cases of countries that encourage or harbor terrorists or protest their incapacity to deal with the terrorists within their borders.
- *Ethically conditional aid.* Economic assistance should be dependent on policies by the recipient that increase the possibility of human freedom and development. The principle that it is not our business what distant states do to their peoples provided they support us in international relations must be rejected.

- *An international system of property rights.* Ultimately, it is absurd that Libya should control Libyan oil when the population lives five hundred miles from the oil fields and has played no part in their development. The claim by Arabs in oil-less countries to a share of oil revenues is no more and no less absurd. Equally, it is wrong to exploit resources without a fair representation of the interests of local people and a fair share for them. We must evolve a consistent system of international property rights that acknowledges and compromises these values and allows growth to occur.

> *"One of the pitfalls of outside enforcement [of Southern stability] is that it is unlikely to work and [is] . . . unlikely to foster democracy."*

North and South Must Cooperate to Maintain Order

S. Neil MacFarlane and Thomas G. Weiss

In promoting international security in the post–Cold War world, cooperative efforts between regional and international bodies are essential, S. Neil MacFarlane and Thomas G. Weiss maintain in the following viewpoint. To illustrate their point, the authors describe the efforts of regional and international organizations in Nicaragua and El Salvador in the 1980s. They conclude that such efforts have the potential not only to resolve conflicts, but also to promote democracy and human rights. MacFarlane is a professor of political science at Queens University in Kingston, Ontario, Canada. Weiss is the associate director and dean of Brown University's Thomas J. Watson Jr. Institute for International Studies in Providence, Rhode Island.

As you read, consider the following questions:

1. What problems do the authors say regional organizations face? What are regional groups' strengths?
2. Why were regional groups in Central America able to initiate a peace process in Nicaragua and El Salvador, according to the authors? What do the authors say was the UN's role in the peace?

Excerpted from S. Neil MacFarlane and Thomas G. Weiss, "The United Nations, Regional Organizations, and Human Security: Building Theory in Central America," *Third World Quarterly*, vol. 15, no. 2, 1994. Reprinted with permission.

Dramatic changes in the international system lend salience to the concept of global governance. The end of the Cold War has increased the incidence of conflict in certain (though not all) regions, continuing an upward trend towards the violent expression of political grievances, in particular by ethnic minorities and other political dissidents. And the disappearance of bipolar confrontation has removed (at least temporarily) the most substantial political barriers to conflict management by the United Nations. One result has been the explosion of peacekeeping and peacemaking activities.

The end of bipolar confrontation has also created space for regional peace and security initiatives as well as a rising rhetorical demand for them. Such considerations informed UN Secretary-General Boutros Boutros-Ghali's comment in his much-publicised 1992 report to the Security Council:

> Under the Charter, the Security Council has and will continue to have primary responsibility for maintaining international peace and security, but regional action as a matter of decentralization, delegation and cooperation with United Nations efforts could not only lighten the burden of the Council but also contribute to a deeper sense of participation, consensus and democratization in international affairs.

There are new partisans for both universal and regional intergovernmental organisation, but the debate about their relative merits is an old one: Is the United Nations the appropriate lead actor in the search for regional security? Does the UN have the necessary financial and technical resources to fulfil this mission globally? If not, how can UN activities be supplemented or complemented by those of other organisations? And how should UN activities relate to those of other (in particular regional) multilateral bodies in the quest for security? In short, could there be an improved division of labour between regional and universal organisations? . . .

The United Nations Under Siege

Both universal and regional organisations have pluses and minuses as mechanisms in the pursuit of human security. The United Nations has substantial technical resources and experience in the area of conflict management and resolution. As a global organisation, it also possesses the advantage—in the absence of fundamental systemic conflict among major powers—of distance from regional conflicts and consequently of greater impartiality based on nonregional perspectives.

Initial euphoria about the prospects for international peace and security in the post-Cold War era have given way to greater realism. As such, it would appear imprudent to rely excessively on the United Nations, given growing problems with ongoing operations in both Somalia and the former Yugoslavia, as well as the aborted one in Haiti. These difficulties reflect a number of deeper difficulties, not the least of which are the burdens that expanded peacekeeping has placed on the organisation. The United Nations is in serious financial difficulty and sorely lacks sufficient and qualified staff. As he was leaving office in winter 1993, former UN Under-Secretary-General for Administration, Dick Thornburgh, characterised the continued expansion of the world organisation's activities in peacekeeping as a 'financial bungee jump'. . . .

The great powers not only appear reluctant to provide troops but also to pay for any substantial expansion of UN conflict management responsibilities. The end of the Cold War diminishes greatly the interest perceived by the West in many regional conflicts. Great power resources are limited, among other things, by the sluggishness of the global economy.

After the Cold War, governing élites and publics are seeking to divert expenditures away from foreign policy and security tasks to long postponed domestic needs. Four years after the official end of the Cold War, a survey of élite and public opinion in the United States indicated that when asked to identity the most urgent foreign policy priority, most Americans named a domestic issue, with a particular emphasis on the economy.

There simply is no political pay-off for Congressional support for the UN. Therefore, while the last two administrations have committed themselves to repaying the substantial American arrears to the United Nations, Congress remains recalcitrant about even normal assessed contributions to the UN budget. In fact, peacekeeping debts and arrears for 1993 were paid with FY 1994 allocations. . . .

The Advantages of Regionalism, in Theory

In this context, regional approaches to crisis management and conflict resolution seem attractive. The members of regional organisations suffer most dramatically from the destabilising consequences of war in their area. They receive the refugees and bear the political, social and economic consequences. They receive, willingly or unwillingly, the combatants of neighbouring countries seeking sanctuary. They face the choice of pacifying and repatriating combatant and noncombatant aliens on their territory or of resisting hot pursuit by those from whom these refugees have fled. Local conflict and the consequent perceptions of regional instability dampen investment flows and retard growth. They divert public resources into defence expenditures. Because regional powers and organisations have the greatest stake in the management and resolution of armed conflicts in their locales, they are more likely than outsiders to react to the outbreak of war.

Moreover, regional actors are perhaps those best suited to mediation in local conflicts. They understand the dynamics of strife and cultures more intimately than do outsiders. Leaders are far more likely to have personal connections to protagonists in local conflicts. Involvement by other regional powers is less likely to be perceived as illegitimate interference than that of extra regional organisations. Finally, issues relating to local conflict are far more likely to be given full and urgent consideration in regional fora than in global ones, since the latter have broader agendas, competing priorities and numerous distractions.

However, regional organisations also display significant shortcomings as a potential replacement for the United Nations. . . . The institutional capacities of many regional organisations are extremely feeble, so much so that they have been notoriously unable to carry out mandates in peace and security. As one respected African observer, Ambassador Olara Otunnu, has summarised:

> I do not believe that it will be possible in the near future for regional organizations to respond effectively to the challenge of conflicts within states. Few regional organizations have relevant traditions . . . Also, regional groups often suffer from the perception of being partisan . . . Moreover, in the case of Third World regional organizations, there is also the problem of resources . . . [F]or the foreseeable future, peacekeeping will have to be the responsibility of the United Nations.

. . . In short, there is good reason to doubt the will and the capacity of regional organisations to perform well in the management of conflict within their areas. The end of the Cold War does little to change this conclusion. Global and regional organisations possess both merits and demerits with regard to the management and resolution of regional conflict and the enhancement of human security. Some disadvantages (for example, financial weakness) are shared. Some . . . are not. Questions thus arise as to whether there is a possible complementarity between global and regional organisations, as well as to whether combined approaches to the question of security might not result in more enduring and positive effects.

The Central American Case

An exploration of these questions in Nicaragua and El Salvador seems salient because Central America is one region whose security to date has improved in the post-Cold War era. These cases are interesting not merely as a means of assessing the role of the principal regional organisation, the Organization of American States (OAS). They also illustrate a creative process of forming and reforming *ad hoc* regional groupings to help solve the area's endemic civil wars. Another aspect of interest in this area lies in the interwoven tapestry of activities by regional groups, the United Nations and nongovernmental organisations. The comparative success of this multilayered approach to regional politico-military security suggests strongly that the analytical web should be cast beyond formal intergovernmental institutions.

Overriding the United Nations' Charter

The onset of the "unipolar" world [after the collapse of the Soviet Union in 1991] signaled that the thrust of North-South relations has finally shifted from "development" to "security," and the Third World nations are now risk zones. . . .

After Iraq's invasion of Kuwait in 1990, the United Nations [Security Council] took the lead in opposing [Iraqi president] Saddam Hussein's occupation of Kuwait. . . .

[However,] Chapter VIII of the UN Charter explicitly calls for reliance on regional arrangements or agencies to resolve regional conflicts. Attempts to use regional agencies were discouraged from the outset by the United States and its allies. Article 42 of the UN Charter authorizes the collective use of force after all other remedies have been exhausted. . . . The UN Security Council had to determine that economic sanctions against Iraq . . . would not work before authorizing the use of force. No such determination was made by the Council. Moreover, if Article 42 is invoked, the collective use of force must be under UN jurisdiction and the UN flag, as was the case in Korea in the 1950s. Again, the UN abdicated its duties in this regard by allowing the application of force under a different command structure than its own.

Nader Entessar, *Journal of Third World Studies*, Fall 1992.

By the mid-1980s it had become clear that neither the contras in Nicaragua nor the Frente Farabundo Martí para Liberación Nacional (FMLN) in El Salvador could hope to evict the governments there by force. Latin American efforts to reach a negotiated solution to the conflict in Central America emerged with the Contadora process in 1983, involving Mexico, Venezuela, Colombia and Panama. They were subsequently joined by a 'support group' of newly democratic governments in Argentina, Brazil, Peru and Uruguay. Washington, which contributes the lion's share of the OAS budget, largely prevented the organisation from dealing with the wars in the area. Hence the Contadora Group outlined a series of initiatives between 1983 and 1986 that sought to isolate the conflict from East-West rivalry. Not surprisingly, this effort floundered in the face of the Reagan administration's view of the problems in Central America as arising from Soviet-Cuban expansionism and Washington's determination to fight back against international communism [which, it felt, was represented in Nicaragua by the ruling Sandinista Party and in El Salvador by the FMLN guerrillas].

Changes in the Soviet Union, in US policy, and in Central American conditions had produced a deadlock in which the parties began to be more open to possibilities for compromise—a change emanating not from Washington or Moscow or even from the rest of Latin America, but from Central America itself. The first summit of Central American presidents was held in Guatemala in May 1986. Known as Esquipulas I, this session set the stage for Central American summits that would ultimately serve as a vehicle for successful regional negotiations.

President Oscar Arias Sánchez of Costa Rica seized the initiative by presenting, in January of 1987, what would become known as the 'Arias Plan'. Initially perceived by Nicaraguans as a US-inspired provocation, the Arias Plan gradually gathered political momentum in Central America. By April, the Nicaraguans had signed on to the plan, accepting it as a true Central American initiative. On 7 August 1987 the Esquipulas II agreement was signed, committing the different states in the region to the implementation of the total Arias Plan. For his vision and extraordinary diplomacy, the Costa Rican president was awarded the Nobel Peace Prize later that year.

Between August 1987 and April 1990, there were six Central American summits, during which agreements were hammered out on free elections, confidence-building measures, disarmament, national reconciliation and international verification. . . .

Military Stalemate

Nineteen-eighty-nine marked a pivotal year in the Central American conflicts. Early in his administration, President George Bush was obliged by Congress to reduce sharply aid for the contras. The ailing President of El Salvador, José Napoleon Duarte, was succeeded by an elected successor, Alfredo Cristiani of the Arena Party. In Nicaragua the contras had failed to regain the initiative; and in El Salvador, the guerrilla offensive of November 1989 failed miserably.

In Nicaragua, the Sandinistas began talks with the opposition about initiating national reconciliation, agreeing to internationally-monitored elections in February 1990 with the Unified Nicaraguan Opposition (UNO) under Violeta Barrios de Chamorro. In February 1990, much to its surprise, the Sandinista government of Daniel Ortega Saavedra lost the elections to the UNO coalition and the new government began the long and arduous process of national reconciliation.

In El Salvador Cristiani proved sincere in his search for peace with the FMLN. Over the course of two years of discussions in Mexico City brokered by the United Nations, the two parties finally agreed to a comprehensive plan for peace and reconciliation in El Salvador on 16 January 1992. It guaranteed the safety of the FMLN, put restrictions on the armed forces and provided for the guerrillas to disarm and to participate in the democratic process.

In Nicaragua, there were several operational activities by outside organisations with special relevance for future regional settlements: small arms control, verification of arms reductions and supervision of elections. The United Nations Observer Group in Central America (ONUCA) conducted the most extensive military operation that can still be categorised as 'observation'. This was established in October 1989 in response to a request by the Central American presidents for UN verification of the security aspects of two unresolved problems in Esquipulas II: the cessation of aid to irregular forces; and the non-use of the territory of one state for attacks on others.

Demilitarisation

The first problem was understood to include the cessation of all forms of military assistance to insurgents, and the second to prevent any act of aggression against one state from the land, territorial sea or airspace of another. Spot checks and *ad hoc* investigations were made by mobile teams of UN military observers based in sensitive border areas. In December 1989, ONUCA's mandate was expanded to include verification of any subsequent agreements about the cessation of hostilities and demobilisation of irregular forces. Following the Nicaraguan elections in February 1990 and agreements concerning the demobilisation of the contras in March, ONUCA thus became responsible for destroying weapons delivered by insurgents and establishing 'security zones' where former contras awaited reintegration into the economy.

After the United Nations had finished this task, and as part of the negotiated settlement, the OAS fielded the International Commission of Support and Verification (CIAV/OEA). Paid for by the United States, the $40 million effort of civilian liaison in the countryside was designed to keep contras from returning to war and the Sandinistas from influencing unduly the reintegration of these former guerrillas into the local economy. In spite of significant demobilisation, remnants of CIAV/OEA remain today in the countryside ostensibly to prevent the return to arms by former guerrillas, now called 'recontras'. This operation is searching for a new mission in the development arena.

Given that disarmament is a central requirement for lasting peace, especially in countries with large numbers of heavily-armed regular and irregular forces, the precedent in Central

America is significant. The fact that the UN—in particular a Venezuelan battalion that was transferred from Namibia to help out immediately—has the experience and credibility in this area, and that the OAS was associated as 'window dressing', reflects the type of operational problems faced by regional institutions. The expansion of UN capabilities to monitor the destruction of Iraq's arsenal of weapons of mass destruction as part of the comprehensive ceasefire imposed by the Security Council after the Gulf war strengthens this operational advantage of the world organisation.

The UN's Observer Role

The United Nations Observer Mission to Verify the Electoral Process in Nicaragua (ONUVEN) was dispatched by the Secretary-General following a decision by Central American presidents that the Nicaraguan elections should be internationally observed. This was the first instance of UN verification of domestic elections in a sovereign state, another precedent that appears significant for future settlements of regional conflicts. Significantly, ONUVEN was an entirely civilian body that spearheaded more numerous observers furnished by private organisations and the OAS. Not only did the UN personnel orchestrate election observation, but they also ensured the liaison between their own and other civilian observers with the military personnel from ONUCA. The distinction between military and civilian components within future UN operations that emphasise elections is likely to be blurred, as has already been the case during elections in Namibia, Angola, Haiti and Cambodia.

Perhaps no issue raises more red flags about sovereignty than human rights, which is why the use of both UN civilian and military personnel in the UN Observer Mission in El Salvador (ONUSAL) was noteworthy. During the long and gruelling civil war, nongovernmental organisations had routinely reported human rights abuses. But there had been virtually no international verification, one of the most significant shortcomings in the human rights regime. The deployment of military and civilian observers prior to the cease-fire was a significant advance, which indicated confidence in the world organisation. Convening a Truth Commission, publishing its findings, and acting upon them was another. These were important task-expansions by the United Nations in relationship to the shibboleth of domestic jurisdiction that is so dear to many recalcitrant governments and enshrined in article 2(7) of the UN Charter. . . .

To summarise, what progress has been made in Central America is the result of a creative blending of the activities of regional and universal intergovernmental and nongovernmental bodies. Each type of organisation at each level played an essential role in complementing those of others. These roles shifted flexibly over time in response to evolving conditions. The result was a dramatic enhancement in human security in much of the region, even if the peace process in both Nicaragua and El Salvador remains tenuous. . . .

A Bottom-Up Approach to Southern Conflicts

It is an open question whether there will be more outside efforts, including intervention, to help quell war and make peace, or rather more efforts to contain armed conflicts and let them run their course with significant expenditures to keep them from spilling over. However, if there are any such efforts by the international community, the Central American case contains . . . additional lessons.

First, successful efforts to enhance human security depend on both regional and international conditions. At the regional level, the critical permissive condition was military stalemate. At the global level, it was the end of the Cold War that reduced the propensity of outsiders to fuel local conflicts and also facilitated American accommodation. The smallness of the region facilitated decisions among a manageable number of governments within the conflict area as well as by outsiders to undertake a relatively do-able task—in contrast with the enormous and expensive operations in Cambodia, Somalia and the former Yugoslavia.

Second, the case also reflects the importance of the role of regional actors in establishing a momentum towards peace. Generally, we conceive of regional international collaboration as a top-down process. This is implicit in the very notion of subcontracting. The Central American case suggests the significance of the bottom-up direction and lends weight to the argument of some observers that one of the pitfalls of outside enforcement is that it is unlikely to work and, moreover, unlikely to foster democracy. The process of conflict resolution was initiated and sustained both politically and diplomatically by regional action. Technical aspects of the process of conflict resolution were in effect subcontracted upwards to the UN (and, to a lesser extent, the OAS).

"Less than 5 percent of legally admitted immigrants . . . [possess] job skills and educational attainments actually needed by the economy."

Immigration from South to North Should Be Curbed

Robert Fox, Wayne Lutton, and John Tanton

Immigrants from North Africa and the eastern Mediterranean are moving into Western Europe in large numbers, reports Robert Fox in Part I of the following viewpoint. There has been much social and political opposition in Europe to these Third World immigrants, who are thought to bring crime and disease with them. Fox is a writer on social and economic issues affecting the Mediterranean. In Part II, Wayne Lutton and John Tanton argue that the United States is being overwhelmed by immigrants who take jobs away from American workers. The authors charge that the bulk of these immigrants have few skills that benefit the American economy. Lutton is a policy analyst who writes on population and immigration issues. Tanton, an eye surgeon, writes on immigration and sustainable development.

As you read, consider the following questions:

1. What do Fox, Lutton, and Tanton all say is bad about the clannishness of immigrants from the developing world?
2. What kind of jobs do Lutton and Tanton say that immigrants are taking away from Americans?

Robert Fox, "The Invasion of Europe," *The Spectator*, August 1991. Reprinted by permission of *The Spectator* (UK). Excerpts from Wayne Lutton and John Tanton, *The Immigration Invasion*, (Petoskey, MI: Social Contract Press, 1994.) Reprinted with permission.

I

The populations of north Africa and the Levant are now expanding exponentially, and as more leave the villages and the land for the cities, the resources for life are becoming scarce. On the other hand, the population of Western Europe, and very likely Eastern Europe too, is static and in several areas actually contracting fast. The dilemma has been summed up in a neat formula of the United Nations Environment Programme (Unep) for the Mediterranean. In 1945, Unep says, two-thirds of the coastal population of the Mediterranean were on the northern European shore (from Gibraltar to the Bosphorus). By the end of the century the position will be exactly reversed, with two-thirds of the peoples of the littoral living on the southern and eastern shores—and still producing only 10 per cent of the industrial wealth of the Mediterranean neighbourhood.

In travels since the mid-1980s to every country on the shores of the Mediterranean researching a book, I have witnessed a scene of astonishing change. Ports, villages, souks and markets, caravanserais and refugee camps swarm with children. Half the population of Tunisia is [as of 1991] under the age of 18, half the Palestinians of Gaza and the West Bank are under 16. Turkey and Egypt are each on course to have 100 million inhabitants by 2025. By then Cairo will be a sprawling megalopolis, a new kind of *rus in urbe* [country in the city], of some 30 million. In Algeria the population is growing at around 3 per cent a year. The command economy of the FLN [National Liberation Front] neo-Marxists has left many on the brink of starvation, hence the rise of opposition in Islamic fundamentalism, and the urge to emigrate.

Northern Europeans have ignored these changes for too long. Now the Mediterraneans are among us as never before. France has more than four million immigrants, 7 per cent of the total population. Illegal arrivals are running at more than 150,000 a year, and it is this that has provoked the alarm of European officials. . . .

Eight Million Migrant Workers

The International Labour Organisation makes a cautious guess that there are some 8 million migrant workers on the move throughout the European Economic Community. This is likely to be a wild underestimate, as the standard formula is that for every visible illegal migrant worker there is one or possibly two escaping detection—and this could mean that 5 per cent of the European working population will be illegal residents.

The signs of change have been greatest in Italy, long a land of emigration (the record year was 1913, when 800,000 Italians left), now a target for North African and, now, Albanian immigration. In the space of five years the piazzas of old cities like

Genoa have become encampments for Moroccans and Tunisians. The biggest May Day demonstration in 1990 in Milan was by Muslim militants. Soon every one of the city's 5,000 bakery workers will be Moroccan. In 1990 the Italian government offered amnesty to illegal workers, guaranteeing residence rights and work permits—more than a quarter of a million came forward in six months.

Now Italy, like Spain, has imposed strict visa regulations on all applying to travel to and from the Maghreb. The signs are that these will not work. . . .

Ramirez/Copely News Service. Used with permission.

Some Italians have reacted with uncharacteristic intolerance. The Lombard League successfully fought 1990's local elections, gaining half the votes in some parts of the north, on an overtly racial ticket. 'It's not a question of race, but a health hazard—they bring AIDS, hepatitis and a different culture,' one of the League's Milan luminaries told me. Africa no longer begins in Calabria, Italy, as Lombards and Piedmontese used to say, but starts at the Appenines—which puts Chiantishire firmly in Berber country. In 1990 Tuscany proved the unlikely setting of serious racial disorder in the centre and outskirts of Florence and the ferry port of Piombino. . . .

With the new arrivals are coming old Mediterranean ways,

the habit of doing business in the tribe and the family, of parallel power and less respect for central and public authority. We have happily embraced Mediterranean manners for years, from espresso coffee, to kebabs and souvlaki and trattorie on the pavement. But beyond our enthusiasm for the warm south under the banners of Benetton and the sunshades from Benidorm lurks the mentality of the mafioso. Mafia networks, criminal syndicates, and *clanisme* as the Corsicans call it, are now rampant from one side of the Mediterranean to the other, and firmly amongst us as a string of bank scandals including the collapse of Bank of Credit and Commerce International have now made apparent. Mafia methods are a means of coping with dynamic chaos natural to the Mediterranean, of putting some 'order in the disorder' as the Italians like to say. It is a phenomenon all Europeans must take seriously and there are signs that the British Government has at last recognised this, and may have to play 'the immigration card'.

II

The United States has been going through economic hard times. The official national unemployment rate in early 1994 stood at just under 7 percent. When "discouraged workers" (those who want to work but have lost just about all hope of obtaining employment) and those who are involuntarily working only part-time are added, the overall rate of unemployment and underemployment probably exceeds 15 percent, or double the official figure.

Yet, despite massive joblessness, the United States intentionally imports a million or more additional job seekers every year—while looking the other way as millions more come in illegally. . . .

The 1990 Immigration Act increased legal immigration by nearly 40 percent. At the time it was being pushed through Congress, it was often described as a "jobs bill." That is because proponents claimed that the United States faced an impending shortage of workers.

Questionable Claims

Ben Wattenberg, of the American Enterprise Institute, asserted that the huge federal budget deficit could be eliminated if more immigrants were admitted. University of Maryland Marketing Professor Julian Simon, a former senior fellow at the conservative Heritage Foundation and favorite of the *Wall Street Journal*, testified that

> Immigrants do not take jobs, they create jobs. . . . My recommendation would be that we simply jump immigration visas to one million per year . . . there is no change [in public poli-

cies] that could have even a fraction of the economic benefit that we can get simply by increasing the number of immigrants by 100 percent.

The exact impact of immigration on employment patterns is debated by many people. But, during a time of high unemployment, we should certainly not add hundreds of thousands of job seekers to already saturated job markets. . . .

Legal immigrants, including relatives of previously admitted aliens, as well as amnestied aliens, have arrived in record numbers with almost no consideration for their possible impact on the U.S. economy.

Unskilled and Uneducated

Less than 5 percent of legally admitted immigrants are certified by the Department of Labor as possessing job skills and educational attainments actually needed by the economy. When illegal aliens are included, the percentage of immigrants entering our work force because of our need for their specific talents is minuscule.

The overwhelming majority of immigrants, both legal and illegal, who have arrived since 1965 are from Third World countries. Many have less than five years of education and are illiterate in their native language, let alone in English.

They compete most directly with those Americans who themselves are experiencing high rates of unemployment—teenagers, women, and racial minorities (including Hispanic-Americans).

Far from contributing to our general economic well-being, massive immigration is hurting the employment prospects of many Americans.

Impact on U.S. Cities

The Center for Immigration Studies confirms that overall unemployment rates in the occupations where immigrants most often compete for work are well above the national average.

Three-quarters of foreign-born job seekers concentrate in just seven states, five of which now have jobless rates above the national average.

Six cities that attract the most immigrants—Miami, Los Angeles, New York, San Diego, Anaheim, and Chicago—all have unemployment rates well above the national average, with New York, Los Angeles, and Anaheim exceeding the national rate by over 40 percent.

Thirty-four metropolitan areas where immigrants settle in large numbers are on the Labor Department's list of "labor surplus" localities and can therefore qualify for federal procurement preferences, based on two or more years of unemployment 20 percent above the national average.

Conversely, the areas that have fared best during the recession do not have large populations of recent immigrants. The states with the largest job gains during 1991 included Nebraska (4.1 percent payroll growth), Arkansas (3.3 percent), South Dakota (2.7 percent), Alaska (2.6 percent), Idaho (2.5 percent), and Utah (2.4 percent).

Commonly Held Misconceptions

The presence of large numbers of recent immigrants in the U.S. work force has yet to spark a national reaction, and there have been few calls to repeal the increase in legal immigration provided for in the 1990 Immigration Act. This is probably due to the persistence of two commonly held, but mistaken, views about participation by aliens in the economy: first, that they are mostly employed as seasonal agricultural workers, and second, that they generally take jobs that Americans simply will not perform.

Despite the fact that they are working here illegally, a considerable body of research has been conducted over the years, which has revealed a great deal about the participation of aliens in the work force. The evidence shows that relatively few immigrants (perhaps 8 to 15 percent) are employed in seasonal agriculture; the vast majority are employed in sectors of the economy where millions of Americans compete for work, frequently holding good jobs that citizens would gladly fill.

In April, 1982, at a time when unemployment was at approximately current levels, the INS [Immigration and Naturalization Service] conducted "Operation Jobs," a major effort that led to the arrest of thousands of illegal aliens on the job. Eighty-two plants in nine metropolitan areas were raided.

Taking Well-Paid Jobs

In Chicago, illegals were discovered holding jobs that paid from $4.82 to nearly $17 an hour. In Denver, illegal aliens were found working at jobs paying over $12 an hour. At that time, the hourly minimum wage was $3.35. The average wage paid to illegals apprehended in San Francisco was $5.19 an hour—55 percent over the minimum wage. Businesses where illegal aliens were removed from the work force were swamped with applications from job-seeking citizens.

Rice University economist Donald Huddle has conducted field studies of the employment of illegal aliens in Houston, during times of both economic growth and recession. He has found that illegals continue to find employment in commercial construction and other sectors of the economy where wages range from the minimum rate to $10 or more an hour. Professor Huddle observed that, "these wages debunk the commonly held notion that illegal aliens are taking only those jobs that Americans do not want because they are lowly paid.". . .

Professor Huddle has in 1992 prepared two studies detailing the impact that immigrants, legal and illegal, are having on the U.S. work force. He found that:

- Based on research by Professors Joseph Altonji and David Card, it is clear that the earnings of low-skilled American workers—black males, black or white females with not more than 12 years of education, and white males with less than 12 years of education—are seriously depressed in areas where they compete in the job market with large numbers of immigrants. A 10 percent increase in the number of immigrants in a particular Standard Metropolitan Statistical Area, results in a 12 percent decline in weekly earnings, with black males' earnings reduced by almost 20 percent.

- Low-skilled American workers are hurt more by illegal immigrants than by legal immigrants. This is because illegals often work for lower wages than legal immigrants and citizens; they enjoy little legal protection from employers who exploit them; and they provide a major cost advantage to employers who hire large numbers of illegals, since employers frequently do not withhold federal and state income taxes, make Social Security contributions, or pay workers' compensation.

- Hundreds of thousands of Americans are being directly displaced from jobs by recent immigrants. . . .

Aliens Recruit Aliens

A major factor in the displacement of Americans is that many jobs are simply not available to them.

In labor-intensive fields, growing numbers of employers have found it profitable to let aliens do the recruiting. As Professor Philip Martin of the University of California at Davis explains, all too frequently job openings are not advertised in newspapers or listed with state employment services. Instead, aliens recruit other aliens by word of mouth.

Over time, the work places become "colonized" by aliens to the degree that Americans are not welcome and would find themselves strangers if employed at these establishments. If aliens leave for other employment, or are expelled by government authorities, employers have been known to contract with "coyotes" [illegal-immigrant smugglers] to hire alien replacements. "The cross-border recruitment system," Martin points out, "provides illegal alien workers with a more sophisticated job search network than is available to many unemployed American workers."

Proponents of increased immigration, notably Julian Simon, argue that, "immigrants not only take jobs, they create (some) jobs." True, but often as not, the new jobs benefit other aliens, not Americans.

Journalist Donatella Lorch describes how this process is transforming important sectors of the economy in the New York metropolitan area. Recent immigrants from the Indian subcontinent now operate about 40 percent of the city's gas stations (Koreans dominate this sector in Los Angeles); over 85 percent of the green-grocer stores are owned and operated by Koreans; Indians and Pakistanis now enjoy a virtual monopoly on newsstands and are now moving into the jewelry trade. Guyanese are a growing presence in drugstore operations and machinery repair. Jamaicans and Irish now compete for control of the child-care business, while Afghans are coming to dominate the fast-food chicken trade.

"Once a niche is found, it creates a snowball effect," she explains, "gathering in labor from that ethnic group and expanding exponentially. . . . The common thread linking all immigrant work niches is the insider's edge on the profession."

Elizabeth Bogan, in her book *Immigration in New York*, writes that, thanks to the "ethnic hiring networks and the proliferation of immigrant-owned small businesses in the city [that] have cut off open market competition for jobs . . . there are tens of thousands of jobs in New York City for which the native-born are not candidates.". . .

Does Our Economy Need Immigrants?

The question that needs to be asked is this: "Does our economy really require large numbers of immigrants?" Given the lower average education and skills of many recent immigrants, as shown by Professor George Borjas in his book *Friends or Strangers: The Impact of Immigrants on the the U.S. Economy*, plus the need to provide education and opportunities for our own citizens, the answer is a resounding, "No." Even Professor Julian Simon, in response to the question, "Is immigration really necessary to the economy?" admits, "We can live nicely without it."

As Benjamin Matta pointed out in *Labor Law Journal*, "The vast majority of the current immigrant supply is substitutable in the workplace with low-skilled native-born labor. Newly arrived immigrant labor is also substitutable with low-skilled immigrant workers who arrived in earlier waves.". . .

In all but a very few instances, foreign professionals are not required for any present or likely future vacancies.

Keep in mind that one of the "Peace Dividends" deriving from the collapse of the Soviet Union is hundreds of thousands of lay-offs of highly trained professionals in defense-related industries, and the U.S. Armed Forces. The Army, Navy, and Air Force plan to eliminate more than 548,000 service and support positions by 1999. An additional 2 million jobs are expected to be lost—over and above the most recent lay-offs in 1994—among civilians working in defense-related industries. There simply will not be a shortage of workers!

The Role of Employer Sanctions

Strict enforcement of employer sanctions (that provision of the 1986 Immigration Reform and Control Act that imposes penalties on employers who knowingly hire illegal aliens) would keep employers from hiring illegal aliens and force them to raise wages and improve working conditions, making these jobs more attractive to natives and recent legal immigrants. This would force sweatshops and those who violate child labor laws out of business.

Furthermore, it would spur technological innovation as industries strive to make workers more productive rather than relying on lowering wages to cut costs. . . .

We in the United States face an alternative. Either we incorporate our own recently displaced workers into an economy that places a premium on high-skill, high-wage enterprises (such as Japan's or Germany's), or we try to compete with Third World countries for low-pay, labor-intensive industries. Increasing immigration can only force us toward the latter alternative.

"In virtually every field in which the United States asserted global leadership in the 1980s . . . one finds immigrants."

Managed Immigration from South to North Should Be Encouraged

Saskia Sassen and Stephen Moore

In Part I of the following viewpoint, Saskia Sassen argues that immigration policies of developed countries are increasingly at odds with the growing integration of today's global economic system. Attempts to open borders to money and goods but close them to immigrants is problematic, she asserts. Sassen teaches urban planning at Columbia University and is author of *The Global City* and *Cities in a World Economy*. In Part II, Stephen Moore points out that contrary to popular belief immigrants are not an economic drain. Their above average entrepreneurial spirit and relatively high educational and skill levels create more jobs and generate more public revenue than they absorb, Moore contends. Moore is a regular contributor to *Insight* magazine, a conservative weekly published by the Washington Times Corporation.

As you read, consider the following questions:

1. What evidence does Sassen cite to support her belief that the world is becoming economically integrated?
2. According to Moore, what special qualities do most immigrants have?

Current immigration policy in developed countries is increasingly at odds with other major policy frameworks in the international system and with the growth of global economic integration. All highly developed countries have received rapidly growing numbers of legal and undocumented immigrants since the early 1980s; none has found its immigration policy effective. These countries are opening up their economies to foreign investment and trade while deregulating their financial markets. In developed countries, the emergence of a new economic regime sharply reduces the role of national governments and borders in controlling international transactions. Yet the framework of immigration policy in these countries remains centered on older conceptions of the nation-state and of national borders.

How can immigration policy account for the facts of rapid economic internationalization and the corresponding transformation of national governments? This is the subject I briefly discuss here.

A Shift in the Global Economy

The 1980s saw a major shift in the global economy. In that decade, the developed countries opened their economies to foreign investment, international financial markets, and imports of goods and services; deregulation and internationalization of a growing range of economic activities became hallmarks of economic policy. As economic doors have opened to others, many developing countries have implemented export-oriented growth strategies. Export-manufacturing zones and the sale of once-public sector firms on world markets became key venues for this internationalization.

Global economic trends engendered a new framework for national economic policy-making. This new framework is evident in the formation of regional trading blocks: the U.S.-Canada Free Trade Agreement, the European Community (EC), the new trading blocks being formed in Southeast Asia as well as the NAFTA [North American Free Trade] agreement. At the heart of this framework is a new conception of the role of national borders. Borders no longer are sites for imposing levies. Rather, they are transmitting membranes guaranteeing the free flow of goods, capital and information. Eighteenth-century concepts of free trade assumed freedom of movement between distinct national economies: 21st-century concepts of free trade are about an economy which is itself global, and about governments that coordinate rather than control economic activities.

To be sure, neither the old border-wall nor the nation-state has disappeared. The difficulties and complexities involved in this transformation are evident in the many obstacles to the ratification of the Uruguay Round of the GATT [General Agreement on Tariffs and Trade] talks, which aims at further opening economies to the circulation of services. But the relentless effort to overcome these difficulties also signals the pressure to depart from an old conception of national economic policy and the emergence of a new conception of how economic activity is to be maximized and governed.

Immigration Policies Rooted in the Past

The framework for immigration policy in the highly developed countries, on the other hand, is still rooted in the past. Immigration policy has yet to address global economic integration in the 21st century and its implications. Border-control remains the basic mechanism for regulating immigration—an increasingly troubled effort given new policies aimed at opening up national economies, such as the lifting of restrictions on foreign investment, the deregulation of financial markets, and the formation of financial free zones in major cities. Those policies amount to a partial denationalizing of national territory for the flow of capital, and they in turn globalize certain sectors of the workforce, notably the high-level transnational professional and managerial class.

Moreover, the policy framework for immigration treats the flow of labor as the result of individual actions, particularly the decision to migrate in search of better opportunities. Such a policy puts responsibility for immigration on the shoulders of immigrants. Policy commentary which speaks of an immigrant "influx" or "invasion" treats the receiving country as a passive agent. The causes for immigration appear to be outside the control or domain of receiving countries; immigration policy becomes a decision to be more or less benevolent in admitting immigrants. Absent from this understanding is the notion that the international activities of the governments or firms of receiving countries may have contributed to the formation of economic linkages with emigration countries, linkages that may function as bridges not only for capital but also for migration flows. That older view emphasizes individual "push" factors and neglects systemic linkages.

Immigration Follows Economic Activity

The worldwide evidence shows rather clearly that there is considerable patterning in the geography of migrations, and that the major receiving countries tend to get immigrants from their zones of influence. This holds for countries as diverse as the U.S., France or Japan. A transnational analysis of immigration contributes to its redefinition and allows us to see migrations as happening within global systems. The periods known as Pax

Britannica and Pax Americana are but two representations of such transnational systems. The formation of systems for the internationalization of manufacturing production, or the formation of regional trading blocs, are other instances. These systems can be characterized in a multiplicity of ways: economic (the Atlantic economy of the 1800s, the EC, NAFTA); politico-military (the colonial systems of several European countries, U.S. involvement in Central America); transnational war zones (formation of massive refugee flows as a result of major European wars); cultural-ideological zones (impact in socialist countries of the image of Western democracies as offering the "good life").

Immigrants Compete with Immigrants

Can't much of the high unemployment among America's troubled urban underclass be pinned on record levels of immigration? No, says Wade Henderson, director of the Washington, D.C., office of the National Association for the Advancement of Colored People: "You can't blame immigrants for the problems of the black poor." Their plight, he says, mainly arises from failures in domestic social policy rather than from immigration policy.

That's not to say that wrenching displacement never occurs. Janitors in Los Angeles and hotel workers in Washington, D.C., to select two instances, were once predominantly black Americans and are now mainly immigrants. But experts agree that in most cases new arrivals replace and compete for low-skilled jobs with other immigrants, not with Americans. The garment industry is a prime example: Men and women from Latin America, the Caribbean, and the Far East sit at machines once operated by Italians and Jews. "The garment district has always been a stepping stone for immigrants, especially those who speak no English," says Thomas Glubiak of New York State's Department of Labor.

Jaclyn Fierman, *Fortune*, August 9, 1993.

Recent developments in Japan capture the intersection of economic internationalization and immigration. They also illuminate the intersection of immigration policy and reality. Japan's closed door policy has not prevented a growing influx of immigrants. Nor has its 1990 immigration law, which opens up the country to high-level foreign workers but closes it to all low-wage workers, kept out the latter. Furthermore, despite a strong anti-immigration culture, immigrants have become incorporated into various labor markets and have begun to form immigrant communities in major cities in Japan. A detailed exploration of the dynamic at work provides useful insights into immigration processes.

What makes the disparity between the framework for immigration policy and the facts of the world economy particularly urgent is that all highly developed countries have experienced sharp increases in migration of both legal and undocumented immigrants. In some countries there is a resurgence of immigration after inflows had fallen sharply in the 1970s: this is the case for Germany and Austria. In other countries, notably the U.S., immigration policy opened up the country in 1965, yet in the 1980s, the number of entries doubled compared with the 1965–1980 period. Still other countries are becoming immigration countries for the first time in their contemporary histories: this is the case with Italy and Spain, long-time emigration countries, and with Japan, a nation of deep anti-immigration beliefs and policies. . . .

Toward New Policies

How should the new reality shape our thinking about immigration? A more comprehensive approach can provide more analytic and empirical footholds towards a better understanding of migration and towards more effective policy. The various transnational economic, cultural, political systems now evident in the world all tend to have very specific geographies. They are not planet-wide events, but occur in the relation of cities to cities, or in production chains linking factories in rather remote areas of developing countries to manufacturing and distribution centers in developed countries. Considerable migration flows within these new geographies for economic transactions. By understanding the nature of these geographies we can understand where to intervene for regulatory purposes. Further, international migrations themselves are patterned in geographic, economic and temporal terms. These two types of patterning provide maps within which to search for new policies to regulate immigration.

If immigration is partly an outcome of the actions of the governments and major private economic actors in receiving countries, the latter could conceivably recognize the migration impact of such actions and make decisions accordingly. For instance, economic policies that facilitate overseas operations of firms, particularly in developing countries, should recognize the migration impact of such operations. Economic internationalization suggests that the responsibility for immigration may not be exclusively the immigrant's. Refugee policy in some countries does lift the burden of immigration from the immigrant's shoulders. U.S. refugee policy, particularly for Indochinese refugees, does acknowledge partial responsibility on the part of the government. Clearly, in the case of economic migrations, such responsibility is far more difficult to establish, and by its nature far more indirect. As governments increasingly coordinate rather than contain economic activity, their role in immigration policy, as in other aspects of political economy, becomes elusive. Despite this complexity, the responsibilities for the consequences of globalization do not disappear. If economic internationalization contributes to migration flows, recognition of this fact can only help in designing more effective immigration policy.

II

Anyone who believes that immigrants are a drain on the U.S. economy has never visited the Silicon Valley in California. Here and in other corridors of high-tech entrepreneurship, immigrants are literally the lifeblood of many of the nation's most prosperous industries. In virtually every field in which the United States asserted global leadership in the 1980s—industries such as computer design and software, pharmaceuticals, bioengineering, electronics, superconductivity, robotics and aerospace engineering—one finds immigrants. In many ways these high-growth industries are the modern version of the American melting pot in action.

Consider Intel Corp. With profits of $1.1 billion in 1992, it is one of the most prolific and fast-expanding companies in the United States, employing tens of thousands of American workers. It is constantly developing exciting, cutting-edge technologies that will define the computer industry in the 21st century.

And it is doing all of this largely with the talents of America's newest immigrants. Three members of Intel's top management, including Chief Executive Officer Andrew S. Grove, from Hungary, are immigrants. Some of its most successful and revolutionary computer technologies were pioneered by immigrants, such as the 8080 microprocessor (an expanded-power computer chip), invented by a Japanese, and polysilicon FET gates (the basic unit of memory storage on modern computer chips), invented by an Italian. Dick Ward, manager of employee information systems at Intel, says: "Our whole business is predicated on inventing the next generation of computer technologies. The engine that drives that quest is brainpower. And here at Intel, much of that brainpower comes from immigrants.". . .

Significant Contributions

Intel . . . is not alone in relying on immigrants. Robert Kelley Jr., president of SO/CAL/TEN, an association of nearly 200 high-tech California companies, insists: "Without the influx of Asians in the 1980s, we would not have had the entrepreneurial explosion we've seen in California." David N.K. Wang, vice president for worldwide business operations at Applied Materials Inc., a computer-technology company in California, adds that because of immigration, "Silicon Valley is one of the most international business centers in the world."

Take away the immigrants, and you take away the talent base that makes such centers operate. Indeed, it is frightening to think what would happen to America's global competitiveness if the immigrants stopped coming. Even scarier is the more realistic prospect that U.S. policymakers will enact laws to prevent them from coming.

New research has begun to quantify the contributions of immigrants to American industry. The highly respected National Research Council reported in 1988 that "a large fraction of the technological output of the United States [is] dependent upon foreign talent and that such dependency is growing." Noting that well over half of all scientists graduating with doctorate degrees from American universities and one in three engineers working in the United States are immigrants, the report states emphatically: "It is clear . . . that these foreign-born engineers enrich our culture and make substantial contributions to the U.S. economic well-being and competitiveness."

The United States' competitive edge over the Japanese, Germans, Koreans and much of Europe is linked closely to its continued ability to attract and retain highly talented workers from other countries. A 1990 study by the National Science Foundation says, "Very significant, positive aspects arise from the presence of foreign-born engineers in our society.". . .

Creating Jobs

Public opinion polls consistently reveal that a major worry is that immigrants take jobs from American workers. The fear is understandable but misplaced. Immigrants don't just take jobs, they create jobs. One way is by starting new businesses. Today, America's immigrants, even those who come with relatively low skill levels, are highly entrepreneurial.

Take Koreans, for example. According to sociologists Alendro Portes and Ruben Rumbaut, "In Los Angeles, the propensity for self-employment is three times greater for Koreans than among the population as a whole. Grocery stores, restaurants, gas stations, liquor stores and real estate offices are typical Korean businesses." Cubans also are prodigious creators of new businesses. The number of Cuban-owned businesses in Miami has expanded from 919 in 1967 to 8,000 in 1976 to 28,000 in 1990. On Jefferson Boulevard in Dallas, more than 800 businesses operate, three-quarters of them owned by first- and second-generation Hispanic immigrants. Just 10 years ago, before the influx of Mexicans and other Central Americans, the neighborhood was in decay, with many vacant storefronts displaying "for sale" signs in the windows. Today it is a thriving ethnic neighborhood.

To be sure, few immigrant-owned businesses mature into an Intel. In fact, many fail completely. Like most new businesses in America, most immigrant establishments are small and only marginally profitable. The average immigrant business employs two to four workers and records roughly $200,000 in annual sales. However, such small businesses, as President Clinton often correctly emphasizes, are a significant source of jobs.

It should not be too surprising that immigrants are far more likely than average U.S. citizens to take business risks. After all, uprooting oneself, traveling to a foreign culture and making it requires more than the usual amount of courage, ambition, resourcefulness and even bravado. Indeed, this is part of the self-selection process that makes immigrants so particularly desirable. Immigrants are not just people—they are a very special group of people. By coming, they impart productive energies on the rest of us.

This is not just romanticism. It is well-grounded in fact. Countless studies have documented that immigrants to the United States tend to be more skilled, more highly educated and wealthier than the average citizen of their native countries.

Thomas Sowell, an economist and senior fellow at the Hoover Institution in Stanford, Calif., reports in his seminal study on immigration, "Ethnic America," that black immigrants from the West Indies have far higher skill levels than their countrymen at home. He also finds that the income levels of West Indies immigrants are higher than those of West Indies natives, American blacks and native-born white Americans.

Surprisingly, even illegal immigrants are not the poverty-stricken and least skilled from their native countries. Surveys of undocumented immigrants from Mexico to the United States show that only about 5 percent were unemployed in Mexico, whereas the average unemployment rate there was about three times that level, and that a relatively high percentage of them worked in white-collar jobs in Mexico. In addition, surveys have found that illiteracy among undocumented Mexicans in the U.S. is about 10 percent, whereas illiteracy in Mexico is about 22 percent. . . .

Making America Great

In the past century, America has admitted roughly 50 million immigrants. This has been one of the largest migrations in the history of the world. Despite this infusion of people—no, because of it—the United States became by the middle of the 20th century the wealthiest nation in the world. Real wages in America have grown more than eightfold over this period. The U.S. economy employed less than 40 million people in 1900; today it employs nearly 120 million people. The U.S. job machine had not the slightest problem expanding and absorbing the 8 million legal immigrants who came to this country in the 1980s. Eighteen million jobs were created.

But what about those frightening headlines? "Immigration Bankrupting Nation." "Immigrants Displacing U.S. Workers." "Foreigners Lured to U.S. by Welfare."

Here are the facts. The 1990 census reveals that roughly 6 percent of native-born Americans are on public assistance, versus 7 percent of the foreign-born, with less than 5 percent of illegal immigrants collecting welfare. Not much reason for alarm. Because immigrants tend to come to the United States when they are young and working, over their lifetimes they each pay about $20,000 more in taxes than they use in services, according to economist Julian Simon of the University of Maryland. With 1 million immigrants per year, the nation gains about $20 billion more than cost. Rather than fiscal burdens, immigrants are huge bargains.

Nor do immigrants harm the U.S. labor market. A comprehensive 1989 study by the U.S. Department of Labor concluded: "Neither U.S. workers nor most minority workers appear to be adversely affected by immigration—especially during periods of economic expansion." In the 1980s, the top 10 immigrant-receiving states—including California, Florida, Massachusetts and Texas—recorded rates of unemployment 2 percentage points below the U.S. average, according to the Alexis de Tocqueville Institution in Arlington, Va. So where's the job displacement?

Selling Fear and Bigotry

We are now witnessing in America what might be described as the return of the nativists. They are selling fear and bigotry. But if any of their allegations against immigrants are accurate, then America could not have emerged as the economic superpower it is today. . . .

By pursuing a liberal and strategic policy on immigration, America can ensure that the 21st century, like the 20th, will be the American century.

Periodical Bibliography

The following articles have been selected to supplement the diverse views presented in this chapter.

Richard Bissell	"Natural Resource Wars: Let Them Eat Trees," *The Washington Quarterly*, Winter 1994. Available from MIT Press Journals, 55 Hayward St., Cambridge, MA 02142.
Francis M. Deng	"Africa After the Cold War: Rethinking Colonial Boundaries," *Current*, September 1993. Available from Helen Dwight Reid Educational Foundation, 1319 18th St. NW, Washington, DC 20036-1802.
Alan Thein Durning	"Guardians of the Land: Indigenous Peoples and the Health of the Earth," *Worldwatch Paper 112*, December 1992. Available from the Worldwatch Institute, 1776 Massachusetts Ave. NW, Washington, DC 20036.
Nader Entessar	"North-South Military Relations in the Post–Cold War Era: Opportunities and Constraints," *Journal of Third World Studies*, Fall 1992.
John Bellamy Foster	"'Let Them Eat Pollution': Capitalism and the World Environment," *Monthly Review*, January 1993.
Francis Fukuyama	"Immigrants and Family Values," *Commentary*, May 1993.
Daniel Hellinger	"Empire Strikes Back," *In These Times*, July 26, 1993.
Paul Johnson	"Colonialism's Back—and Not a Moment Too Soon," *The New York Times Magazine*, April 18, 1993.
Robert E. Neumann	"This Next Disorderly Century: Some Proposed Remedies," *The Washington Quarterly*, Winter 1993.
Stephen John Stedman	"The New Interventionists," *Foreign Affairs*, vol. 72, no. 1, 1992/1993.
Crispin Tickell	"The World After the Summit Meeting at Rio," *The Washington Quarterly*, Spring 1993.
Pete Wilson et al.	"Immigration: Boon or Bane to the U.S.?" *The World & I*, September 1994. Available from 2800 New York Ave. NE, Washington, DC 20002.

For Further Discussion

Chapter 1

1. Malcolm W. Brown begins his viewpoint with a discussion of the trade in human body parts and then likens the growth in the human population to that of bacteria and cancer. What is Brown's purpose in employing such graphic and shocking examples? Does it help or harm his case against overpopulation, in your opinion? Explain your answer.

2. In their viewpoints, Ivy George and Jeremy Seabrook both argue that capitalist development has failed its stated purpose and damaged the lives of Third World peoples. With reference to colonialism and human values, what do these authors' arguments have in common? How are their arguments different?

Chapter 2

1. How do Walden Bello, Shea Cunningham, and Bill Rau evaluate the structural adjustment policies of the World Bank and the International Monetary Fund (IMF)? How does Amy L. Sherman view the same austerity measures? Which analysis is more convincing? Why?

2. José Goldemberg maintains that modern technology transfer to the Third World will help the environment. The *Ecologist* editors argue that imported technology is damaging to the environment. Are the authors·arguing on the same theoretical level? Which is more convincing? Why?

3. Fred L. Smith Jr. is president of the Competitive Enterprise Institute, an organization that promotes environmental protection through private ownership of natural resources. How is this affiliation reflected in the points of his argument?

Chapter 3

1. In their viewpoints, Francis Fukuyama and Jim Petras attempt to show the strengths of their preferred political-economic systems. Undermining their opponents' position is an important part of their arguments. Give examples of how they do this.

2. Both Samuel P. Huntington and Amartya Sen make essentially economic arguments in favor of their respective positions on which should come first, economic liberalization or democratization. Which argument is more convincing? Why?

3. Larry Diamond approaches the subject of civil society's power to effect democratization from a theoretical perspective. Anthony W. Pereira discusses the failed attempts of one society's members to organize. What are the strengths and weaknesses of each author's approach?

Chapter 4

1. Warren Christopher is U.S. secretary of state. Richard Schifter is head of the U.S. delegation to the UN Human Rights Commission. The author who opposes their viewpoint, Noam Chomsky, is a well-known critic of American politics and foreign policy. Explain how their affiliations and backgrounds are reflected in the tone and substance of their arguments.

2. Show how the viewpoints of Shyam J. Kamath and John Cavanagh, Robin Broad, and Peter Weiss are in essential agreement over the past failures of American aid to the Third World. What opposite conclusions do they reach about the continuation of U.S. aid in the future?

Chapter 5

1. What is the significance of the fact that Malaysian logging firms are currently working in South American forests, according to Eugene Linden? Does this fact undermine Mahathir Mohammed's contention that such activity is necessary for Malaysia and the rest of the South to achieve economic development? Explain.

2. How do Robert Fox, Wayne Lutton, and John Tanton support their charge that immigrants are taking away American jobs and that most immigrants have no skills that would benefit the U.S. economy? What evidence do Saskia Sassen and Stephen Moore offer to counter these charges? Which type of documentation seems more convincing? Why?

Organizations to Contact

The editors have compiled the following list of organizations concerned with the issues debated in this book. The descriptions are derived from materials provided by the organizations. All have publications or information available for interested readers. The list was compiled on the date of publication of the present volume; names, addresses, and phone numbers may change. Be aware that many organizations take several weeks or longer to respond to inquiries, so allow as much time as possible.

Africa Faith and Justice Network (AFJN)
PO Box 29378
Washington, DC 20037
(202) 887-0528

AFJN advocates economic justice in the Third World, primarily in Africa. Its publications include a bimonthly newsletter in which an issue paper is presented, quarterly reports on African countries, and the book *Africa Faces Democracy*.

Association for Women in Development (AWID)
Virginia Polytechnic Institute
1060 Litton Reaves Hall
Blacksburg, VA 24061-0334
(703) 231-3765
fax: (703) 231-6741

AWID is a professional association concerned with international development and gender issues. It also works to ensure that women fully and actively participate in, and share in the benefits of, a more equitable development process. AWID's publications include a bimonthly newsletter, an AWID Special Paper Series, conference and workshop reports, and the books *The Global Empowerment of Women* and *The Future of Women in Development: Voices from the South*.

Association of Third World Studies (ATWS)
Georgia Southern University
Landrum Box 8106
Statesboro, GA 30460-8106
(912) 681-5668
fax: (912) 681-0824

Founded in 1983, ATWS works to enhance the quality of life of Third World peoples and encourages research and teaching in Third World Studies. ATWS publishes the biannual *Journal of Third World Studies* and the *International Perspectives* newsletter.

Cato Institute
1000 Massachusetts Ave. NW
Washington, DC 20001
(202) 842-0200
fax: (202) 842-3490

The institute is a libertarian public policy research organization that recommends minimal government interference in domestic affairs and noninterventionism in foreign affairs. Its publications include the triannual *Cato Journal* and the books *Perpetuating Poverty: The World Bank, the IMF, and the Developing World*; *Prosperity Versus Planning: How Government Stifles Growth*; *Africa Betrayed*; and *Economic Reform in China*.

Council on Hemispheric Affairs (COHA)
724 Ninth St. NW, Rm. 401
Washington, DC 20001
(202) 393-3322
fax: (202) 393-3423

COHA is a nonpartisan education and research organization that monitors United States-Canadian, U. S.-Latin American, and Canadian-Latin American relations. It publishes the *Washington Report on the Hemisphere*, a biweekly newsletter dealing primarily with U.S. relations with Latin America.

Human Rights Watch (HRW)
485 Fifth Ave.
New York, NY 10017
(212) 972-8400
fax: (212) 972-0905

HRW works with international organizations such as the United Nations to promote and monitor human rights worldwide. It reports rights abuses and stresses enforcement of U.S. laws that require governments receiving U.S. economic, military, or diplomatic support to adhere to appropriate human rights practices. It publishes the *Human Rights Watch Quarterly Newsletter*, the annual *Human Rights Watch World Report*, and a semiannual publications catalog.

Indigenous Women's Network (IWN)
PO Box 174
Lake Elmo, MN 55042
(612) 770-3861

IWN works to enhance visibility of indigenous women in the Western Hemisphere and encourages the resolution of contemporary problems through traditional values. IWN publishes the biannual *Journal of Indigenous Women*.

Institute for Food and Development Policy (Food First)
398 60th St.
Oakland, CA 94618
(510) 654-4400
fax: (510) 654-4551

Food First is a nonprofit research and educational center that focuses on issues of hunger and democracy around the world. It promotes participatory, equitable, and ecologically sustainable development in the Third World. Food First publishes the quarterly newsletter *Food First News and Views* and the books *Basta! Land and the Zapatista Rebellion in Chiapas*, *Chile's Free-Market Miracle: A Second Look*, and *Dark Victory: The United States, Structural Adjustment, and Global Poverty*.

International Monetary Fund (IMF)
700 19th St. NW
Washington, DC 20431
(202) 623-7000
fax: (202) 623-6278

IMF's purpose is to promote international economic cooperation, to help keep a balance of trade among nations so that all benefit from the expansion of trade, and to lend its member nations money when necessary. It acts as a depository of information and statistical data regarding the economic affairs of its members. The fund publishes pamphlets, brochures, fact sheets, the semimonthly *IMF Survey*, and an *Annual Report*.

Maryknoll Fathers and Brothers
PO Box 308
Maryknoll, NY 10545
(914) 941-7590
fax: (914) 941-0670

As part of the Catholic Foreign Mission Society of America, this religious order works with poor and oppressed people in the Third World. The order distributes educational materials and publishes the monthly *Maryknoll* magazine, the bilingual monthly magazine *Revista Maryknoll*, and videotapes as well as sponsoring radio broadcasts.

Oxfam America
115 Broadway
Boston, MA 02116
(617) 482-1211
fax: (617) 728-2594

Oxfam is a development and disaster-assistance organization that funds self-help projects in the poorer countries of Asia, Africa, and the Americas. It advocates economic and agricultural self-reliance. Its publications include the *Oxfam America* quarterly newsletter as well as pamphlets related to the development of the Third World.

Population Council
1 Dag Hammarskjöld Plaza
New York, NY 10017-2220
(212) 339-0514
fax: (212) 755-6052

The Population Council is an international organization that seeks to achieve a sustainable balance between people and resources. It provides social and health programs and conducts research, including biomedical research to develop improved contraceptive technology. The council publishes numerous journals, booklets, publications, and the books *Resources, Environment, and Population: Present Knowledge, Future Options*; *The New Politics of Population: Conflict and Consensus in Family Planning*; and *Directory of Surveys in Developing Countries: Data on Families and Households 1975–92*.

Population Renewal Office (PRO)
36 W. 59th St.
Kansas City, MO 64113
(816) 363-6980

PRO is a privately funded think tank that conducts research on population and related issues such as teen pregnancy, abortion, and AIDS. It provides demographical information and research findings to individuals who wish to challenge the viewpoint of those who advocate population controls. PRO publishes a variety of position papers, including "Population and the Environment." There is no charge for materials.

Third World Resources (TWR)
464 19th St.
Oakland, CA 94612
(510) 835-4692
fax: (510) 835-3017

TWR collects, organizes, evaluates, and publicizes print and audiovisual resources on Third World regions and issues. It publishes annotated directories that include supplementary lists of resources and information on organizations, books, periodicals, pamphlets, and audiovisual resources. TWR also publishes *Third World Resources: A Quarterly Review of Resources from and About the Third World*.

United Nations Development Programme (UNDP)
1 United Nations Plaza
New York, NY 10017
(212) 906-5000
general information: (212) 906-5330

The UNDP grants funding for development cooperation. It works with 174 governments to build the social and economic resources of developing countries. Its publications include the annual *Human Development Report*, the human development magazine *Choices*, the newsletter *Update*, and the *UNDP Annual Report*.

Bibliography of Books

W.M. Adams   *Green Development: Environment and Sustainability in the Third World.* London: Routledge, 1992.

Haleh Afshar and Carolyne Dennis, eds.   *Women and Adjustment Policies in the Third World.* New York: St. Martin's Press, 1992.

Anil Agarwal et al.   *For Earth's Sake: A Report from the Commission on Developing Countries and Global Change.* Ottawa: International Development Research Center, 1992.

Samir Amin   *Re-reading the Postwar Period: An Intellectual Itinerary.* New York: Monthly Review Press, 1994.

Anita Anand et al.   *The Power to Change: Women in the Third World Redefine Their Environment.* London: Zed, 1993.

Kenneth E. Bauzon, ed.   *Development and Democratization in the Third World: Myths, Hopes and Realities.* Washington: Crane Russak, 1992.

Boutros Boutros-Ghali   *An Agenda for Peace: Preventative Diplomacy, Peacemaking, and Peace-Keeping.* New York: United Nations, 1992.

Rosi Braidotti et al.   *Women, the Environment and Sustainable Development: Towards a Theoretical Synthesis.* London: Zed, 1994.

Robert Cassen et al.   *Population and Development: Old Debates, New Conclusions.* New Brunswick, NJ: Transaction, 1994.

Jorge G. Castaneda   *Utopia Unarmed: The Latin American Left After the Cold War.* New York: Knopf, 1993.

Noam Chomsky   *Year 501: The Conquest Continues.* Boston: South End Press, 1992.

Yih-chyi Chuang   *Learning by Doing, Technology Gap, and Growth.* Taipei, Taiwan: Institute of Economics, 1993.

David Louis Cingranelli   *Ethics, American Foreign Policy and the Third World.* London: Macmillan, 1993.

Humphrey Dalton   *Will America Drown? Immigration and the Third World Population Explosion.* Washington: Scott Townsend, 1994.

Constantine P. Danopoulos, ed.   *Civilian Rule in the Developing World: Democracy on the March?* Boulder, CO: Westview Press, 1992.

Michael C. Desch	*When the Third World Matters: Latin America and United States Grand Strategy.* Baltimore: Johns Hopkins University Press, 1993.
Paul Ekins	*A New World Order: Grassroots Movements for Global Change.* New York: Routledge, 1992.
Daniel Faber	*Environment Under Fire: Imperialism and the Ecological Crisis in Central America.* New York: Monthly Review Press, 1993.
Rosemary Galli	*Rethinking the Third World.* New York: Crane Russak, 1992.
David Glover	*The Developing Countries in World Trade: Policies and Bargaining Strategies.* Boulder, CO: Lynne Rienner, 1993.
Calvin Goldscheider, ed.	*Fertility Transitions, Family Structure, and Population Policy.* Boulder, CO: Westview Press, 1992.
Paul Harrison	*The Third Revolution: Environment, Population, and a Sustainable World.* London: I.B. Tauris, 1992; distributed in U.S. by St. Martin's Press.
Jeff Haynes	*Religion in Third World Politics.* Boulder, CO: Lynne Rienner, 1993.
Wil Hout	*Capitalism and the Third World: Development, Dependence and the World System.* Brookfield, VT: E. Elgar, 1993.
Charles Humana, ed.	*World Human Rights Guide.* 3rd ed. Oxford: Oxford University Press, 1992.
Robert H. Jackson	*Quasi-States: Sovereignty, International Relations and the Third World.* Cambridge: Cambridge University Press, 1993.
Brian L. Job, ed.	*The Insecurity Dilemma: National Security of Third World States.* Boulder, CO: Lynne Rienner, 1992.
Antonio Jorge, ed.	*Economic Development and Social Change: United States—Latin American Relations in the 1990s.* New Brunswick, NJ: Transaction, 1992.
Azizur Rahman Khan	*Structural Adjustment and Income Distribution: Issues and Experience.* Geneva: International Labour Office, 1993.
William Korey	*The Promises We Keep: Human Rights, the Helsinki Process and American Foreign Policy.* New York: St. Martin's Press, 1993.
John Madeley	*Trade and the Poor: The Impact of International Trade on Developing Countries.* New York: St. Martin's Press, 1993.

281

Russell McGurk

U.S. Economic Policy and Sustainable Growth in Latin America. New York: Council on Foreign Relations Press, 1992.

Robert Miller, ed.

Aid as Peacemaker: Canadian Development Assistance and Third World Conflict. Ottawa: Carleton University Press, 1992.

Janet Henshall Momsen and Vivian Kinnaird, eds.

Different Places, Different Voices: Gender and Development in Africa, Asia and Latin America. New York: Routledge, 1993.

Ralph Nader et al.

The Case Against Free Trade: GATT, NAFTA, and the Globalization of Corporate Power. San Francisco: Earth Island Press, 1993.

A.S. Oberai

Population Growth, Employment, and Poverty in Third World Mega-Cities: Analytical and Policy Issues. New York: St. Martin's Press, 1993.

Robert Pinkney

Democracy in the Third World. Boulder, CO: Lynne Rienner, 1993.

Susan Place, ed.

Tropical Rainforests: Latin American Nature and Society in Transition. Wilmington, DE: Scholarly Resources, 1993.

Helena Ribe et al.

How Adjustment Programs Can Help the Poor: The World Bank's Experience. Washington: The World Bank, 1990.

Jamil Salmi

Violence and Democratic Society: New Approaches to Human Rights. London: Zed, 1993.

Jean-Jacques Salomon and André Lebeau

Mirages of Development: Science and Technology for the Third Worlds. Boulder, CO: Lynne Rienner, 1993.

Roger D. Stone

The Nature of Development: A Report from the Rural Tropics on the Quest for Sustainable Economic Growth. New York: Knopf, 1992.

Vito Tanzi, ed.

Transition to Market: Studies in Fiscal Reform. Washington: International Monetary Fund, 1993.

Victor E. Tokman, ed.

Beyond Regulation: The Informal Economy in Latin America. Boulder, CO: Lynne Rienner, 1992.

Kate Young

Planning Development with Women. New York: St. Martin's Press, 1993.

Index

283

287

South Korea
  democratization of, 175
  success under authoritarianism, 146-47
Sowell, Thomas, 271
statism, 57, 218, 220
  beneficial factors of, 69
  move to mercantilism, 61-62
Strategic Defense Initiative, 198
structural adjustment programs (SAPs), 40,
  65-70
Summers, Lawrence, 111, 129
Suriname, deforestation of, 230-31, 232
sustainable development, 102

Tanton, John, 258-63
technology
  as social process, 50-51
  technological leapfrogging, 76
  transfer
    helps the South, 71-77
    hurts the South, 78-86
  vernacular science, 79-80
  see also energy
Thatcher, Margaret, 123
Third World
  as bacterial culture or cancerous tumor,
    21
  characteristics of, are affecting the
    North, 24-25
  as collective state of mind, 20
  domestic instability in, 191
  see also democracy; development;
    poverty; statism
Thurow, Lester, 67
Tocqueville, Alexis de, 138-39, 152, 155,
  158
totalitarianism. See authoritarianism
trade barriers
  are counterproductive, 106
  Circle of Poison theory, 106
  green, 104-105
  protectionist, 99
Truth Commission (El Salvador), 178, 253

Unified Nicaraguan Opposition (UNO),
  251
United Nations
  Conference on Trade and Development,
    70
  Economic Commission for Africa, 69
  Environment Programme (UNEP), 103,
    256
  First Committee, 200, 202-204
  Food and Agriculture Organization
    (FAO), 28, 44, 82
  Human Rights Center, 176
  Human Rights Commission, 173
  Observer Mission in El Salvador
    (ONUSAL), 253

Observer Group in Central America
    (ONUCA), 252-53
  Observer Mission to Verify the Electoral
    Process in Nicaragua (ONUVEN), 253
  Security Council, 203-204, 253
    under siege, 247-48
  Universal Declaration of Human Rights,
    173-74, 178, 180, 214
United States
  aid to Third World
    causes harm, 216-24
    must be given, 208-15
  allows Chinese rights violations, 184-87,
    209-10
  backed terror in Indonesia, 182-84
  directly intervened in
    Grenada, 240
    Libya, bombing of, 240
    Panama, 188-89, 240
  new imperialism of, 239-42
  and nuclear weapons
    should disarm itself, 199-207
    should forbid in South, 190-98
  supports human rights and democracy,
    172-80
    con, 181-84
  war with Iraq, as hypocrisy, 185
  see also foreign aid
Universal Declaration of Human Rights
  (UN), 173-74, 178, 180, 214
U.S. Agency for International Development (USAID), 82, 88, 210-12, 222

vernacular science, 79-80

Walesa, Lech, 142
Wang, David N. K., 269-70
war(s)
  intranational disputes, 176-77, 193
  probability of, 195-96
  recent frequency of, 191
Wattenberg, Ben, 258
WEC (World Energy Conference), 73-74
Weiss, Peter, 208-215
Weiss, Thomas G., 246-54
Workers Party (Brazil), 129, 165
World Bank
  acknowledges traditional farming
    methods, 84-85
  aggravates Third World poverty, 65-69,
    210-13, 219-20
  failure of aid to India, 221-22
  on causes of environmental damage, 79
  see also structural adjustment programs
    (SAPs)
World Court, 200, 202-204
World Health Organization, 203-204

Zunes, Stephen, 155